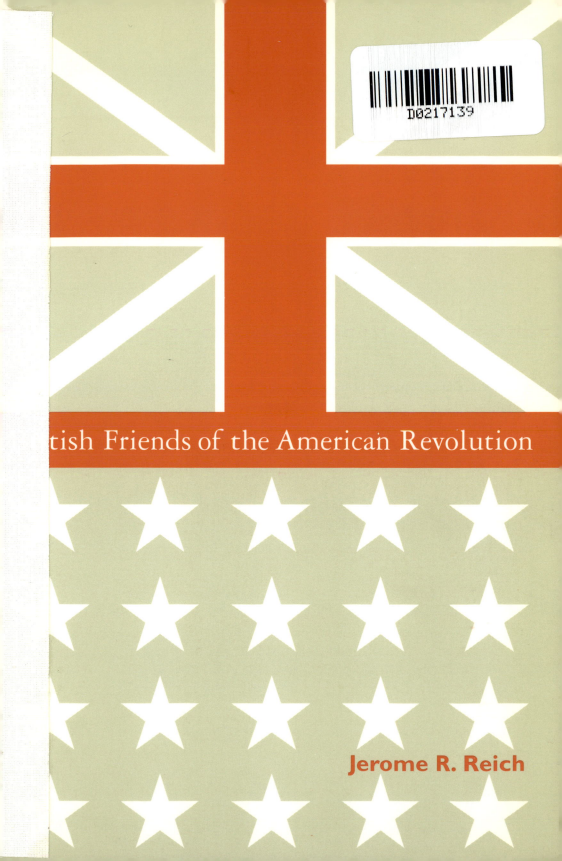

tish Friends of the American Revolution

Jerome R. Reich

WITHDRAWN

British Friends of the American Revolution

British Friends of the American Revolution

Jerome R. Reich

M.E. Sharpe
Armonk, New York
London, England

Library of Congress Cataloging-in-Publication Data

Reich, Jerome R.
British friends of the American Revolution / Jerome R. Reich
p.   cm.
Includes bibliographical references (p.   ) and index.
ISBN 0-7656-0073-0 (hardcover : alk. paper).—ISBN 0-7656-0074-9 (pbk. : alk. paper)
1. United States—History—Revolution, 1775-1783—Influence.
2. United States—History—Revolution, 1775-1783—Foreign public opinion, British.
3. Public Opinion—Great Britain—History—18th century. I. Title.
E209.R35   1997
973.3—dc21
97-14520
CIP

Printed in the United States of America

The paper used in this publication meets the minimum requirements of the
American National Standard for Information Sciences—
Permanence of Paper for Printed Library Materials,
ANSI Z 39.48-1984.

BM (c)   10   9   8   7   6   5   4   3   2   1
BM (p)   10   9   8   7   6   5   4   3   2   1

To my son Michael
whose commitment and insight
have been indispensable at all stages
in the production of this volume.

Contents

British Friends of the American Revolution

The Stage and the Players

"Let our *patriots* [italics mine] therefore, if they would arrive at eminence by their conduct, go over to America, and demand the confidence of the colonies. They may have real merit to plead there in their attempts to overthrow the Constitution of Great Britain; they may have merit there by endeavoring to render the impudent resolutions of a provincial committee, superior to our lawful ordinances. But here, my lords, I trust they will ever be held contemptible, that their characters will be as mean, as their proceedings have been flagitious, and that their machinations to destroy the importance of the British empire, will always make them detestable to every good Englishman."[1]

Against whom was this diatribe, delivered by the earl of Hillsborough in the House of Lords on May 18, 1770, directed? Who were these villainous individuals, ironically termed "patriots" by the secretary of state for America? As this volume will indicate, they included, among others, William Pitt, "the Great Commoner," the most popular statesman of his time; that "devil" (as King George III termed him) John Wilkes, the key person in the radical reform movement, as well as Reverend John Horne Tooke, his rival in the same movement; Dr. Richard Price, a distinguished dissenting clergyman with a mathematical bent; two old enemies who joined together as leaders of the Whig party, the earnest and eloquent Edmund Burke and the rakish descendant of King Charles II, Charles James Fox; one of the few true "colonial experts," former governor of Massachusetts Thomas Pownall; James Burgh, a schoolmaster-turned-political-reformer; a sensation in her time, republican historian Catherine Macauley; David Hartley, a distinguished scientist who meddled in politics; John Cartwright, a naval officer who felt that the British empire had grown unwieldy and corrupt; and Josiah Tucker, an Anglican dean who was economically sophisticated enough to realize that Great Britain would actually benefit if it granted the North American colonies their independence; and the duke of Richmond, whose efforts on behalf of America and parliamentary reform earned him the sobriquet, "the Radical Duke."

What did this diverse group of individuals have in common to draw down upon themselves the ire of Lord Hillsborough? Very little, except that for disparate, sometimes even contradictory motives and utilizing varying techniques, they opposed the policy of the British government toward its Thirteen Colonies.

Our understanding of these "British Friends of the American Revolution" will be enhanced by a brief survey of political developments in eighteenth-century Great Britain and America. During the reigns of the first two Georges (1714–1760), the Whig Party dominated the British government. The Whigs were not a party in the modern sense of the term. They were a conglomeration of competing factions each led by a nobleman. Years of power brought about a significant change in Whig political thinking. No longer did they accept the Lockean theories of natural rights and the contractual origin of government, which they had espoused during the Glorious Revolution of 1688. Well before the accession of George III, they had come to believe in a conservative doctrine that posited a balanced government of King, Lords, and Commons. In practice, however, sovereignty rested in Parliament or, in other words, in themselves—the landed aristocracy that dominated both Houses of Parliament. A corollary of this belief was that sovereignty was indivisible and thus Parliament had unlimited power to legislate for the British colonies as well as the home country.

Not all Whigs accepted these new doctrines. A small minority called themselves Real Whigs or Commonwealthmen (because many of their ideas dated back to the period 1649–1660).[2] They also believed in a balanced form of government, but one in which the powers of all three branches were circumscribed by an unwritten constitution, a body of fundamental laws many of which, they claimed, antedated the Norman Conquest. They retained the Lockean concept of a social contract; believed that the Glorious Revolution had not sufficiently limited the power of the Crown (particularly its ability to "pack" the House of Commons and maintain a standing army); and felt that more frequent elections, a broader franchise, and a reapportionment of seats in the House of Commons were necessary to make that body less corrupt and more independent. Closely allied with the Real Whigs were the Dissenters, those Englishmen not affiliated with the Church of England, who sought to remove the legal and political disabilities under which they suffered. During the 1760s, a third group—urban (largely London) radicals energized by the John Wilkes affair—also joined the reformist ranks. This often uneasy coalition provided the most consistent and zealous supporters of the American point of view. This should come as no surprise because the leaders of the American cause were themselves Real Whigs (though they did not use the adjective).

This is clearly illustrated by the statements made in two court cases that took place in the colonies even before serious problems arose between Great Britain and its American colonies. According to John Adams's contemporary notes, in 1761, in a losing court battle against writs of assistance (general search warrants), James Otis declared, "As to Acts of Parliament, an Act against the Constitution is void; an Act against natural equity is void."[3] And two years later, after the Privy Council disallowed Virginia's Two-Penny-Act, which effectively lowered clergymen's salaries, an Anglican clergyman sued his vestry for back salary. In his exhortation to the jury, Patrick Henry, the attorney for the vestry, claimed "that a King, by disallowing Acts of this salutary nature, from being the father of his people, degenerated into a Tyrant and forfeits all right to his subjects' obedience."[4] But the gulf in political outlook between Great Britain and the colonies was even deeper than these quotations indicate.

The Glorious Revolution also exerted significant influence on colonial political practice and theory. Americans assumed that the Revolution had won for the individual colonial assemblies all the rights gained by the English House of Commons and, conversely, that the English Parliament had no power over the colonies except in the area of imperial affairs. In spite of the opposition of the British government, by 1763 the first assumption had been largely realized: Members of the colonial assemblies had the right of freedom of discussion on the floor of the legislature; they were immune from arrest while the legislature was in session; they could make their own rules, settle disputed elections, and elect their own speaker; and finally, they won the exclusive right to initiate money bills and to oversee the expenditure of public funds. Only the governor's power to veto (and the Privy Council's to disallow) acts of the colonial legislature and the governor's power to prorogue or dissolve it differed from English practice, in which the king no longer exercised these powers over Parliament.

As to the second assumption, colonial affairs were technically under royal control and, though Parliament claimed ultimate power over the colonies, it rarely chose to exercise it. The years between Walpole's rise to power in 1721 and 1763 were later termed by Edmund Burke the period of "salutary neglect," when Parliament passed laws for the colonies that dealt only with imperial affairs—regulation of trade and manufacturers; the establishment of a postal service; control of the naturalization process; and supervision of coinage, currency, defense, and foreign affairs.

Sir Francis Bernard, governor of Massachusetts from 1760 to 1769, was exaggerating only slightly (or had a presentiment of the colonial position ten years in the future) when he wrote in 1765

> In Britain the American governments are considered as corporations empowered to make bylaws, existing only during the pleasure of Parliament, who have never yet done anything to confirm their establishment and hath at any time a power to dissolve them. In America they claim . . . to be perfect States, no otherwise dependent upon Great Britain than by having the same king, which having compleat legislatures within themselves are in no ways subject to that of Great Britain; which in such instances as it has heretofore exercised a legislative power over them has usurped it.[5]

Only two of our "friends," Thomas Pownall and Josiah Tucker, had the background and experience to draw logical conclusions from Governor Bernard's assessment. We shall meet them and John Cartwright, a man who combined their ideas, in the next chapter.

Notes

1. R.C. Simmons and P.D.G. Thomas, eds., *Proceedings and Debates of the British Parliaments Respecting North America, 1754–1783*, III, p. 335.
2. Caroline Robbins, *The Eighteenth Century Commonwealthman*, provides the best study of this group.
3. Charles Francis Adams, ed., *The Works of John Adams*, II, p. 522.
4. John P. Kennedy, ed., *Journals of the House of Burgesses of Virginia, 1761–1765*, p. 211.
5. Edward Channing and Archibald Cary Coolidge, eds., *The Barrington-Bernard Correspondence and Illustrative Matter, 1760–1770*, p. 96.

Governor Pownall, Dean Tucker, and Major John Cartwright: Practical Idealists or Wishful Thinkers?

Theory and practice rarely coincide. As already noted, British statesmen insisted that they ruled a unitary empire with all power residing in king and Parliament. In practice, however, the home government had concerned itself only with imperial affairs while the colonial legislatures dealt with the regulation of marriage and divorce, the provision of relief to the poor, the maintenance of roads and bridges, the organization of a militia, and, most crucial, the levying of taxes. In other words, without intending to—in fact quite contrary to the desires of its leaders—the British had developed (to use modern terms) a federal empire in which the colonies held dominion status.

Most Americans took this situation for granted but the opposite was true of their British counterparts. One of the few exceptions was Thomas Pownall.

Thomas Pownall was born in 1722 of a Lincolnshire family of more prestige than pelf.[1] He attended Lincoln grammar school and graduated from Trinity College, Cambridge, in 1743. While in college, he developed a taste for philosophy and literature and did the preliminary work on a treatise on government, *Principles of Polity*, which was later published in 1752. His younger brother, John, who was already an important functionary of the Board of Trade, obtained a clerkship there for Thomas. However, Thomas came to realize that, for those of his social class, fame and fortune were only to be won in the colonies. In 1753, therefore, he became private secretary to Sir Danvers Osborne, the newly appointed governor of New York.

Pownall's career in the New World was over almost before it began, when Sir Danvers committed suicide within a week of his arrival in New York. However, Pownall was not inclined to retreat to his insignificant position with the Board of Trade. He was determined to become an expert on the colonies by exploring them thoroughly. During the years 1754 and 1755, Pownall traveled through New England, the middle colonies, and down to Maryland and Virginia. In all these travels he managed to ingratiate himself with the leading men of each colony, including Governor Shirley of Massachusetts, Governor Sharpe of Maryland, and, most important of all, Benjamin Franklin, with whom a lasting relationship was forged.

Pownall had arrived in the colonies at an auspicious time. It was obvious to all that the conflict between Great Britain and France for the hegemony of North America was soon to climax. Pownall knew that the Board of Trade had resolved to call an intercolonial conference to discuss Indian and military affairs. In his travels he diligently prepared himself for participation in this conference. When the Albany Congress was held in 1754, Pownall delivered a paper in which he outlined a plan of defense for the colonies that relied upon British naval control of the Great Lakes.[2] However, for most of the Congress, he found himself more a student than a teacher. And the main lesson that he learned was that imperial regulation of land purchases and the fur trade was an absolute necessity for the healthy economic development of the colonies.

Immediately following the conclusion of the Albany Congress, Pownall drew up a plan for western settlement. Many of his ideas were later embodied in a similar proposal by Benjamin Franklin, which was drafted in 1756.[3] Both plans recommended the New England style of settlement in which the land was divided up into townships and sold in an orderly manner. Although the outbreak of the French and Indian War precluded any action on these plans, many of their features were incorporated in the postrevolutionary land laws of 1785 and 1787.

In 1755, Pownall was named lieutenant governor of New Jersey. However, he was hoping for a more important position and returned to England in February 1756. There he obtained the post of "secretary extraordinary" and advisor on civil affairs to Lord Loudoun, who had just been appointed commander in chief of the British forces in North America. Pownall preferred this position to the governorship of Pennsylvania, which was offered to him by the Penn family. His choice proved fortunate because his relationship with Loudoun led to a commission as governor of Massachusetts in 1757.

The position of wartime governor of Massachusetts was a delicate one. Pownall was repeatedly caught between the demands for men and supplies from the British military commanders and the reluctance of the Massachusetts legislature to vote him the necessary funds and powers. Although sensitive to military needs, Pownall always took the position that the rights and privileges of the legislature must be respected even in wartime. Apparently he was successful in pleasing all parties because when he resigned his governorship in 1760, he left with the promise of the governorship of South Carolina and the respect of most of the leading men in Massachusetts, including both Sam and John Adams. As John Adams wrote in 1774, "Mr. Pownall seems to have been a friend to liberty and to our constitution, and to have had an aversion to all plots against either."[4]

Pownall, however, had higher ambitions than the governorship of South Carolina. He felt that his rightful place was in London, helping to formulate policy for the entire empire. Knowing that this could not come about at least until the conclusion of the war, Pownall accepted a position as supply officer in Germany where he remained from 1761 to 1763. Even in Germany, his thoughts remained on colonial affairs and in 1764 he produced the first edition of a study that he entitled *Administration of the British Colonies.*[5] Succeeding editions, enlarged and revised to meet changing conditions, followed in the years between 1765 and 1777.

To capsulize what came to be two closely written volumes, Pownall finally recommended essentially the formation of a dominion form of government—albeit one almost completely dominated by the home country. As Pownall expressed it in the second edition, Great Britain should not be thought of merely "as the kingdom of this Isle only, with many appendages of provinces, colonies, settlements, and other extraneous parts, but as a grand marine dominion consisting of our possessions in the Atlantic, in America, united in one empire."[6]

As early as 1764, Pownall suggested the creation of a colonial department headed by a secretary of state, which would have sole and complete jurisdiction over all colonial affairs. One of the top priorities of the colonial department was to send a commission to the colonies to examine the political realities of colonial government and commerce in order to draw up a plan of government that would preserve colonial "rights and liberties" yet still keep them dependent "upon Great Britain as the center." Pownall felt that "an actual system of dominion" already existed and that it was only necessary to formalize it and to grant the colonists representation in Parliament as well as their local legislatures (though he gradually came to realize that neither the colonists nor the British government were willing to adopt this measure).[7]

Pownall also had many suggestions in regard to monetary, judicial, Indian, military, and mercantile affairs.[8] As indicated by his advice to Parliament to authorize a limited and regulated amount of paper money and to "enlarge the spirit of our commercial laws" to make the administration of Navigation Acts more flexible, Pownall was concerned with the welfare of the colonies as well as with the interests of the mother country. Pownall came to accept the distinction between internal and external taxation and hoped that the pre-1763 situation would return, in which Great Britain had avoided the former and the colonies had accepted the latter.[9] (An excise tax collected within the colonies fell into the category of an internal tax; customs duties on goods or products entering or leaving the colonies were deemed to be external taxes.) Yet in spite of the authorship of this work on colonial administration, or perhaps because of it, Pownall was never again appointed to any position in which he might have influence on colonial affairs. From 1767 to 1780, however, Pownall served in the House of Commons where, as we shall see later, he remained a friend of colonial interests.

The other Englishman in the 1760s who had the background to suggest a solution—albeit an even more radical one—to the controversy between Great Britain and its North American colonies was Josiah Tucker, an Anglican minister who served as dean of the cathedral of Gloucester. Tucker was born in Wales in 1713 and, although from modest background, obtained Bachelor of Arts, Master of Arts, and Doctor of Divinity degrees from Oxford.[10] Early in his career, Tucker exhibited a propensity for putting his ideas in print. His first publication (1742) attacked the tenets of Methodism. Three years later, the Jacobite Rebellion inspired Tucker to write a pamphlet defending the Hanoverian succession and warning of perils facing England if the Stuarts were to return to the throne. These publications were soon followed by many others on religion, education, and the naturalization of foreigners—a subject on which Tucker had, for that time, extremely liberal and unpopular views.

Many of Tucker's writings dealt with trade and commerce—an area in which he proved to be both knowledgeable and innovative. His main work on economics, *The Elements of Commerce and Theory of Taxes* (1755), anticipated, and may even have influenced, the thinking of the French physiocrats and Adam Smith.[11] Although he did not advocate free trade, Tucker did oppose commercial monopolies such as those of the East India Company. His economic studies probably led to his anti-imperialist stance. In his earliest economic publication, *An Essay on Trade,* which first appeared in 1749, Tucker was already predicting that colonies that realized they no longer needed the assistance of the mother country would soon seek their independence. But at this date, he still felt that colonies were potentially of great economic benefit to the mother country and that a firm but fair policy would retain their loyalty. However, further study convinced Tucker that colonies were unnecessary, or even an impediment, to a nation's prosperity and he objected to the Seven Years' War.

In 1763, Tucker advised Lord Shelburne that the West Indian islands acquired from France were not "worth the Costs both of Men and Money, which had been, and would be, bestowed on them."[12] In that same year, he wrote an antiwar essay entitled *The Case of Going to War for the Sake of Procuring, Enlarging or Securing of Trade, Considered in a New Light.* In it he attempted to prove that "Neither Princes nor People can be Gainers by the most successful wars: Trade in particular will make its Way to the Country where Goods are manufactured the best and cheapest:—But conquering Nations neither manufacture well nor cheap:—And consequently must sink in trade as they extend in Conquest."[13]

Tucker was an active leader in local Whig politics but he did not approve of his party's stand on the Stamp Act. In 1766, he published *A Letter from a Merchant in London to His Nephew in North America, Relative to the Present Posture of Affairs in the Colonies.* This pamphlet began by attempting to refute the American claim that Parliament had no right to levy an internal tax upon them because they were not represented in that body. Like so many other Englishmen, Tucker believed that the colonial legislatures were subordinate to Parliament and could only be compared with bodies such as London's common council. He also presented the standard case for virtual representation in Parliament, the doctrine that a member of Parliament represents the interests of the whole empire, not just the district that elected him. Tucker even claimed that Parliament had shown undue partiality toward the colonies by granting them a monopoly of the sale of tobacco in England and by paying overgenerous bounties to stimulate colonial production of hemp, silk, rice, indigo, and naval stores.[14]

Tucker next joined the chorus that tried to demolish the American complaints against the "excessiveness" and "unseasonableness" of the Stamp Tax by contrasting the Englishman's high tax burden and the relative prosperity, with the general freedom from taxation of the average American.[15] But from this point, Tucker's approach differed markedly from that of all other English writers on the Stamp Act crisis. Tucker claimed that American opposition to the Stamp duties was "a mere Sham and Pretense." He felt their basic objectives were: (1) a desire to escape all British regulation of their trade, (2) a desire to evade the payment of their debts to English merchants, and (3) a desire to be independent.

Thus, long before any American had written, spoken, or even dreamed of independence, Tucker told them that "you wish to be an Empire by itself, and to be no longer the Province of another. This Spirit is upper most; and this Principle is visible in all your Speeches, and all your Writings, even when you take some pains to disguise it."[16] But even more surprising was his advice to the British government. As Tucker viewed the situation, the government had three alternatives: (1) coercion, (2) procrastination, or (3) separation. Although he was absolutely certain that Great Britain had the power to coerce the colonies into obedience, Tucker opposed this course of action: "What Fruits are to result from making, you [the colonists] a conquered People?—Not an Increase in Trade; that is impossible: For a Shop-keeper will never get the more Custom by beating his Customers: and what is true of a Shop-keeper is true of a Shop-keeping nation."[17]

Nor could Tucker see any advantage to procrastination. He felt that the clash between the colonies and mother country was inevitable and the delay would only increase the strength of the colonies and make the eventual struggle "more obstinate and the Determination the more bloody."[18] This left only the third alternative—"cast them off, and . . . exclude them forever from the manifold Advantages and Profits of Trade, which they now enjoy by no other Title but that of being a part of the British Empire."

Tucker predicted that the dire consequence to the colonists of such a course would include damage to their entire economy, high taxation, Indian attacks, and even internecine warfare. He was certain that "Under all these Pressures and Calamities, [Americans] will certainly open their Eyes at last . . . they will curse their ambitious Leaders, and detest those Mock Patriots who involved them in so many Miseries. And having been surfeited with the bitter Fruits of American Republicanism, they will heartily wish, and petition to be again united to Mother Country."[19]

Events between 1766 and 1774 only confirmed Tucker's opinion that American independence was inevitable. In the latter year he reissued *The Case for Going to War* and *A Letter from a Merchant in London,* and added a new pamphlet, *The True Interest of Great Britain Set Forth in Regard to the Colonies.* In this latest work, Tucker reiterated much of what he had already written but somewhat softened his punitive attitude toward the colonies. By 1774, he had come to the conclusion that it was natural and proper for colonies "to aspire after Independence and to set up themselves as soon as ever they find that they are able to subsist, without being beholden to the Mother Country." Tucker felt that "the sovereignty of the Mother Country over her colonies" could no longer be effectively exercised because of the extensive political freedom it had allowed them and the removal of the "fear from a foreign enemy" resulting from the British conquest of Canada.[20]

In this pamphlet, he not only dismissed procrastination and conquest of the colonies as viable alternatives but also argued against two other "straw men" that he set up: allowing the colonies representation in Parliament and shifting the seat of empire from the Old to the New World.[21] By this time, Tucker was absolutely convinced that granting independence to the colonies, even supporting them militarily against any foreign attack, if necessary, would be definitely advantageous for the mother country. He was confident that the high prices they would still obtain in England for their raw materials and the cheapness of English manufactured goods would induce Americans to continue to trade with Great Britain. He was also confident that they could not be conquered by France or any other European power. In addition, he listed other possible benefits from American independence such as:

- stopping the migration of skilled workers to America, which had been impossible while they were still colonies;
- saving the costs of colonial civil and military administration;
- saving the costs of the bounties that had been paid to stimulate colonial production of raw materials;
- facilitating the collection of debts owed to British merchants because refusal to pay would no longer serve as an effective lever on Parliament;
- increasing the dependence of the West Indian colonies on the mother country;
- improving the status of the Anglican Church in America because it would no longer be handicapped by political ties with Great Britain; and even
- maintaining influence in North America as he expected the colonies to quarrel among themselves and appeal to Great Britain for support.

Tucker admitted that he saw little possibility of either the Tories' or the Whigs' accepting his advice but nevertheless felt that "right will prevail at last" and predicted that American independence was inevitable.[22]

The *True Interest of Great Britain* had been printed in a volume entitled *Four Tracts and Two Sermons,* but early in 1775 Tucker felt that still another pamphlet was necessary to explain his views. This *Tract V* was subtitled *Respective Pleas and Arguments of the Mother Country and of the Colonies, Distinctly Set Forth.* Interestingly enough, it began with a dedicatory epistle, one-third the length of the *Tract* proper, addressed to the members of the Continental Congress whom Tucker thanked for helping to prove him right because he viewed their gathering as proclaiming "that you renounce all Subjection whatever to the Legislature of the Parent-State."[23] The dedication then chided the Americans for not granting the same freedoms they desired to their slaves or to the Indians, and for continuing to demand all the privileges of British citizenship for themselves without willingness to assume any of its burdens. Next, it warned members of Congress not to expect the French Catholics of Canada to join their revolution (although Tucker expected that Canada, too, would ultimately demand its independence) and not to ignore the many problems being faced by the Swiss Confederation, which Americans seemed to be taking as their model. Finally, the dedication concluded by expressing the hope that after independence America would "behave better and more justly" toward Great Britain.[24]

The *Tract*'s main aim was to prove that the claims of the mother country and its colonies were so contradictory and so mutually exclusive that "any Scheme for a Compromise is absolutely impracticable."[25] His entire argument was based on the opposing views of the power of Parliament over the colonies. Unlike Pownall, Tucker was unable to accept the concept of divisible sovereignty: "In all Societies there must be a dernier Resort and *Ne plus ultra* of ruling power. . . . Here in Great Britain it is King, Lords and Commons, when in Parliament assembled." By Great Britain, he meant Scotland, Ireland, and all the colonies whether they had local legislatures or not. According to this line of reasoning, Parliament had always, and still possessed, unlimited authority throughout the British empire.[26]

Tucker next presented the colonial view of the powers of Parliament as expressed in a Declaration of Rights passed by the Continental Congress itself in October 1774. He included all ten of the resolutions contained in that Declaration but the most relevant to his argument was the fourth, which stated

> That the foundation of English liberty, and of all free Government, is a Right in the People to participate in their Legislative Council: And as the English Colonists are not represented and from their local and other circumstances cannot properly be represented in the British Parliament, they are entitled to a free and exclusive Power of Legislatures, where their Right of Representation can alone be preserved, in all Cases of Taxation and internal Polity, subject only to the Negative of their Sovereign, in such a Manner as has been heretofore used and accustomed: but from the necessity of the case, and a regard to the mutual interests of both countries, we cheerfully consent to the Operation of such Acts of the British Parliament as are *bonafide* restrained to the Regulation of our external Commerce, for the Purpose of securing the commercial Advantages of the whole Empire to the Mother Country, and the commercial Benefits of its respective Members, excluding every idea of Taxation internal or external, for raising a Revenue on the Subjects in America without their consent.[27]

In the remainder of the *Tract,* Tucker reiterated his main thesis that the English and American views "hold no Grounds for a Compromise," declaring that "the Parent-State grounds her present claim of Authority and Jurisdiction over the colonies on Facts and Precedents . . . the colonists, who are all the Disciples of Mr. Locke, have Recourse to what they call immutable Truths—the abstract Reasonings, and eternal Fitness of Things,—and in short to such Rights of

Human Nature which they suppose to be unalienable and indefeasible."[28]

Tucker had no illusions that the Americans would be satisfied with, or obey, parliamentary regulation of its trade. He quoted Benjamin Franklin to prove that Parliament's authority must be recognized completely or not at all. As Tucker saw it, the colonies would not recognize the power of Parliament, therefore Great Britain's choice was simple: "Quarrel perpetually—or to separate peacefully. Surrender the disobedient Colonies entirely up . . . Or to become their Tributaries and Vassals?"[29] Tucker was not a man to equivocate!

Although Fred Hinkhouse, in his survey of the reaction of the British press to the events leading to the American Revolution, quotes a few articles favorable to his views, Tucker was well aware that they were anathema to the party in power, its opponents, and the public in general. Nevertheless, as we shall see later in this volume, he persisted in his efforts.[30]

Combine the ideas of Pownall and Tucker, mix well, and you have *American Independence the Interest and Glory of Great Britain* written by John Cartwright. Cartwright, more famous for his lifelong battle for parliamentary reform, was born in 1740.[31] He joined the navy at the age of eighteen and was on inactive duty in London at the time of the Boston Tea Party. The passage of the Coercive Acts (see chapter 6) and the publication of Tucker's *True Interest of Britain* impelled him to propose a solution to the problem of Anglo-American relations. *American Independence* appeared originally as a series of ten anonymous letters addressed to Parliament from March 20 to April 14, 1774.

Cartwright began his first *Letter* by stating that his aim was to "establish a principle of lasting union between our colonies and the mother country" and to avoid the "mutual jealousy, animosity, and strife" that would result from the ministerial policy.[32] He then posed two questions: Does the British Parliament have sovereignty over America and does it have a right to tax the colonists? With a brief review of English constitutionalism culminating with Locke's emphasis on life, liberty, and property, Cartwright emphatically answered the second question in the negative. Obviously, Parliament had no right to tax (take away the property of) colonists who were not represented in it, were too far away from England to send representatives, and, even if they did, would be too few to protect colonial interests.[33]

In the second *Letter,* Cartwright tackled the thornier question of parliamentary sovereignty over the colonies. But here, too, he was adamant: "Parliament hath not the rights of sovereignty over his Majesty's American subjects." He reached this unorthodox conclusion because he claimed that sovereignty lies in the people and the Americans had established governments of their own, which made them "no longer dependent colonies; they are independent states."[34]

In the third *Letter,* Cartwright explained that if Parliament renounced its sovereignty over the colonies, they would voluntarily join with the mother country in a "family union" and pay their fair share of imperial expenses.[35] If not, Great Britain would be "an over-grown empire" and must eventually "fall to pieces."[36]

In the fourth *Letter,* Cartwright again dismissed the possibility of American representation in Parliament and answered the charge of American ingratitude by pointing out how the colonies had benefited British commerce and industry.[37] He reiterated that colonies were entitled to their independence "whenever they shall think proper to demand it." He did not disapprove, however, if conditions such as were found in the West Indies made it expedient for these colonists to accept parliamentary sovereignty voluntarily.[38]

The fifth *Letter* repeated Cartwright's hope for an Anglo-American union before our minister could "pull down upon our devoted heads the mighty ruins of an over-grown empire."[39] He reminded his readers of the bloody demise of ancient empires but felt Great Britain could avoid their fate because of its "perfect constitution." Nor did he fear that a rising American empire would threaten Great Britain; on the contrary, they would strengthen each other.[40]

The sixth *Letter* offered Britons only two choices: "relinquish at once our claims to sovereignty, or fix on their [the Americans] neck with strong hand the galling yoke of slavery"; no middle course was possible. Cartwright predicted that the second choice "must finally be ineffectual" and end in attacks on Great Britain by its European rivals.[41] In this *Letter,* Cartwright made his first reference to Dean Tucker's writings. Though he differed strongly with Tucker on the concept of parliamentary sovereignty, Cartwright heartily agreed that America must be independent.[42]

Letters seven, eight, and nine consist of a detailed refutation of Tucker's political assumptions with copious quotations from his works. He concurred with Tucker that the economic maturity of the colonies made their independence inevitable and that economic ties between the two nations would remain firm. However, he disagreed with Tucker on the question of complete independence, identifying closely with Pownall in advocating a dominion-like arrangement. He lastly complimented Tucker for stumbling on the correct solution to the American problem, even though for the wrong reasons.[43]

In the tenth *Letter,* Cartwright suggested the text of a parliamentary act, which would state that the colonies "are all held and declared to be free and independent states." Another clause of the act would provide that Parliament and the colonial legislatures would sign a treaty

> in order that a firm brotherly and perpetual league may be concluded between Great Britain and them for their mutual commercial benefit, and their joint security against all other kingdoms and states, as well as for the preservation of the warm affection and harmony which ought ever to subsist between a mother country and her offspring.[44]

The tie binding the two countries together was to be the king, "the father of the three millions of happy subjects instead of reigning joint tyrant over so many discontented slaves, or losing by revolt so many of his people."[45] Cartwright painted a glowing picture of a prosperous Anglo-American union as opposed to a ramshackle empire wracked by internal dissension and foreign wars. He concluded his *Letter* with the warning: Americans "must either be our deadly foes, or our steadfast friends.—Great Britain, take thy choice!"[46]

These ten *Letters* were reprinted in pamphlet form, which was distributed to all members of Parliament. A second edition appeared in 1775 with two additional *Letters* (in which he summarized the arguments and conclusions of his original pamphlet) and a lengthy *Postscript*.[47]

Cartwright noted that he had been termed "a traitorous fomentor of rebellion" but predicted that his proposal for American independence would soon prove to be in the best interests of Great Britain.[48] After he recapitulated his rationale for American independence, Cartwright concluded his *Postscript* with a detailed draft of a bill to grant American independence and to form "The Great British League and Confederacy." His plan was for Britain to ally itself with eighteen independent American states and remain in complete control of foreign and military policy.[49] He, like Pownall, envisioned an orderly process of American westward settlement, with new independent states being formed and joining the Confederacy as soon as they reached a population of fifty thousand. Ultimately, he foresaw a total of at least thirty-six states extending all the way to the Mississippi River.[50] Cartwright was so sure of the soundness of his proposals that he concluded by expressing his willingness to approach the king, alone if necessary, and "to propose them in the most earnest manner; content should they be found to fail or even to fall short . . . to be branded as a traitor."[51]

In his *Postscript,* Cartwright had differed with Lord Chatham (Pitt) because of the latter's insistence upon parliamentary sovereignty over America and referred in passing to Burke's speech on American taxation.[52] Cartwright was so dismayed by this speech that he felt it necessary to address a separate *Letter* to Burke to refute his argument that Parliament had the right (though it should not exercise it) to tax the colonies. It was Cartwright's admiration for Burke's abilities and eloquence that impelled this attempt to convert Burke to his views. He denied Burke's contention that a constitution of the British empire existed or that Parliament had any sovereignty over America. Cartwright declared, "where *there is no such participation* [in Parliament] *no subjection is due*" and Americans were not, and could not be, represented in Parliament. The Declaratory Act was, therefore, unjustified and certainly in 1775 "a flight of madness not to be accounted for."[53] (See chapter 3.)

Cartwright compared America to a youthful apprentice who probably would have eventually expected a partnership (albeit a junior one) but who might, because of ill-usage, be provoked into setting up a completely different establishment. He felt that America had not as yet reached this stage and never would if Parliament accepted his proposals. The alternative (and this was written before news of Lexington and Concord reached Great Britain) was war in which Great Britain would "wade up to the eyes in blood" and "finally terminate in the independence of America." He castigated Burke, when his speech was published, for not omitting "all erroneous, fallacious and fatal doctrines" such as the concept of an "imperial parliament with boundless powers." He challenged Burke to "lay aside every party prejudice" and fight for the true interests of America.[54] Cartwright ended his missive to Burke with a lyrical comparison of a young man (Great Britain) gently wooing a damsel (America) who would become his lovely wife and partner and hoped that Burke would "merit and attain the name of patriot" by his efforts to bring this "marriage" to fruition.[55]

Parliament, as might be expected, paid as little attention to Cartwright as it did to Tucker or Pownall. As he had pledged in his *Postscript,* Cartwright turned to the king and, in 1777, Cartwright presented him an address containing the proposal for an imperial union. He hoped that George III might be "wise enough and good enough to pay attention to it" as it could lead to "happiness and peace."[56] Unfortunately, the king paid no more attention to it than did the members of Parliament. Cartwright remained consistent to his principles. In 1775, he was appointed a major of the Nottinghamshire militia in which he served faithfully for seventeen years. However, in the following year, when Admiral Lord Howe requested him to be one of his lieutenants for the American campaign, Cartwright, despite his love for the navy and the opportunity for rapid promotion, reluctantly refused. His reason, as he wrote Lord Howe, "thinking as I do on the most unhappy contest between this kingdom and her colonies, it would be a desertion from my principles . . . were I to put myself in a situation that might probably cause me to act a hostile part against them."[57] Moreover, Cartwright, when invited to enter the naval service of the United States, refused on the grounds that "nothing could absolve a man from the duty he owed his own country."[58] John Cartwright spent the remainder of his long and productive life doing his duty to his country by spearheading the cause of parliamentary reform.

Notes

1. The major sources on Pownall's life include John A. Schultz's *Thomas Pownall—British Defender of American Liberty* and the older Charles A.W. Pownall volume, *Thomas Pownall.*

2. Thomas Pownall, *The Administration of the British Colonies,* 5th ed., contains the full text of this proposal. Hereafter referred to as *Administration of Colonies.*

3. Albert H. Smyth, ed., *The Writings of Benjamin Franklin,* III, pp. 358–366.

4. Charles Francis Adams, ed., *The Works of John Adams,* IV, p. 21. Adams still wrote effusively about Pownall in 1817. See vol. X, pp. 241–243.

5. T. Pownall, *Administration of Colonies,* I, p. 10. A more detailed analysis of this work may be found in G.H. Guttridge's article in the *William and Mary Quarterly,* 3d ser., XXVI (January 1969): 31–46, and the chapter by John Shy, "Thomas Pownall, Henry Ellis, and the Spectrum of Possibilities, 1763–1775" in *Anglo-American Political Relations, 1675–1775,* ed. A.G. Olson and R.M. Brown, pp. 155–186.

6. T. Pownall, *Administration of Colonies,* I, p. 40.

7. Ibid., p. 166.

8. Ibid., p. 252.

9. Ibid., II, pp. 64–69.

10. The best modern sources for Tucker's life and thought are Robert Livingstone Schuyler, ed., *Josiah Tucker: A Selection from His Economic and Political Writings,* and Walter E. Clark, *Josiah Tucker: Economist.*

11. Schuyler, *Josiah Tucker,* pp. 11–17.

12. Josiah Tucker, *Four Letters on important National Subjects; Addressed to the Right Honorable the Earl of Shelburne,* p. 2.

13. Josiah Tucker, *Four Tracts on Political and Commercial Subjects,* 2d ed., p. 96.

14. Ibid., pp. 103–121.

15. Ibid., pp. 122–131.

16. Ibid., pp. 131–136.

17. Ibid., pp. 138–141.

18. Ibid., pp. 141–143.

19. Ibid., pp. 143–149.

20. Ibid., pp. 159–161.

21. Ibid., pp. 164–202.

22. Ibid., pp. 202–224.

23. Josiah Tucker, *The Respective Pleas and Arguments of the Mother Country and of the Colonies, Distinctly Set Forth: and the Impossibility of a Compromise of Differences or a Mutual Concession of Rights Plainly Demonstrated,* pp. iii-iv.

24. Ibid., pp. iv-xvi.

25. Ibid., p. 10.

26. Ibid., pp. 12–32.

27. Ibid., pp. 33–37.

28. Ibid., pp. 38–39.

29. Ibid., pp. 41–48.

30. Fred Junkin Hinkhouse, *The Preliminaries of the American Revolution as Seen in the English Press, 1763–1775,* pp. 114–115.

31. The best modern treatment of Cartwright is John W. Osborne, *John Cartwright.* An older work is F.D. Cartwright, ed., *The Life and Correspondence of Major Cartwright,* 2 vols.

32. John Cartwright, *American Independence the Interest and Glory of Great Britain,* pp. 1–2.

33. Ibid., pp. 2–5.

34. Ibid., pp. 6–9.

35. Ibid., p. 13.

36. Ibid., p. 15.

37. Ibid., pp. 19–20.

38. Ibid., pp. 21–24.

39. Ibid., p. 26.

40. Ibid., pp. 27–29.

41. Ibid., pp. 30–31.

42. Ibid., pp. 32–34.

43. Ibid., pp. 38–57.

44. Ibid., p. 63.

45. Ibid., p. 64.

46. Ibid., pp. 65–68.

47. Ibid., appendix, pp. 9–14.

48. Ibid., postscript, p. 10.

49. Ibid., pp. 35–42.

50. Ibid., pp. 42–48.

51. Ibid., pp. 50–51.

52. Ibid., pp. 25–30.

53. John Cartwright, *A Letter to Edmund Burke, Esq. Controverting the principals of American Government laid down in the lately published Speech on American Taxation Delivered in the House of Commons on the 19th of April, 1774,* pp. 5–6, 9, 10–11, 15.

54. Ibid., pp.15–17, 20–25.

55. Ibid., pp. 26–31.

56. F.D. Cartwright, Major Cartwright, I, p. 101.

57. Ibid., p. 75.

58. Ibid., pp. 80–81.

Pitt, Burke, and American Policy, 1763–1770

Whig domination under the first two Georges was made possible because the kings played a relatively passive role in government and placed their substantial patronage resources at the disposal of their chief minister. In practice, this meant that the "Court and Treasury" members of Parliament (or King's Friends or Placemen, as they came to be called), who gave their loyalty to the king out of respect, gratitude, or hope for appointments, pensions, or other sinecures, could be counted on to support the government in power unless the king indicated otherwise. This group occupied about one-third of the seats in the House of Commons, outnumbered only by the Independents who controlled about one-half the seats. The Independents, predominantly country gentlemen, also tended to support the government in power unless it adversely affected their own interests, or its policies were obviously bankrupt. All this changed with the accession of George III to the throne in 1760. He reversed the policy of his predecessors and determined to free himself from Whig influence and to play a much more active role in governmental affairs. This resulted in the end of the era of Whig supremacy and (unintentionally) ushered in a decade of political instability, during which relations between Great Britain and the Thirteen Colonies deteriorated to such an extent that compromise became virtually impossible for either party in spite of all the efforts of our "friends."

King George III made his first foray into politics in 1761, when he forced the resignation of William Pitt, the architect of British victory in the Seven Years' War, and replaced him as chief minister in the following year with his favorite, Lord Bute. Because of Bute's unpopularity, this experiment failed in less than a year and the king reluctantly accepted Bute's suggestion that George Grenville, whom Bute thought he could control, be made head of the government.

By this time, the war had come to a conclusion and British politicians realized that the conquest of Canada, Florida, and the Ohio Valley required an end to the policy of "salutary neglect." Pontiac's Uprising of 1763 only reemphasized the need for new guidelines regarding westward settlement, the regulation of the fur trade, the stationing of military and naval forces in America, and the modification of the acts of trade so that they not only increased benefits for the home country but produced a revenue to support the expenses entailed in defending the colonies against Indian attack. This last element was particularly crucial because English landowners were already objecting to the escalation of the national debt during the war and the attendant weight of their tax burden.

Grenville attacked all these problems with dispatch. The Proclamation of 1763 temporarily limited settlement to the area east of the Appalachians and placed numerous restrictions on the fur trade. An army of ten thousand was stationed on the frontier and a naval squadron in Halifax (soon also to be a site of a vice-admiralty court); and the customs service was enlarged and reinvigorated. Then, in 1764, Grenville proposed the Sugar Act, which was designed not only to curtail colonial smuggling but to raise a revenue "for defraying the Expences of defending, protecting, and securing the said [American] colonies."[1] The Sugar Act raised the tax on sugar, placed duties on various European products that had not previously been taxed, and reduced the prohibitive 1763 six-pence-a-gallon tax on foreign molasses to three pence but made it clear that it would now be enforced. The bill sailed through Parliament with only one member, William Beckford, a Jamaican merchant, questioning whether colonial rights were being infringed upon, but he ultimately voted for the bill. Even the agents of the North American colonies only fought unsuccessfully for the reduction of the molasses tax to two pence (only two years later, however, it was lowered to one penny). Though the Sugar Act was blamed in America for the (actually postwar) depression that struck the northern colonies in 1764 and evoked challenges to Parliament's right to raise a revenue by means of an act of trade, attention in both England and America was soon diverted to a more serious crisis.

Grenville's second attempt to raise an American revenue was through the passage of a Stamp Act. Stamp duties had been in effect in England continuously since the reign of William III and had been suggested for America numerous times (most recently during the Seven Years' War) before Grenville proposed it in 1764. The vehemence of colonial protest against such a tax confirmed Grenville's view of the necessity of passing a Stamp Act bill. It was no longer only a matter of raising a revenue; it was now a test of

Parliament's authority to levy a tax, even an internal tax, on its colonies.

During the opening debate on the measure, twelve members of the House of Commons spoke against the Stamp Act but most of them opposed it only on the grounds of political inexpediency. Even Colonel Isaac Barré, the most eloquent, pro-American speaker at this session, who referred to the colonists as "Sons of Liberty," hinted perhaps but never explicitly denied Parliament's right to levy an internal tax on the colonists. Only Beckford (by one account of the debate) made this accusation. The vote of 245 to 49 in favor of the bill discouraged its opponents, and the Stamp Act became law in March 1765 with little further resistance.[2]

In May of that same year, Parliament passed a Mutiny, or Quartering, Act, which dealt with the billeting of troops stationed in America. Originally, the bill allowed the quartering of soldiers in private homes if they could not be accommodated in barracks or public houses. However, the colonial agents, with the assistance of Governor Pownall (and King George), were able to convince Grenville to avoid a political battle and have soldiers billeted in uninhabited houses, barns, or other buildings rather than in private homes. The colonists were required, however, to provide these troops with "fire, candles, vinegar and salt, bedding, utensils for dressing their victuals, and small beer, cider, or rum."[3] This obligation was to become a major colonial grievance particularly in New York, the headquarters of the British army in America.

Two months later, the king dismissed Grenville for reasons completely unrelated to his American policy and replaced him with the marquis of Rockingham, the leader of another Whig faction. At first glance, the change of administration did not suggest any change in British policy toward America. The Rockingham Whigs had not actively opposed the passage of the Stamp Act, but the fact that they were not responsible for it became critical when the storm of colonial opposition burst. This opposition took place on several levels: colonial assemblies voted protests, and the Stamp Act Congress of October 1765 drew up a dignified "Declaration" and sent petitions to the king, the House of Lords, and the House of Commons. In the meantime, well-organized "mobs" had used force, or the threat of force, so effectively that by November 1765 no stamp master (the official in charge of distributing the stamps) remained on duty in any colony. And finally, the colonists organized a boycott of English goods, which was so effective that English merchants and manufacturers suffered severe losses. Their ensuing lobbying and petitioning efforts persuaded the Rockingham ministry to either suspend, modify, or repeal the Stamp Act. He ultimately chose repeal, but, unfortunately as it turned out, linked it to a declaration of Parliament's unlimited control over the colonies. That Rockingham was

...ament to repeal the Stamp Act owes much to the ...grizzled veteran, William Pitt, and a new recruit,

...ps the best description of William Pitt, the Elder. ...he assumed a family-controlled seat in the House of Commons in 1735, where he helped bring about Walpole's downfall. In 1746, he received his first office and proved to be an able and—a rarity—honest paymaster general. He was in and out of various offices between 1751 and 1757, until popular support (unusual for that period) and the government's mismanagement of the Seven Years' War put him in control of the government. During the next four years, he masterminded British victories all over the world and became "the Great Commoner," a popular hero in England and throughout the English-speaking world. As already noted, he was forced out of power in 1761 and, although he remained an icon of the Whigs, his actions became ever more eccentric and unpredictable. The gout that plagued him since his youth became almost unbearable and Pitt was absent from Parliament all during 1765.

But he was present and at his most eloquent on January 14, 1766, when the fate of the Stamp Act was discussed. After Grenville called for its enforcement, Pitt responded that "every capital measure they [Greenville's ministry] have taken, has been entirely wrong!" Though agreeing that Parliament was "sovereign and supreme [over the colonies], in every circumstance of government and legislation whatsoever," he insisted that "Taxation is no part of the governing or legislative power." As to the doctrine of virtual representation, Pitt described it as "the most contemptible idea that was entered into the head of a man." Declaring "I rejoice that America has resisted," he concluded with the demand that

> the Stamp Act be *repealed absolutely, totally and immediately*. That the reason for appeal be assigned, because it was founded on an erroneous principle. At the same time let the sovereign authority of this country over the colonies, be asserted in as strong terms as can be devised, and be made to extend to every point of legislation whatsoever. That we may bind their *trade*, confine their *manufactures*, and exercise every *power* whatsoever, except that of taking their money out of their pockets without their consent![4]
> [italics in original]

As soon as news of Pitt's January 14 speech reached John Adams, he noted in his diary that Pitt must be considered the "genius and guardian angel of Britain and British America."[5]

Three days later, Edmund Burke made his maiden speech in Parliament. Born in Ireland in 1721, Burke moved to England in 1750 to study law but found journalism more congenial. In 1765, he became private secretary to Rockingham and, later that same year, was rewarded with a seat in the House of Commons. As he himself related, he began his maiden speech haltingly but when Grenville challenged him, he then "spoke some minutes poorly, but not quite as ill as before."[6]

On January 27, the petition of the Stamp Act Congress was presented to the House of Commons. The ministry was split on the question because the Congress was considered an illegal body and it had denied Parliament's right to tax the colonies, but Pitt had no such qualms. He agreed with American theories of taxation, felt the Stamp Act Congress was as innocuous as a London club, and described its petition as "innocent, dutiful, and respectful." Burke supported him but the Rockingham administration utilized a technical procedure to prevent a vote on the question lest it be embarrassed.[7] On February 3, a new resolution was brought to the floor by the ministry. It was a statement declaring that Parliament "had, hath, and of right ought to have, full power and authority to make laws and statutes, of sufficient force and validity, to bind the colonies and people of America, subject to the crown of Great Britain in all cases whatsoever."[8] Rockingham felt that such an affirmation was necessary if he were to secure enough votes to repeal the Stamp Act. He had deliberately adopted Pitt's phraseology, hoping that Pitt and his followers would assume that taxation was not included and support it.

Burke supported the declaration in a subtle speech in which he made a distinction between an "active" constitutional right and a "sleeping" right, giving as an example the king's right to veto an act of Parliament that he no longer exercised. He implied that, as far as taxation was concerned, the Declaratory Act would fall into this latter category.[9] Pitt, however, was not impressed by this circumlocution. He demanded the words "in all cases whatsoever" be omitted to make clear that taxation was not included in the declaration. Pitt concluded his remarks with these prophetic remarks:

> Bind them with the golden cords of equity and moderation. Cords of iron will never hold them. If you have this [declaratory] resolution like an eagle hanging over them I believe they will never go to rest. Lenity, humanity, magnanimity. They held the world by more than their legions.[10]

Unfortunately Pitt's warning was not heeded. The Declaratory Act passed with the understanding that it included the right to tax the colonies. But the repeal of the Stamp Act was still not assured. On February 5, Grenville's followers attempted delaying tactics but when Pitt and Burke led the opposition, Grenville himself gave the order to retreat in order to

xt battle, which took place on February 7, when he
n to enforce the Stamp Act.[11] Burke responded that
ᵤuid be a disaster for both the colonies and Great Britain.
ᵣₑdicted that if the motion passed, "the streets of Boston, Philadelphia, and New York should run with blood."[12] The futility of attempting
to enforce the Stamp Act was obvious and Grenville's motion was defeated 274 to 234.

With enforcement no longer a possibility, the Grenvillites next attempted
to secure a modification rather than a repeal of the Stamp Act. The ministry
countered with a barrage of witnesses (including Benjamin Franklin) who
testified that the economic suffering in Great Britain caused by the American boycott could only be alleviated by a complete repeal. On February 21,
the decisive debate was held. Grenville asked for a postponement but Pitt
objected and the session continued. Burke was unambiguous: "The system
of government with respect to the plantations effectually excludes taxation.
[Through] the monopoly of their trade . . . we get all that we can have from
the plantations."[13]

Pitt reiterated Burke's point that the British economy benefited far
more from the Navigation Acts than it ever could from American taxation.
Otherwise he was much more conciliatory than usual. He explicitly announced that he did "not blame the first proposers of this [Stamp Act] Bill.
He applauds the intention. But if there has been error, the next merit after
error is a timely and dignified retreat." He expressed the hope that repeal
would cause America to "subside not only into peace but into perfect
harmony, duty and gratitude." But if not, and America continued to deny
the lawful authority of Parliament, Pitt promised to "give his vote for
employing the last ship and the last man in this country to force them to
perfect obedience."[14]

At about 2:00 A.M., the exhausted members of the House voted to repeal
the Stamp Act by a vote of 275 to 167. Most reports of the session agreed
that Burke's remarks were the highpoint of the debate. Pitt himself paid
tribute to Burke and is reported to have said that Burke spoke "with a Degree
of precision which he believed was never before heard in this house."[15] But
as usual, Pitt was the popular hero. Applause greeted him as he left the
House of Commons and a crowd followed him through the streets. (In contrast, Grenville was greeted with a chorus of hisses.) The March 18 issue of
the *London Chronicle* contained an effusive tribute to Pitt:

> Englishmen, Scottishmen, Irishmen, Colonists, Brethren. Rejoice in the wisdom
> of *one* man, which hath saved you from civil war and your enemies! Erect a
> Statue to that Man in the Metropolis of your dominions! Place a garland of oak
> leaves on the Pedestal, and grave on it Concord.[16][italics in original]

A few months later, Pitt received a letter from the Massachusetts assembly informing him that he had received a vote of thanks for "your noble and generous efforts in support of the common rights of mankind, and liberties of Great Britain and her colonies."[17] And not to be outdone, South Carolina erected a statue in his honor.

The Rockingham ministry did not have much time to celebrate its victory. The king had never been enthusiastic about Rockingham personally or about complete repeal of the Stamp Act. He may also have been impressed by a speech made by Pitt in April 1766, in which he expressed the hope for "such a ministry as the King himself should choose, the people approve, and who should be eminent above others for their ability and integrity,"[18] in other words a blue-ribbon coalition cabinet. In any case, after some hesitation in July, the king allowed Pitt to form a ministry with the duke of Grafton as its titular head, and Pitt himself was elevated to the House of Lords as the earl of Chatham. Upon accepting Pitt as his chief minister, George III wrote him expressing the royal agreement with his aim of "destroying all party distinctions."[19] Instead of a "model," however, the new cabinet proved to be a disaster. Burke was obviously disgruntled when he described it as a "diversified mosaic," a composite of "patriots and courtiers; king's friends and republicans; whigs and tories; treacherous friends and open enemies," but he was not too far off the mark.[20] Burke, himself, might have been in the cabinet as the duke of Grafton considered him "the readiest man upon all points perhaps in the whole House."[21] Burke, however, chose to remain with the Rockinghamites. But Pitt's acceptance of a title was his most serious error. First, it severely damaged his popularity because the general public suspected that the king had coopted him by the offer of a title. Second, his absence from the House of Commons, the basic area of political activity, left his ministry leaderless, contentious, and ineffectual. And most tragic of all, his longstanding physical problems were complicated before the end of 1766 by a mental breakdown, which resulted in an absence from Parliament of over two years.

His absence was severely felt when the assembly of New York refused to obey the Mutiny Act of 1765. Pitt, who was in Bath at the time, never committed himself to any definite course of action. He did, however, write to Shelburne, the secretary of state in charge of American affairs, that "the stamp act ... has frightened those irritable and umbrageous people [New Yorkers] quite out of their senses. I foresee that, determined not to listen to their *real* friends, a little more frenzy and a little more time will put them into the hands of their enemies"[22] [italics in original]. The cabinet proposed all types of punishments (including billeting troops in private homes) but the final decision was to refuse to approve any legislation passed by the

New York assembly.[23] Edmund Burke opposed this measure, calling it "another proof . . . of that confusion of Ideas and imbecility of Counsel . . . of the present administration" and, in itself, "violent; unjust; and ineffective."[24]

Thomas Pownall, making his first speech as a member of Parliament, declared that the Mutiny Act itself was faulty and that the attempt to punish the New York assembly was impracticable because Americans viewed the requirement of furnishing supplies to the soldiers as an internal tax to which they "universally, unitedly, and unalterably . . . resolved not to submit." He concluded his remarks with the hope that Great Britain would return to its older policy of allowing colonial assemblies to determine how to quarter troops and hinted at the necessity of eventually adopting his favorite scheme of "political union" between Great Britain and the colonies.[25] The opposition to the measure was disunited, however; the proposal became law in July and was to take effect on October 1, 1767. Ironically, it immediately became superfluous, because in June the New York assembly had capitulated and voted the necessary funds to meet the requirements of the Mutiny Act.

Now that the Mutiny Act problem was settled, the British government resumed its efforts to solve the basic dilemma: How much and in what form were the colonies to contribute to the over £400,000 cost of their defense? In January 1767, Charles Townshend, the Chancellor of the Exchequer, announced that he had plans to raise a revenue for this purpose, "which would not be heavy in any manner upon the people in the colonies."[26] On February 18, he was more specific. Although not accepting the colonial distinction between internal and external taxes, he expressed willingness to "indulge" them and therefore recommended the levying of duties on certain items (eventually on lead, paper, paints, silk, glass, and tea) imported into the colonies. By May, however, Townshend changed his mind on the purpose of the revenue, now reviving a plan he had been considering for many years to pay the salaries of the governors, judges, and other royal officials in the colonies rather than to support the army.[27]

Burke spoke against these new American duties, predicting that they would "unsettle America" and have an adverse effect on its commerce.[28] However, he found almost no support in Parliament, in his own party, or even among the colonial agents. The Townshend Acts were passed in July 1767; Townshend, himself, passed away suddenly in September of the same year just as news of his enactments reached America. American reaction to the Acts was gradual but firm. John Dickinson, a well-trained lawyer, wrote twelve *Letters from a Farmer in Pennsylvania to the Inhabitants of the British Colonies,* which argued that Parliament had no right to levy any type of tax on the colonies. The Massachusetts assembly followed with a circular letter to the other colonies, urging united opposition to the Townshend Acts (an act for which the governor later dissolved it). The Massachusetts assembly also sent a letter to the earl of Chatham, thanking him for his past support and imploring him to use his influence to repeal the Townshend duties.[29] And once again nonimportation of British goods was employed to convince Parliament that the Acts should be repealed.

Early in 1769, Burke composed a pamphlet, *Observations on the Late State of a Nation* (in response to a tract that championed Grenville's policies), in which he defended the record of the Rockingham ministry and attempted to convince the public of the necessity of the repeal of the Townshend Acts by reminding them that the colonies suffered under a double monopoly: "1. a monopoly of their whole import, which is to be altogether from Great Britain; 2. a monopoly of all their export, which is to be nowhere but Great Britain as far as it can serve any purpose here." How then, he queried, can they become "a just object of revenue?"[30]

Thomas Pownall made a motion to repeal the Townshend Acts on April 19, 1769, arguing that the duties were damaging the British economy rather than raising a revenue in the colonies.[31] Burke agreed, although he felt that repeal had to be delayed to the next session of Parliament.[32]

Although no action was taken on the motion at the time, in May the ministry agreed to repeal all the duties except (fatally) the tax on tea, which was to be retained as a symbol of parliamentary supremacy. It was March 5, 1770, before this motion was brought before Parliament. During the intervening ten months, a crucial change had occurred on the political scene: Lord North had recently replaced Grafton as chief minister. After ten years of experimentation, King George III found a man who accepted him as more than the titular ruler of the nation. From 1770 until 1782, the king essentially dictated governmental policy—particularly in regard to America. Fortunately for him, North was an experienced politician, most recently serving as Chancellor of the Exchequer, and an able manager of the House of Commons, who with the support of the "king's friends" and Independent members, was easily able (even though Chatham returned to Parliament) to defeat a disunited and dispirited opposition.

The continuing debate on the Acts focused on the question of whether the duty on tea should also be repealed. Pownall and others advocated this addition, but the government defeated them by a vote of 204 to 142.[33] Burke reacted to this defeat by proposing, on May 9, 1770, a series of resolutions censuring the present government and its predecessor for their mismanagement of American affairs between 1767 and 1770. He described their policies as "a continuous series of such Madness, inconsistency, folly, Negligence as has no parallel in any time."[34] But once again, the ministry prevailed. Nevertheless, the repeal of all but one of the Townshend duties defused the tension between the mother country and the Thirteen Colonies, and until the passage of the Tea Act of 1773, relations between the two were relatively peaceful.

Earlier in 1769, when the Mutiny Act of 1765 came up for review, the threat of billeting in private homes again arose. Pownall led the attack against this proposal, repeating the arguments he had advanced two years earlier. This time he was successful in convincing the House of Commons to accept two amendments to the bill: the Mutiny Act would not be in effect in the colonies that passed laws to provide for the troops (though they had to agree to having these laws approved by the Privy Council) or where the British commanding officer and local officials could come to terms on mutually agreeable accommodations.[35] Though disappointed in the clause requiring Privy Council approval, the American colonial agents agreed that the new act strengthened the hand of colonial legislatures and "may be advantageously applied to the case of taxation."[36]

Pownall, disappointed by what he considered the lack of support from the colonial agents, suggested replacing them with a "patron," obviously himself, whose prestige would carry weight in Parliament. However, although one Massachusetts correspondent wrote to him that "Ev'ry American . . . is indebted to you for your Speech in Parliament [which was] regarded as a Proof of . . . your Zeal for the Welfare of both countries,"[37] when the Massachusetts assembly dismissed its agents in 1770, it selected Benjamin Franklin to replace them.

By April 26, 1770, the news of the Boston Massacre reached Great Britain and one of the London members of the House of Commons requested a review of American affairs to which Lord North agreed. Edmund Burke followed with a scathing tirade on the government, inviting its members "to walk out of their places" [resign].[38] When full-scale debate began on May 8, Pownall was the first to speak. He vouched for the loyalty of the people of Massachusetts on the basis of his own experience and because of their cooperation in all the previous colonial wars. He blamed their current unrest on threats to their government and the unwise and unconstitutional actions of the military authorities. He warned his fellow legislators that unless the British government restored the authority of the colonial civil governments over the military, "you may drive the [American] people to rebellion." He moved that steps be taken to remedy this situation; a long debate followed but no action was taken on his motion.[39]

In that same month, Burke published a pamphlet, *Thoughts on the Present Discontents,* which was to have little immediate, but crucial long-term, impact. In this pamphlet, Burke recommended that the British government should be conducted by political parties, "a body of men united for promoting by their joint endeavors the national interest upon some particular principle in which they are all agreed."[40] However, he warned that clandestine royal influence over the House of Commons must be eliminated if this party system were to operate successfully. Though indicating his support for granting Wilkes his seat (see chapter 4), Burke advised against shortening the duration of Parliaments (from seven to three years) and, surprisingly, excluding placemen from the House of Commons. He implied that the overthrow of the North ministry and the return of the Rockinghamites to power would solve all the nation's problems. As Burke summarized,

> If the reader believes that there really exists . . . a Faction ruling by the private inclinations of a Court [note, not the king], . . . and that this Faction, whilst it pursues a scheme for undermining all the foundations of our freedom, weakens . . . all the powers of executory Government, . . . he will believe also, that nothing but a firm combination of public men against this body . . . can possibly get the better of it.[41]

As noted, Burke's pamphlet failed in its immediate object: the North administration remained firmly in power. In the next chapter, we shall meet two people who basically agreed with Burke's American policy but who were outraged by Burke's refusal to support more basic parliamentary reform.

Notes

1. R.C. Simmons and P.D.G. Thomas, eds., *Proceedings and Debates of the British Parliaments Respecting North America, 1754–1783* (hereafter referred to as *Parliament Debates*), I, p. 500.
2. Ibid., II, pp. 9–17.
3. As quoted in John Braeman, *The Road to Independence*, p.124.
4. Simmons and Thomas, *Parliament Debates*, II, pp. 84–91.
5. Charles Francis Adams, ed., *The Works of John Adams*, II, p. 191.
6. Thomas W. Copeland et al., *The Correspondence of Edmund Burke*, I, pp. 232–233. Hereafter referred to as *Burke Correspondence*.
7. Simmons and Thomas, *Parliament Debates*, II, p. iii.
8. Ibid., p. 125.
9. Ibid., p.143.
10. Ibid., p. 150.
11. Ibid., p. 168.
12. Ibid., p. 170.
13. Ibid., p. 284.
14. Ibid., pp. 284–285.
15. Copeland et al., *Burke Correspondence*, I, p. 243.
16. As quoted in Fred Junkin Hinkhouse, *The Preliminaries of the American Revolution as Seen in the English Press, 1763–1775*, pp. 69–70.
17. John Almon, ed., *Anecdotes of the Life of the Right Honorable William Pitt, Earl of Chatham*, III, p.262. Hereafter referred to as *Pitt Anecdotes*.

18. Simmons and Thomas, *Parliament Debates,* II, p. 374.

19. William Stanhope Taylor and Captain John Henry Pringle, eds., *Correspondence of William Pitt, Earl of Chatham,* III, p. 21. Hereafter referred to as *Pitt Correspondence.*

20. Almon, *Pitt Anecdotes,* III, p. 369.

21. Taylor and Pringle, *Pitt Correspondence,* III, p.110.

22. Ibid., pp. 193–194.

23. Simmons and Thomas, *Parliament Debates,* II, p. 464.

24. Paul Langford, ed., *The Writings and Speeches of Edmund Burke* (hereafter referred to as *Burke's Speeches*), II, p. 59.

25. Simmons and Thomas, *Parliament Debates,* II, pp. 480–485.

26. Ibid., p. 411.

27. Ibid., p. 470.

28. Langford, ed., *Burke's Speeches,* II, pp. 61–62.

29. Almon, *Pitt Anecdotes,* III, pp. 265–269.

30. Langford, ed., *Burke's Speeches,* II, p.192.

31. Simmons and Thomas, *Parliament Debates,* III, p.149.

32. Ibid., p.151.

33. Ibid., pp. 240–242.

34. Langford, ed., *Burke's Speeches,* II, p. 326.

35. Ibid., III, pp. 135–136.

36. Ibid., p. 140.

37. "Letters of Samuel Cooper to Thomas Pownall, 1769–1777," *American Historical Review* VIII (January 1903): 305–306. Other details may be found in Albert Matthews, "Letters of Dennys de Berdt 1757–1770," *Publications of the Colonial Society of Massachusetts* XIII (1910–1911): 368–378.

38. Simmons and Thomas, *Parliament Debates,* III, pp. 257–259.

39. Ibid., pp. 271–275.

40. Langford, ed., *Burke's Speeches,* II, p. 317.

41. Ibid., p. 321.

"Birds of a Feather": John Wilkes and John Horne Tooke

As mentioned in the introductory chapter, the London radicals were prominent among the friends of America. Two of the most conspicuous of them were John Wilkes[1] and John Horne Tooke (born John Horne, he added Tooke to his name in 1782 at the request of his wealthy benefactor, William Tooke).[2] Both London-born (Wilkes in 1725, Tooke in 1736), Wilkes was the son of a wealthy distiller, Tooke of a prosperous poultry dealer. Tooke attended Westminster and then Eton. At Eton, embarrassed by his father's lack of title, he claimed to be the son of "an eminent Turkey merchant." At Eton, he suffered more than embarrassment, he lost the sight of his right eye in a scuffle with one of his classmates but this injury never seemed to have handicapped him. After leaving Eton, Tooke studied with private tutors and then earned his Bachelor of Arts with honors from Cambridge University. His family wished him to become an Anglican clergyman but Tooke preferred the legal profession. After a brief career as a schoolmaster, he was ordained a deacon in 1759. Within a few months he became ill and, using this as an excuse, he resigned his position and entered the Inner Temple to study law. However, parental pressure and financial persuasion won out and, in 1760, he was ordained a clergyman of the Church of England.

Wilkes's life took a very different direction. Wilkes attended, but did not graduate from, the University of Leiden, a favorite school for Dissenters who were barred from Oxford and Cambridge (though, later, Wilkes joined the Church of England). Married at twenty-one to a wealthy woman ten years his senior (and from whom he was soon separated), he spent much of his time at the infamous Hell Fire Club, best known for its members' profligacy and licentiousness. He also had a more serious side and, after several unsuccessful attempts, won a seat in Parliament (1757) where he became a supporter of William Pitt. Though remaining in Parliament after Pitt's fall, Wilkes realized he could be more effective as a journalist. His newspaper, the *North Briton,* printed vitriolic attacks on Lord Bute, which stopped just short of being libelous. But on April 23, 1763, in the soon to become notorious *North Briton, Number 45,* after attacking the ministry, he added his regret "that a prince of so many great and amiable qualities . . . can be brought to give the sanction of his sacred name to the most odious measures."[3]

King George III was furious at the insinuation that he was a mere tool in the hands of his ministry and insisted that anyone who was connected with the authorship, printing, or publication of *Number 45* be arrested. Because not all these people were known, the government issued a general warrant, rather than warrants with specific names for their arrest. Wilkes, though a member of Parliament, was taken into custody, released on a writ of habeas corpus, rearrested, and placed in the Tower of London, then discharged in May because his confinement was a breach of parliamentary privilege.

The welcoming cries of "Wilkes and Liberty" were premature. In November 1763, when Parliament reconvened, Grenville asked it to declare *Number 45* a seditious libel (and as such, not protected by parliamentary privilege) and to expel Wilkes. This strategy proved effective particularly after Wilkes became known as the author (a few years earlier) of a purportedly obscene *Essay on Woman.* And in November of 1764, after conviction in absentia of "seditious and scandalous libel" (Wilkes had fled to France in 1763), he was officially outlawed. Though still in exile, Wilkes did have the satisfaction of having the courts, in 1764 and 1765, and the House of Commons, in 1766, ban the use of general warrants in cases such as his.

In spite of his reluctance to become a clergyman, Tooke seemed to have been as conscientious, if not more, as many of his colleagues. He read medical books so that he might tender to the physical as well as the spiritual needs of his parishioners. He preached regularly and defended the Church of England against both Catholics and Dissenters. But the Wilkes affair distracted Tooke from his clerical duties. He was appalled at the expulsion of Wilkes from Parliament and his subsequent outlawry. Although the path to clerical preferment was primarily through political patronage, Tooke felt that he must express his indignation. In 1765, this expression took the form of a pamphlet entitled "The Petition of an Englishman." In it, two Scotsmen, Lord Bute and Lord Mansfield, the chief justice of the King's Bench, were arraigned in violent language as violators of English liberty. Tooke defended his attack on them by quoting John Dryden to the effect that "bad men . . . may and ought to be upbraided for their crimes and follies."[4] He alluded to the official reaction against *North Briton, Number 45,* and warned the objects of his attack that

> though it is possible for an infamous royal favourite, by corruption of
> _____ and with the assistance of an iniquitous prerogative judge, to
> harass and drive insulted Liberty from our arms, yet still she finds a refuge
> from which she can never be expelled—a freeman's breast.[5]

Tooke invoked the "Spirit of Hampden, Russel, and Sidney" (heroes of the
seventeenth-century Puritan Revolution) and predicted that he, too, would soon
be "beggard, vilified, imprisoned"[6] but nothing of the sort happened.

Before the end of the year, he was escorting a young gentleman on a tour of
the continent that lasted almost two years. It was on this trip that Tooke first
met Wilkes. A warm friendship grew between them and they promised to
correspond. Tooke's first letter to Wilkes was destined to become an embarrassment to him later. In it he warned Wilkes that he was a clergyman and that

> I have suffered the infectious hand of a bishop to be waived over me, whose
> imposition, like the sop given to Judas, is only a signal for the devil to enter .
> . . but I hope I have escaped the contagions; and, if you should at any time
> discover the black spot under the tongue, pray kindly assist me to conquer the
> prejudices of education and profession.[7]

Notwithstanding this depreciation of his, however unwillingly chosen, profession, Tooke returned to England in 1767 and resumed his clerical obligations. He seemed once again on the road to a successful career when
Wilkes, though still an outlaw, returned to England in 1768. Raising the old
battle cry "Wilkes and Liberty," he ran for Parliament as a candidate from
the city of London. Failing to get elected, he attempted to represent the
county of Middlesex in which Tooke resided.

Although the friendship between the two men had already cooled, Tooke
immediately channeled all his energies into Wilkes's campaign. He spoke
for him, attacked his opponents, raised and contributed money for the cause,
and probably deserved more credit for Wilkes's victory than any other
individual.[8] The term victory is perhaps misleading because the House of
Commons refused to allow Wilkes to take his seat, and, though his outlawry
was reversed, he was fined £1,000 and sentenced to twenty-two months in
prison for his publication of both the *North Briton, Number 45,* and the
Essay on Woman. In fact, although repeatedly reelected from Middlesex,
Wilkes was not seated in Parliament until 1774.

Wilkes's imprisonment and the attempts to seat other candidates in his
place in the House of Commons precipitated numerous riots. During one of
the most famous of these, the so-called Massacre of St. George's Fields, a
young man named William Allen was killed. Tooke attempted to secure the
conviction of the soldiers who had shot at the crowd and of the magistrate

who had ordered them to fire. However, although a trial was held, all those responsible were acquitted.[9] Nor would Tooke tolerate violence against his opponents. On one occasion, he was responsible for the rescue from a mob of Henry Lewes Luttrell, the man who was eventually allowed to take the Middlesex seat in Parliament after Wilkes had been elected to it. Tooke also fought for Wilkes's return to Parliament by means of remonstrances to the throne. In March 1770, he participated in the composition of a remonstrance from the city of London, which called for the dissolution of Parliament and the removal of the present ministers. When the king failed to take this remonstrance seriously, Tooke publicly compared him to Nero. Although barely escaping prosecution for this allusion by publicly apologizing, Tooke immediately authored another remonstrance. It, too, was rejected but Tooke had thoughtfully prepared an additional brief speech for the Lord Mayor of London to deliver so that the reformers might have "the last word."[10]

That same year, Tooke became the target of a libel suit filed by George Onslow. Onslow was a member of Parliament who had deserted the cause of reform and joined the king's party. Tooke wrote a series of newspaper articles in which he accused Onslow of numerous acts of corruption. Onslow responded by filing suit against Tooke. Tooke's attorney was able to prove that one of the printed articles misquoted Tooke's original manuscript and this forced a mistrial. A second trial followed at which Lord Mansfield awarded Onslow £400 in damages. However, on appeal, the verdict was set aside on technical grounds. The voters also vindicated Tooke by defeating Onslow at the ensuing parliamentary election.[11]

In 1771, Tooke and Wilkes cooperated in organizing a campaign to defy the House of Commons's ban on the printing of its debates. This longstanding ban had been formalized when the ruling party had been embarrassed by the publication of the debates occasioned by the expulsion of Wilkes. Tooke persuaded two printers to print the debates. When they were arrested, the Lord Mayor of London and two aldermen freed them and even arrested the parliamentary messenger who attempted to seize a third printer. The House of Commons then briefly committed the Lord Mayor and one of the aldermen to the Tower of London (the other alderman, Wilkes, was left undisturbed), but the two were soon freed, the printers were never prosecuted, and the debates of the House of Commons were henceforth printed regularly.[12]

Earlier in 1769, to further the cause of parliamentary reform, Tooke had helped found an organization that became known as the Society for the Supporters of the Bill of Rights. The immediate aim of the Society was to discharge Wilkes's financial obligations. Its ultimate goals were annual Parliaments, equal representation in Parliament, and removal from the House of Commons of those who accepted any type of emolument from the crown. The Society also worked for the amelioration of the grievances of the people of Ireland, and for the restoration of the sole right of taxation by their own elected representatives for the people of the American colonies. Whatever effectiveness the Society might have had was soon vitiated by a struggle between Tooke, who wished it to pursue the above goals, and Wilkes, who hoped to turn it into a personal organ to improve his financial situation and regain his seat in Parliament. The dispute was won by Wilkes and his supporters, and Tooke and his followers were forced to form a new group, the Society for Constitutional Information. [13]

The split was accompanied by a vitriolic and abusive exchange of letters between Tooke and Wilkes, which began in 1770 and continued through the first half of 1771. Although Tooke gave a good account of himself, he was undoubtedly the loser in the exchange. "Wilkes and Liberty" had already become inextricably intertwined and anyone who attacked Wilkes was immediately suspected by all reformers. Tooke's sincerity, if not integrity, was stripped from him when Wilkes disclosed the letter to him in which Tooke had denigrated his own calling. Moreover, Wilkes was supported in this controversy by the mysterious "Junius," the leading political writer of the period. Junius claimed that Tooke's attacks on Wilkes served the interest of the king's party and did a grave disservice to the cause of reform. At the conclusion of the correspondence, Tooke himself admitted that the "parson of Brentford [Tooke] is at length defeated." [14]

But a dual question arises: What was the attitude of these two men toward America and what was the American attitude toward them? In common with most reformers, Tooke had opposed the Stamp Act and the Townshend Acts. In 1770, at a meeting of the voters of Middlesex, he warned his listeners that "when people of America are enslaved, we can not be free." [15] In 1771, among the principles to which he felt every candidate to the House of Commons should subscribe was the restoration to the colonies of

> the essential right of taxation, by representatives of their own free election, repealing the acts passed in violation of that right since the year 1763, and the universal excise, so notoriously incompatible with every principle of British liberty, which has been lately substituted in the colonies, for the laws of customs. [16]

In February 1770, just prior to the split between Tooke and Wilkes, and as it turned out an added reason for the split, the Society for the Supporters of the Bill of Rights received a gift of £1,500 from the lower house of the South Carolina legislature. The purpose of the gift was to support "the just and Constitutional Rights and Liberties of the People of Great Britain and

America."[17] Wilkes was extremely disappointed that the gift was made to the Society rather than directly to him. It took a great deal of maneuvering on Tooke's part to prevent the sending of an extremely perfunctory letter of appreciation, which Wilkes and his supporters favored. Discussion of Tooke's other contributions to the American cause, however, must wait till a later chapter. Whatever doubts Tooke had of the sincerity of Wilkes's support for the American cause, it is undeniable that, particularly during the years 1768–1770 when Wilkes was imprisoned, these doubts were not present in America.

Americans saw close relationships between Wilkes's arrest on a general warrant and the writs of assistance that had been used in the colonies to conduct searches of possibly smuggled goods. Later, the Boston Massacre was compared to the Massacre of St. George's Fields. John Adams (among other Americans) was elected to the Society for the Supporters of the Bill of Rights because of his sympathy "with the Friends of Liberty in England for our mutual safety and defence."[18] The Boston Sons of Liberty opened a correspondence with Wilkes in June 1768, congratulating him on his election to Parliament and expressing the hope that he might "perhaps save a tottering Empire."[19] Wilkes responded promptly, pledging to give "particular attention to whatever respects the interests of America which I believe to be immediately connected with, and of essential moment to our parent country."[20] A series of letters followed during the next two years, all of which anticipated his release from prison and return to the House of Commons. As William Palfrey, a partner of John Hancock and the secretary of the group, affirmed, "*the fate of Wilkes and America* must stand or fall together."[21] [italics in original]. Wilkes's letters were fewer but consistent in their espousal of the colonial cause, even promising not to "rest till the *declaratory bill,* as well as *all the late* [Townshend] *duties,* are absolutely repealed."[22] [italics in original].

While strongest in New England, Wilkes was extremely popular in all thirteen colonies. South Carolina's donation has already been noted. A town was named for him (and Barré) in Pennsylvania, as well as counties in North Carolina and Georgia. Engravings and pipes made in his image were popular all over America, and Paul Revere designed a silver cup in his honor. When Arthur Lee, an American member of the Society for the Supporters of the Bill of Rights, backed Wilkes against Tooke, he justified it to his brother, Richard Henry Lee, on the basis of Wilkes's support of America.[23] However, after 1770, American ardor cooled. The calm following the repeal of the Townshend Acts and Wilkes's failure to regain his parliamentary seat were probably factors, but perhaps even more important was the general feeling of Americans that neither Wilkes nor any of their other

British sympathizers was in a position to defend their interests.[24] As Arthur Lee wrote his brother in 1772, the North ministry has "no opposition now, nor any forming."[25] John Wilkes, however, did not despair and we will hear from him in later chapters.

Notes

1. The best modern study of Wilkes is Peter D.G. Thomas, *John Wilkes: A Friend to Liberty.*

2. The basic source for Tooke's life is the 1813 study by Alexander Stephens, *Memoirs of John Horne Tooke*, 2 vols. The best modern account is Minnie Claire Yarborough, *John Horne Tooke.*

3. As quoted in P.D.G. Thomas, *John Wilkes*, pp. 27–28.

4. Stephens, *Tooke Memoirs*, I, p. 59.

5. Ibid., p. 61.

6. Ibid., p. 66.

7. Ibid., p. 76.

8. Ibid., pp. 218–221.

9. These events are described in John Horne Tooke, *An Oration Delivered by the Rev. Mr. Horne at a Numerous Meeting of the Freeholders of Middlesex.* Hereafter referred to as *Oration.*

10. Stephens, *Tooke Memoirs*, I, pp. 146–158.

11. Accounts of this trial may be found in Joseph Gurney, ed., *The Whole Proceedings in the Cause of the Action Brought by the Rt. Hon. Geo. Onslow, Esq. Against the Rev. Mr. John Horne*, and Stephens, *Tooke Memoirs*, I, pp. 120–144.

12. Stephens, *Tooke Memoirs*, I, pp. 330–351.

13. Ibid., pp. 163–166, 175.

14. This correspondence has been printed in the *Controversial Letters of John Wilkes, Esq., the Rev. John Horne, and their Principal Adherents*, and Stephens, *Tooke Memoirs*, I, pp. 179–319. Tooke's admission of defeat is from his thirteenth letter. The *Letters of Junius* contain that writer's view of the controversy.

15. Tooke, *Oration*, p. 36; Yarborough, *Tooke*, p. 78.

16. Stephens, *Tooke Memoirs*, I, p. 166.

17. Yarborough, *Tooke*, pp. 79–83.

18. Charles Francis Adams, ed., *The Works of John Adams*, II, p. 325.

19. W.C. Ford, ed., "John Wilkes in Boston," *Massachusetts Historical Society Proceedings* XLVII (1913–1914): 191–192.

20. Ibid., p. 192.

21. Ibid., p. 197. The remainder of the letters are to be found on pp. 197–215, and in George M. Elsey, ed., "John Wilkes and William Palfrey," *Publications of the Colonial Society of Massachusetts* XXIV (1937–1942): 411–428. In addition to Palfrey, John and Sam Adams were among the correspondents.

22. Ibid., p. 415.

23. Richard Henry Lee, ed., *The Life of Arthur Lee, LLD.*, I, pp. 186, 189. Hereafter referred to as *Arthur Lee.*

24. An overview of the relations between Wilkes and America during this period may be found in Pauline Maier, "John Wilkes and American Disillusionment with Britain," *William and Mary Quarterly*, 3d series (July 1963): 373–395.

25. Lee, *Arthur Lee*, I, p. 207.

5

The "Honest Whigs"

Upon receiving the first two volumes of *Political Disquisitions* by James Burgh in 1774, John Adams waxed lyrical: "I cannot but think those Disquisitions the best service that a citizen could render his country at this great and dangerous crisis, when the British empire seems ripe for destruction and tottering on the brink of a precipice."[1] What was so unusual about these volumes to draw such extravagant praise from the usually restrained John Adams? And who was the hitherto relatively unknown author, James Burgh?

Burgh was one of the members of an informal group calling themselves "Honest Whigs," who met regularly to enjoy light refreshments and discuss science, philosophy, and political developments. Most were Dissenters, several were ministers, and all were well educated. Though the members included Benjamin Franklin, James Boswell, and some twenty others, we shall concentrate in this chapter only on James Burgh and Catherine Macauley.

Burgh was born in Scotland in 1714. He attended St. Andrews University with the aim of becoming a Presbyterian minister but ill health made this impossible. Instead, he followed a lifelong teaching career. (By mid-century, he had his own school a few miles outside of London.) Ever the moralist, Burgh's first written work was *Britain's Remembrancer* in which he portrayed the Jacobite uprising of 1745 as a warning to the British people to reform their way of life. In later years, he wrote other works on education, morals, economics, politics, public speaking, and religion. Disillusioned by George III's failure to live up to the high hopes he had for him, Burgh took up Wilkes's cause (though finding Wilkes's lifestyle repugnant).[2] Beginning in 1769, Burgh wrote a series of articles under the pseudonym "Constitutionist," calling for thoroughgoing parliamentary reform.

In the following year, this time calling himself "the Colonist's Advocate," he penned eleven articles challenging Parliament's right to tax the

colonies and demanding total repeal of the Townshend Acts. In these articles, Burgh used a wide variety of arguments to buttress his case. He began
by asserting that taxation without representation violated the Lockean principle that "I have truly no property in that which another can, by Right, take
away from me, when he pleases, against my consent."[3] The second article
attacked the theory of virtual representation. "To an American Colonist our
Parliament is (as far as concerns the giving and granting of his Property) the
same as the parliament of Paris. He has as much Representation in one as in
the other."[4] Next, he recommended that colonial taxation be left to their
own "Provincial Assemblies of Representation [which] have always had a
power, analogous to that of our House of Commons, of laying taxes for
bearing the Expences of each respective Government."[5] The fourth article
pointed out that the colonies "have made our Merchants Princes . . . employed our Hands [workers], increased our People, consumed our Manufactures, improved our Navy, maintained our Poor, and doubled, or trebled our
Riches."[6] Was all this to be jeopardized by the small amount of revenue
these duties were to bring in? Burgh then went on to question the use to
which the revenue from the Townshend duties was to be put. He predicted
that governors supported by these duties would make colonial assemblies
"useless" and judges unresponsive to colonial interests.[7]

In the sixth article, Burgh made two related points: "the Colonists have
never been wanting to their own Defence" and Great Britain came to the
defense of the colonies out of its own interest—"Could we have been en-
riched by our Colonies, if we had not defended them from the common
Enemy?"[8] He then claimed that the lack of specie made it almost impossible for Americans to pay the taxes levied by their own legislatures yet now
Parliament is proclaiming "you shall pay us additional Taxes."[9] In the
eighth article, Burgh recommended that Parliament tax "Luxury and Vice"
among ourselves rather than harass the colonists who were formerly so
attached to the mother country.[10] He then reiterated the distinction between
the power to legislate and the power to tax; described the "Stagnation of
Trade" caused by the Townshend Acts; and threatened that if they were not
repealed the colonists would "apply to Manufactures, by which they may
enable themselves to pay the Mother Country Taxes, and lessen the Demand for her Tax-loaded Manufactures."[11]

Sorely disappointed by the lack of total repeal of the Townshend Acts,
Burgh commenced writing what was to be his major, and final, work (he
died in 1775), which appeared (1774–1775) under the title *Political Disquisitions.* In these three long volumes, Burgh first accused recent ministries of
subverting the British constitution by the maintenance of a standing army
and by controlling the House of Commons through corruption and manipu-

lation made possible because of its unrepresentative character. Next, he called for a national association that would campaign for annual parliaments with rotating membership; the exclusion of placemen from the House of Commons; an almost universal franchise; and the secret ballot. Burgh accused Burke of political opportunism because of his refusal to endorse this reform platform in his *Thoughts on the Cause of the Present Discontents.*[12]

Political Disquisitions immediately became a standard reference work not only for British reformers for whom it was intended, but also for American Whigs. We have already read of John Adams's reaction. Other subscribers to an American edition included George Washington, Thomas Jefferson, John Hancock, and John Dickinson. *Political Disquisitions* was utilized later in the debate over the ratification of the Constitution. Madison quoted it in *Federalist Paper Number 56,* but more often antifederalists used it to attack what they viewed as the centralizing tendency of the proposed federal government.[13]

The reason for this popularity is not difficult to discover. To Burgh, one of the two most blatant manifestations of the suppression of English liberties was the mistreatment of the American colonies (the other was the Wilkes affair). Burgh tended to compare the "temperate way of living" found in the colonies with the decadence of the mother country and, as he had earlier recommended, governmental economies and taxes on British "luxury, gaming, and public diversions" rather than taxes on America.[14] He thought the Boston Tea Party was "inexcusable" but compared the harshness of the Coercive Acts to the lenient treatment of the city of Edinburgh (a mere £2,000 fine) in which a riot had taken place in 1737.[15] Burgh, of course, opposed any type of American taxation: It was unconstitutional; it would damage British commerce and manufacturing; and any money raised would only find its way into the pockets of British politicians and their underlings.[16]

Burgh hammered away at the taxation problem. Virtual representation was "ominous to the liberty of the British empire, unjust in its principles, rigorous in its execution, and pernicious in its operation alike to the mother country and its colonies." And why should the colonists have to support British troops in America? The people of the several European nations in which British troops were at times deployed were never expected to subsidize them.[17] Surprisingly, though, Burgh clung to the possibility that "an adequate representation in parliament would probably be acceptable to the colonists." Alternatively, he had two suggestions: (1) the colonists should send temporary representatives to the House of Commons to set a quota of taxes (based upon a percentage of

British taxes) to be paid by the colonies, or (2) an intercolonial convention be held in America that would perform a similar function.[18]

Burgh claimed that "no people ever were more peaceable, or better affected" to their mother country than Americans until 1763. Then began a series of persecutions that included, in addition to taxation, general warrants, quartering of troops, unfair enforcement of the acts of trade, despotic governors, suppression of legislatures, and revocation of charters.[19] He predicted that unless these grievances were remedied, the best that can happen is "a diminution of our trade and revenues" and at worst the loss of America and/or the possible "enslaving" of Great Britain.[20]

Burgh was very circumspect about his republican ideals. On the one hand, though he resented the power of the monarch and the House of Lords, he expressly denied any desire "to establish republican principles" [in Great Britain]. On the other hand, in theory he felt a republic was "preferable" even to a limited monarchy. And, in any case, the choice was up to the people.

> If the people of the country think that they should be in any respect happier under a republican government, than monarchical, or under monarchical than the republic, and find, that they can bring about a change of government without greater inconveniences than the future advantages are likely to balance; why may we not say, that they have a sovereign, absolute and uncontrollable right to change or new-model their government as they please.[21]

We may be certain that Burgh would have approved of the Declaration of Independence but whether he would have approved of the Constitution, we shall never know!

In his *Political Disquisitions,* Burgh referred to an "incomparable female historian" who wrote "for the purpose of inculcating in the people of Britain the love of liberty and their country."[22] Earlier in August 1770, Edmund Burke wrote a friend about the reaction to his pamphlet, *Thoughts on the Cause of the Present Discontents.* On the whole, he was gratified but did mention the unfavorable reaction of "the Bill of rights people" (the Wilkites), particularly "the Amazon . . . our republican Virago. I have been afraid to answer her."[23] Both were referring, Burgh with deference, Burke obviously with tongue in cheek, to Catherine Sawbridge Macauley. It is not surprising that Burke was "afraid" to respond. Mrs. Macauley's reaction to his pamphlet was incisive and contemptuous. It was a "pernicious work" that "endeavors to mislead the people" about the "dangerous maneuvres of Aristocratic faction and party" and prevent "an effectual reformation in the vitiated parts of our constitution and government."[24] She pretended amazement at the "corruption of heart, and the deception of the head of the present writer [Burke]" who recognized the problems facing the nation but who nevertheless, opposes the "return of power in the peoples' hands."[25] She then briefly reviewed the reform program: annual parliaments, rotation in office, redistricting of seats in the House of Commons; expansion of the suffrage to all taxpayers, and the exclusion of placemen from the House of Commons. And, finally, she posed the rhetorical question, "when the corruption of every salutary principle in the constitution calls instantly and loudly for a speedy and effectual reformation, should the contention be reduced to mere endeavors to advance party or friends to superiority and power?"[26]

This was not Mrs. Macauley's first venture into political pamphleteering. In 1767 she wrote a tract entitled *Loose Remarks on certain Positions to be Found in Mr. Hobbes's Philosophical Rudiments of Government and Society, with a Short Sketch of a Democratical Form of Government, In a Letter to Signor Paoli.* (Pascal Paoli was a Corsican leader in exile in England after France occupied his island. He was supported by the Wilkites and Honest Whigs but also accepted a royal pension.) In the pamphlet proper, she attacks Hobbes's advocacy of absolute monarchy, declaring succinctly that "political equality and the laws of good government, as so far from incompatible, that one can never exist to perfection without the other."[27] In the *Short Sketch,* which she addressed to Paoli, however, Mrs. Macauley went into more detail. She suggested a constitution for Corsica that provided for a two-house legislature: a Senate of no more than fifty and a Representative Assembly of the People numbering at least 250. Civil and military officers were to be selected by the Representative Assembly from men who had served in the Senate and were limited to a term of only one year. All laws had to be approved by both houses. One-third of the members of each house were to be retired every three years and were not eligible for reelection for another three years. If an executive were needed, he was to be named by the Representative Assembly on a month-to-month basis. Division of estates among all sons was required to ensure that Corsica would remain an agrarian society.[28] As Arthur Lee wrote at this time, English politicians fell into three categories: (1) the court party; (2) the opposition (Chatham and the Rockinghamites), who merely wanted to replace the court party; and (3) the constitutionalists (among whom included Mrs. Macauley), who were "for appealing to the people at large, and effecting a change of measures as well as men."[29]

Catherine Sawbridge was born in 1731 to a wealthy Kentish family. Largely self-educated, she married Dr. George Macauley, a widower fifteen years her senior, in 1760. (He died six years later.) By 1763, she produced the first volume of a series originally titled *History of England from the*

Accession of James I to that of the Brunswick Line (later delimited to the Revolution of 1688–1689). Four other volumes followed by 1771, and the remaining three were written between 1781 and 1783. In between, in 1778, she penned a volume of a projected *History of England from the Revolution to the Present Time,* which covered the period between 1689 and 1733.

Mrs. Macauley did not write her *History* for purely scholarly purpose (though she did utilize previously unused primary materials). Through conviction and through her brother John Sawbridge, a wealthy London hop merchant (and after 1768, a member of Parliament), she became a member of the Wilkite circle. She was on intimate terms with Wilkes himself and his daughter Polly. She also was virtually an "honorary" member of the Honest Whigs group. Her primary motive for writing her *History* was to refute the Tory interpretation of the same period by David Hume in his *History of England,* which appeared between 1754 and 1762. Her *History* paid tribute to the mythical Anglo-Saxon constitution, glorified the period of the Commonwealth (though not Oliver Cromwell), and lamented the failure of the Glorious Revolution to fully restore English liberties.[30]

The *History* was a sensation. Obviously her friends were complimentary, but even an ordinarily severe critic such as Horace Walpole called it the "most sensible, unaffected and best history of England that we have yet."[31] Her *History* also appealed to an American audience. John Adams testified to its popularity, and in 1770 he extolled the author "as one of the brightest ornaments, not only of her sex, but of her age and country."[32] William Palfrey, in one of his letters to Wilkes, enclosed historical material relating to Massachusetts that he thought "may be of use to Mrs. Macauley," whose *History* he had read with "the greatest satisfaction."[33]

It was not only her *History* that won her esteem in America. In 1769, Mrs. Macauley had written to an American that she did not feel the necessity of writing a pamphlet on behalf of the American cause because "I think the general principles of the rights of mankind inculcated in my great work [*History*], is of more advantage to them than the more suspected arguments framed for the service of a particular purpose."[34] Nevertheless, she welcomed almost every American who resided in London (Arthur and William Lee; Stephen Sayre, later arrested in an alleged plot to kidnap the king; and, of course, Benjamin Franklin) as well as visitors (Benjamin and Jacob Rush; the Reverend Ezra Stiles, later president of Yale College; Henry Marchant, the Rhode Island attorney general at the time to whom she gave copies of her *History;* and Joseph Quincy, Jr., of Massachusetts, who called her "a most extraordinary woman"). In addition, she corresponded with, among others, John and Abigail Adams, James Otis, and Mercy Otis Warren.[35]

Mrs. Macauley was greatly discouraged by the passage of the Coercive Acts (see chapter 6) and reports of their effects in Massachusetts. Perhaps an emotional letter from Abigail Adams, in which she described "thousands reduced to want, or dependent upon charity" but conscious of their "righteous cause" are determined to secure "an ample redress of our Grievances—or a redress by the Sword,"[36] impelled Mrs. Macauley, in 1775, to direct *An Address to the People of England, Scotland, and Ireland, on the Present Important Crisis of Affairs.* In this *Address,* she appealed to the self-interest of the British people. She claimed that Great Britain was "on the eve of a civil war" that was completely unnecessary because the Navigation Acts, to which "the Americans declare they will ever readily submit," bring in much more revenue than any American tax might raise. And this civil war could have only two possible results: Great Britain might win but it would "ruin both herself and America" or America might win and become "a new, a flourishing, and an extensive empire of freemen," while Great Britain would fall under the sway "of a domestic despot, or . . . become the province of some powerful European state." Rather than face this painful choice, Mrs. Macauley urged her readers to "Rouse! and unite in one general effort . . . draw the attention of every part of the government to their own interests and to the dangerous state of the British empire."[37] Unfortunately, the British public did not react as she had hoped.

The next few years were not happy ones for Mrs. Macauley. In failing health, she had moved to Bath in 1774, where she shared the home of Thomas Wilson, an Anglican clergyman twenty-eight years her senior. This arrangement gave rise to a certain amount of gossip, which was only eclipsed by her marriage to William Graham, a surgeon's mate twenty-six years younger than she. That she had married "beneath" her was bad enough but to have married a younger man was, for a woman, considered far worse. Her British friends snubbed her. Moreover, the reputation of her *History* had plummeted—more for political than scholarly reasons. The Whigs, who had once embraced her as a counterweight to Hume, now decided that she was too radical, too much of a republican, and too pro-American for their taste.

As noted, however, in America, as might be expected, her writings were still held in high regard. It was for these reasons that a year after she completed the eighth volume of her *History* (1783), she and her husband embarked for the United States. They arrived in Boston where they spent a great deal of time with Mercy Otis Warren, who was impressed with Mrs. Macauley-Graham's "brilliance of thought" and who was later to follow her example by writing a history of the American Revolution. Actually, Mrs. Macauley-Graham had been in correspondence with the Otis family since

1769, when she had sent James Otis (Mrs. Warren's brother) a copy of her *History*. Mrs. Warren was also one of the few individuals who refused to criticize her friend for marrying a younger man. So pleasant was the Boston stay that Mrs. Macauley-Graham reported that "had I resided in America I should undoubtedly have made Boston the seat of my residence."[38]

In April 1785, the Grahams left for New York to visit with Richard Henry Lee, at that time president of the Continental Congress. Lee, in turn, arranged for the couple to visit the Washingtons at Mount Vernon. The visit must have gone well because at its conclusion Mrs. Macauley-Graham described it as a "friendly and engaging" visit and Martha Washington called her company "agreeable."[39] Washington himself wrote, "A Visit from a Lady so celebrated in the Literary world [he had read her *History*] could not but be very flattering to me," and thanked Richard Henry Lee for introducing her to him, particularly since Mrs. Macauley-Graham agreed with him that the powers of the federal government had to be strengthened.[40]

Upon her return home, Mrs. Macauley-Graham continued to correspond with both Mrs. Warren and George Washington. In March 1787, she wrote the former expressing satisfaction at the failure of Shays's Rebellion and in November expressing the hope that the Constitution would be approved. She favored it partly because it was "grounded on simple Democracy" and partly because she feared that the anarchy that existed under the Articles of Confederation would lead to a European-type government "at variance with the rights of man."[41]

In November 1787, Washington wrote affirming his guarded hope for the approval of the Constitution and, in January 1790, he wrote a lengthy letter explaining his reasons for assuming the presidency and his satisfaction with the operation of the new government.[42] Mrs. Macauley-Graham did not disagree with Washington, but to Mrs. Warren she wrote somewhat ominously that the Constitution might "give a larger trust to that faithless ambitious animal man" than might be conducive to democracy.[43] One might hazard a guess that she would have been a very reluctant federalist.

The American trip temporarily reinvigorated Mrs. Macauley-Graham. Upon her return to England, she wrote *Letters on Education* and, when Edmund Burke published his *Reflection on the Revolution in France* (1790), she once again responded with a spirited refutation of his basic premises, entitled *Observations on the Reflections of the Rt. Hon. Edmund Burke on the Revolution in France*. One wonders whether her initial admiration for the revolution would have survived its later developments. We can be sure, however, that she would have welcomed Washington's letter of July 1791, which reported the "prosperity and tranquility" of the United

States.[44] Unfortunately, our "republican Virago" passed away a month earlier.

But we are getting ahead of our story. To understand the reaction of our British "friends," it is necessary to review the policies of Lord North's administration.

Notes

1. Charles Francis Adams, ed., *The Works of John Adams* (hereafter referred to as *J. Adams Works*), IX, p. 351. Fifteen years later, however, Adams felt the *Political Disquisitions* (as well as *Common Sense* and Mrs. Macauley's *History*) were "extremely mistaken"(read, too radical) in their political theories.

2. The best modern account of the life of James Burgh is Carla H. Hay, *James Burgh, Spokesman for Reform in Hanoverian England.* Hereafter referred to as *Spokesman Burgh.*

3. Verner W. Crane, ed., *Benjamin Franklin's Letters to the Press, 1758–1775,* p.169. Crane mistakenly credited these articles to Franklin.

4. Ibid., p. 173.

5. Ibid., p. 174.

6. Ibid., p. 177.

7. Ibid., p. 181.

8. Ibid., pp. 183–184.

9. Ibid., p. 194.

10. Ibid., pp. 195–196.

11. Ibid., pp. 201, 205, 208.

12. James Burgh, *Political Disquisitions,* I, p. 173. Hereafter referred to as *Disquisitions.*

13. Hay, *Spokesman Burgh,* pp. 42–43.

14. Burgh, *Disquisitions,* III, p. 30; II, p. 313.

15. Ibid., pp. 289, 322.

16. Ibid., pp. 274–290.

17. Ibid., pp. 308–310, 313, 328.

18. Ibid., pp. 279, 315–317.

19. Ibid., pp. 291–299, 303.

20. Ibid., pp. 327–328.

21. Ibid., I, pp. 9, 116–117; II, pp. 18, 277.

22. Ibid., I, p. viii.

23. Thomas W. Copeland et al., *The Correspondence of Edmund Burke,* II, p.150.

24. Catherine Macauley, *Observations on a Pamphlet entitled "Thoughts on the Cause of the Present Discontents,"* p. 6.

25. Ibid., pp. 14–15.

26. Ibid., pp. 17–18.

27. Catherine Macauley, *Loose Remarks on certain Positions to be Found in Mr. Hobbes's Philosophical Rudiments of Government and Society,* 2d ed., p. 12. Hereafter referred to as *Loose Remarks.*

28. Ibid., pp. 21–27.

29. Richard Henry Lee, ed., *The Life of Arthur Lee, LLD,* I, pp. 195–196.

30. The best modern work on Macauley is Bridget Hill, *The Republican Virago: The Life and Times of Catherine Macauley, Historian.* Hereafter referred to as *Republican Virago.*

31. W.S. Lewis and Grover Cronin, Jr., eds., *Horace Walpole's Correspondence,* XXVIII, p. 3.

32. Adams, *J. Adams Works*, X, p. 202; IX, p. 332. Though, again, as in the case of Burgh's *Political Disquisitions*, he later lowered his opinion of her political acuity. See p. 559.

33. *Controversial Letters of John Wilkes, Esq., the Rev. John Horne, and Their Principal Adherents*, p. 211.

34. Macauley, *Loose Remarks*, pp. 34–35.

35. Hill, *Republican Virago*, pp. 193–197, 201–202; Mark Anthony DeWolfe Howe, ed., "English Journal of Josiah Quincy, Jr. 1774–1775," *Massachusetts Historical Society Proceedings*, L, (1916–1917): 454.

36. L.H. Butterfield, ed., *Adams Family Correspondence*, I, pp. 177–178.

37. Catherine Macauley, *An Address to the People of England, Scotland, and Ireland, on the Present important Crisis of Affairs*, 2d ed., pp. 20, 27, 28–29, 31.

38. Worthington Chauncey Ford, ed., "Warren-Adams Letters," *Massachusetts Historical Society Collections, 72–73 (1917–1925):* I, 7–8; II, 254, 258.

39. Ibid., pp. 259, 257.

40. John C. Fitzpatrick, ed., *The Writings of George Washington*, XXVIII, pp. 169, 159, 174, 370–371. Hereafter referred to as *Washington Writings*.

41. Ford, "Warren-Adams Letters," II, pp. 282–283, 299.

42. Fitzpatrick, *Washington Writings*, XXVIII, pp. 316–317; XXX, pp. 495–498.

43. Ford, "Warren-Adams Letters," II, pp. 303–304.

44. Fitzpatrick, *Washington Writings*, XXXI, pp. 316–317.

6

The Coercive Acts and Their Opponents: A Study in Futility

In August 1773, Arthur Lee wrote to Sam Adams about a "scheme" to help the East India Company out of its financial difficulties by allowing it to sell tea directly to America. Even if the colonists paid the tea tax (the one unrepealed Townshend duty), he pointed out that it would still come "cheaper to the consumer" than the smuggled Dutch tea common in the colonies. But, as he continued, paying the tax "may lead to a thousand other ways of enslaving us."[1] Lee was referring to the Tea Act passed by Parliament in May. Although, during the debate, some members of Parliament requested that the tea duty be repealed, Lord North optimistically (and, as it turned out, unrealistically) replied that the tea would be "cheap enough to find a market in America, and preserve the duty."[2]

The consequences are well known. Reports of the Boston Tea Party reached Great Britain in January 1774. The news could not have come at a worse time. Copies of letters from Governor Hutchinson of Massachusetts and his deputy, Andrew Oliver, to Lord Grenville's secretary, which contained statements critical of the colony's leaders, were obtained by Benjamin Franklin and made public in Massachusetts. The Massachusetts assembly petitioned for the removal of the governor and his deputy. The committee of the Privy Council for plantation affairs considered the petition on January 29, 1774. The committee rejected the petition; exonerated Hutchinson (though he was replaced shortly after, at his own request, by General Thomas Gage); and humiliated Franklin, who was immediately removed from his position as deputy postmaster of America.

Not surprisingly, then, the royal message to Parliament on March 7 instructed it to do whatever "may be necessary . . . for better securing the Execution of the Laws, and the just dependence of the Colonies upon the

Crown and Parliament of Great Britain."[3] At first, the ministry considered trying individuals for treason, but its own law officers advised that this would be impossible because of lack of evidence. North then responded by sending to Parliament a measure the cabinet had already been considering: the Boston Port Bill, which closed the port to all shipping (except coastal ships carrying food or fuel) and moved the custom house to Salem until Boston compensated the East India Company for its tea, and law and order were restored.[4]

John Sawbridge, Mrs. Macaulay's brother, was one of the few to announce himself as "heartily against this bill" but could barely be heard over the protests of his colleagues.[5] Governor Pownall tried to explain that the Boston Tea Party "was the act of the mob not of the people" and that Americans "love *order* and peace" (italics in original), which earned him a bout of laughter.[6] As soon as he heard the royal message, Burke warned that past punitive measures had been ineffectual and it would be far better to "remove ... discontents" because "no troops under heaven [can] bring them [the Americans] to obedience."[7] However, he did not speak against the Boston Port Bill until just prior to its certain passage.

To understand his strategy, it is necessary to understand his dual position; he was not only a member of Parliament but, since 1771, also the agent for the colony of New York. His view of an agent's responsibility is illustrated by what he wrote to James Delancey, a leader of the New York assembly.

> The provinces ought ... to have a *direct* intercourse with Ministry and Parliament here, by some person who might be truly confidential with them who appoint him. Who might be entrusted with the strength and weakness of their Cause in all controverted points; and who might represent their own Sentiments in their own way.[8] [italics in original]

And when informed that his appointment (which had been made by the New York assembly alone) would have to be approved by the governor and his council, Burke was ready to decline the position. He felt that a colonial agent must represent "the interests of *the people* of the province as *contradistinguished from its executive Government"* [italics in original]. He also pointed out that the assembly and the governor often differed, which would make the agent's position untenable if he were to represent both of them.[9] Fortunately, however, the Board of Trade postponed its insistence on gubernatorial approval and Burke faithfully carried out his duties for five years.[10]

It was then partially for the sake of his honor rather than, as he wrote New York, for any approval of the Boston Tea Party that he attacked the

Boston Port Bill as "one of the most dangerous Bills that ever were passed in this House, the most unjust in its nature and principle, and most probably in effects." Unjust, he maintained, because it punished the innocent with the guilty, ineffective because every American town had refused to accept the East India Company's tea. Nevertheless, as Burke expected, the bill passed without even a division (formal vote).[11]

Not waiting to see the effect of the Boston Port Bill, Lord North next introduced the Massachusetts Government Bill, which transferred the power of appointing council members from the House of Representatives to the Crown; gave the governor the power, without the consent of the council, to appoint and remove all lower court judges; limited town meetings to one a year (to elect town officials), except those specifically authorized by the governor; and granted the power of summoning juries to county sheriffs (the governor's appointees) rather than by locally elected constables. Pownall once again tried to convince his fellow members that Americans were a "peaceable set of people." More to the point, he predicted that if this act and its predecessor (and its successors, which had already been introduced but will be discussed below) were to be passed, they will be met at first "not by force . . . but by a regular united system of resistance." But if British policy remained punitive, "they are going to rebel."[12]

As with the Boston Port Bill, Burke waited until the third reading of the Massachusetts Government Bill. He began speaking at 11:45 P.M. and did not conclude until 1:00 A.M. with frequent interruptions from an unfriendly audience. After a review of the administration's policy, he warned, "You will lose America. . . . [You] breed in them final despair . . . which will not break out at the time you wish, but when they will be most destructive to you."[13] But once again, the ministry won by a vote of 239 to 64.

Even before the passage of the Massachusetts Government Bill, North brought in the Administration of Justice Bill to protect soldiers, judges, and customs officials, who worked for "the execution of the law or, for suppression of riots," from trial for murder by almost certainly prejudiced colonial juries through relocating their trials to another colony or to Great Britain. Sawbridge and others described the bill as "pernicious," Burke opposed it as liable to "destroy the whole system of jurisprudence," but it passed by a large majority.[14]

On April 29, an American Quartering Bill, the fourth of the so-called Coercive Acts (termed by the colonists as Intolerable Acts) was introduced.[15] This bill amended the Mutiny Act so that troops could be quartered wherever needed—even in private homes, if no other facilities were available. This act passed virtually without debate in the House of Commons. Lord Chatham, however, whose gout had made it impossible for him to attend the debates on the Coercive Acts, rose (though leaning on a crutch) on May 26 to express his opposition to this bill and to the three previous acts. True, he proclaimed, "I cannot help but condemn in the severest terms . . . the late riots of Boston. But the mode which has been pursued to bring them back to a sense of duty to their parent state has been diametrically opposite to the fundamental principles of sound policy." He assumed that the destruction of the tea "was the effect of despair" at the renewed attempt (the Tea Act) to "tax them without their consent." Chatham reiterated his "unalterable" belief that "this country has no right under heaven to tax America." He then complained that "a well-concerted effort" should have been made to identify and punish the "real offenders" rather than punish "the whole body of the inhabitants." He implored his colleagues to abandon their punitive policy because Americans "understand the constitution of the empire . . . and consequently, they will have a watchful eye over their liberties."[16] The House of Lords, however, was as, if not more, determined to assert British sovereignty over the colonies, and Chatham's advice and warning went unheeded.

On April 19, in the midst of the debates on the Coercive Acts, Rose Fuller, a Jamaican and longtime opponent of North's American policy, took the offensive and brought up the possiblilty of repealing the duty on tea. The attempt proved abortive but it did evoke one of the most famous orations of its, or any, period: Burke's speech on American taxation. In this speech, Burke reminded his listeners that the purpose of the Townshend Acts was to support civil government officials in the colonies, and the tea duty alone was obviously inadequate to accomplish this end. Yet the ministry for "so paltry a sum . . . have shaken the pillars of a commercial empire that circled the whole globe." Burke went on to call the tea tax "a tax of war and rebellion" because "two millions of people are resolved not to pay." Burke quoted from Lord Hillsborough's circular letter of May 1767, in which Hillsborough pledged not to levy any further taxes on America for the purpose of raising a revenue and announced the repeal of the Townshend Acts in order to "preestablish *that mutual* confidence and affection *upon which the glory and safety of the British empire depend*" [italics in original]. Why, he queried, have you "not done what you have given the colonies just cause to expect?" I am sure the natural effect of fidelity, clemency, kindness in governors, is peace, good-will, order, and esteem on the part of the governed."[17]

Burke then embarked on a review of the commercial regulations, under which both Great Britain and the colonies prospered and which were accepted by the colonists because America enjoyed "the sole disposal of her own internal government." Only after 1763 did Great Britain attempt to "join together the restraints of a universal internal and external monopoly, with a universal internal and external taxation ... an unnatural union," giving as examples the passage of the Sugar and Stamp Acts.

Next, Burke lauded the actions of the Rockingham ministry in totally repealing the Stamp Act and refusing to be intimidated by Chatham's insistence that Parliament's right to tax be excluded from the Declaratory Act. He defended the latter decision by claiming that no restrictions could be placed on the "legislative rights of this country, with regard to America," but "taxes of this kind [internal] were contrary to the fundamental principles of commerce on which the Colonies were founded."[18] Burke was understandably sensitive on the subject of the Declaratory Act and he returned to it later in his peroration. He made a distinction between Parliament as "the local legislature of this island" and Parliament as an "imperial" legislature that "superintends all the several interior legislatures ... without annihilating any." In this latter capacity, Parliament only "acts if the inferior legislatures fail to perform their duties properly." But in order to fulfill this function, Parliament's "powers must be boundless." "This," Burke insisted, "is what I meant when I have said at various times, that I consider the power of taxing in parliament as an instrument of empire, and not as a means of supply."[19] To answer those who blame all the disturbance in America on the repeal of the Stamp Act, Burke quoted from the letters of Governor Francis Bernard of Massachusetts and General Thomas Gage, the commander in chief of British troops in North America, both referring to a state of "insurrection" in the colonies before the repeal of the act, with the gratitude and cooperation of the colonists after repeal.[20]

Burke next turned to the unfortunate Chatham ministry, which, without his guiding hand, violated his principles as evidenced by the passage of the Townshend Acts. Burke implored the House to repeal the tea duty and to forego the Coercive Acts. "Let us act like men, let us act like statesmen" was his final appeal.[21] One hundred eighty-two members of the House of Commons rejected it; only forty-nine voted for repeal. As Burke wrote to New York, "the Ministry appears stronger than ever.... My advice has little weight anywhere."[22]

One of the forty-nine who did take his advice, Charles James Fox, was to be a notable addition to the British "friends" of America. Fox was an unlikely candidate for membership in this coterie. He was the great-great-grandson of Charles II, the grandson of the second duke of Richmond, and the son of Lord Holland (better known as Henry Fox), one of the leading politicians of the mid-eighteenth century and an inveterate enemy of William Pitt. Charles James Fox attended Eton and Oxford, then completed his education with the customary tour of the continent. In 1768, at the tender age of nineteen, his father provided him with a seat in the House of Commons. Perhaps Lord Holland hoped that politics would distract his son from the gaming tables.[23] If so, he was to be sorely disappointed.

Nevertheless, Fox proved to be an eloquent speaker and his support of the government against Wilkes and his opposition to parliamentary reform won him an appointment to Lord North's ministry, first as a Lord of the Admiralty and then as a member of the Treasury Board. However, he did not always vote with the ministry and, early in 1774, he was removed from office. Any hope of reconciliation between North and Fox vanished soon after the Boston Tea Party and the British government's reaction to it.

Fox was willing to support the Boston Port Bill if the Tea Act were repealed. (Others, according to Burke, voted for it on the same basis.) He opposed the Massachusetts Government Bill, terming it "violent because it is useless, useless because weak." He protested against the Massachusetts Justice Bill on the ground that "Americans have a right to the same laws as we [Englishmen] have." And in all these deliberations, he expressed the same sentiment as he did during the debate on the repeal of the Tea Act: "By leaving America untaxed she would be useful and obedient and by taxing her . . . she would be contrary."[24]

Before going further, we should meet Fox's uncle, another descendant of an illegitimate son of King Charles II, Charles Lennox, the third duke of Richmond.[25] Born in 1735, he enlisted in the army at seventeen, served with distinction in the Seven Years' War, and, by 1765, was the British ambassador to France. He returned to England, however, because he felt his vote might be needed in the House of Lords for the repeal of the Stamp Act. Burke was impressed with Richmond's "shrewdness" in this debate and predicted he would become "a considerable man."[26] He did become secretary of state for the Southern Department during the last seven weeks of the Rockingham administration but was not retained by Lord Chatham. The records of debates in the House of Lords are scanty, but it is clear that Richmond favored the repeal of the Townshend Acts and he took an active role in opposing the Coercive Acts.[27] He attacked the Boston Port Bill "with much more warmth than had appeared in the Commons," and again he spoke "warmly" against the Massachusetts Government Bill, which he felt the colonists "*would be in the right to resist*" (italics in original). He protested against the Massachusetts Justice Bill with "his usual spirit" and demanded a formal vote on the Quartering Bill—which he lost 57 to 16.[28] The duke was nothing if not tenacious; as late as February 1775, he was still inveighing against the Coercive Acts.[29]

It is not surprising, however, that the government was able to pass the Coercive Acts so easily. In the House of Commons, the Rockinghamites numbered about forty; Chatham's followers were down to about a dozen and the only additional votes they could count on came from a scattering of city radicals and independents. The highest opposition vote, on the Massachusetts Government Bill, was sixty-four. The situation in the House of Lords was even more discouraging. In addition, British merchants were no longer as concerned with a disruption of the American trade as they had been in the 1760s. Trade with other European nations had burgeoned in the early 1770s, while colonial trade had declined because of political instability. They, therefore, gave the opposition no meaningful support. As Burke wrote in September 1774, "the insensibility of the merchants of London is of a degree and kind scarcely to be conceived. Even those who are the most likely to be overwhelmed by any real American confusion are amongst the most supine."[30] The Quebec Act, because it was "technically" or strictly speaking not one of the Coercive Acts (though Americans considered it one of the Intolerable Acts), will not be discussed here. It was resented in America (and in England) because it: (1) allowed Quebec to be ruled only by a governor and council with no elected legislature; (2) gave Roman Catholics the right to exercise their religion and recognized their clergy; (3) retained French civil law and land tenure, though English criminal law was introduced; and (4) extended Quebec's boundaries west and south to include most of the Ohio Valley, thus impeding western settlement.

Across the Atlantic, the colonists remained adamant. Popular opinion in Boston was strongly against indemnifying the East India Company and certainly against prosecuting any of the alleged leaders of the Boston Tea Party. In September 1774, at the First Continental Congress, the other colonies made it clear that they supported Massachusetts by voting for nonimportation of British goods beginning December 1, 1774, and nonexportation of goods to Great Britain after September 10, 1775, as well as by organizing a network of committees to enforce these boycotts.

Partly because of this reaction from America and partly for unrelated reasons, King George suggested an early dissolution of Parliament in September 1774 (it was not scheduled to terminate until March 1775). The ensuing election, if anything, strengthened Lord North's position in the House of Commons. The results of this election should not, however, necessarily be considered an endorsement of his American policy, although he and the king took it as such. As Burke complained, "the disorder and discontent of all America . . . operate [as a political factor] as little as the division of Poland."[31] In most constituencies, local rather than national issues decided the elections. A specifically American issue, as well as other features of the radical program, was raised only in London, Bristol, and a few other port towns. A pledge, composed by John Wilkes, promised to pass an act for the repeal of the four late [Coercive] acts respecting America ... being fully persuaded that the passing of such an act will be of the utmost importance for the security of the excellent constitution, and the restoration of the rights and liberties of our fellow-subjects in America.[32]

One friend of America (though not necessarily for this reason), Governor Pownall, lost his seat in this election. However, Lord North, possibly to win him over and/or to take advantage of his expertise, quickly found him another seat. Even though this meant deserting the Whig opposition, Pownall still hoped to play a role in settling the American conflict. Toward the end of 1774, he attempted to convince Benjamin Franklin that a commission headed by him (Pownall) might be sent to America to "settle the differences" between the colonists and Great Britain, but Franklin had little faith in the project ever materializing.[33] Pownall had discussed such a proposal with Lord Dartmouth, the colonial secretary who tended to take a somewhat more conciliatory attitude toward America than his colleagues. As Dartmouth noted, Pownall "had a mind to go to America and be the King's Representative and preside over all the colonies." Dartmouth broached the scheme to his ministerial colleagues but, as Franklin had predicted, "it was scouted at."[34]

Instead, the cabinet decided to present more repressive measures to Parliament: Military and naval reinforcements were to be sent to America and colonial trade was to be limited to Great Britain, Ireland, and the West Indies; all foreign ports were to be off-limits. The only "conciliatory" proposal was the promise that Parliament would not tax any colony that promised to provide adequate support of its military and administrative needs. But the discussion, and the results, of these measures must await another chapter.

Notes

1. Richard Henry Lee, ed., *The Life of Arthur Lee, LLD*, I, p. 237.
2. R.C. Simmons and P.D.G. Thomas, eds., *Proceedings and Debates of the British Parliaments Respecting North America, 1754–1783* (hereafter referred to as *Parliament Debates*), III, p. 490.
3. Ibid., IV, p. 31.
4. Ibid., p. 117.
5. Ibid., p. 66.
6. Ibid., p. 142.
7. Ibid., p. 44.
8. Thomas W. Copeland et al., eds., *The Correspondence of Edmund Burke* (hereafter referred to as *Burke Correspondence*), II, p. 291.
9. Ibid., pp. 290–293.
10. Ibid., p. 313.

11. Ibid., p. 528; Simmons and Thomas, *Parliament Debates,* IV, pp. 123–126.

12. Ibid., pp. 152, 278, 280.

13. Ibid., p. 370.

14. Ibid., pp. 261, 386.

15. Ibid., p. 318.

16. Simmons and Thomas, *Parliament Debates,* IV, pp. 438–440.

17. Ibid., pp. 202–206, 208–209.

18. Ibid., pp. 210–211, 216–217.

19. Ibid., p. 227.

20. Ibid., pp. 219–221.

21. Ibid., pp. 222–228.

22. Copeland et al., *Burke Correspondence,* II, p. 534.

23. Charles James Fox has been the subject of numerous biographies; among the more recent are Loren Reid, *Charles James Fox: A Man of the People,* and John W. Derry, *Charles James Fox.*

24. Simmons and Thomas, *Parliament Debates,* IV, pp. 77, 232, 273; Copeland et al., *Burke Correspondence,* II, p. 533.

25. The best modern work on Richmond is Alison Gilbert Olson, *The Radical Duke: Career and Correspondence of Charles Lennox, third Duke of Richmond.*

26. Simmons and Thomas, *Parliament Debates,* II, p. 339; Copeland et al., *Burke Correspondence,* I, p. 244.

27. Simmons and Thomas, *Parliament Debates,* III, pp.49–50.

28. Ibid., IV, pp. 146, 420, 434, 441.

29. Ibid., V, p. 335.

30. Copeland et al., *Burke Correspondence,* III, p. 31.

31. Ibid.

32. From the *Annual Register* of September 26, 1774, as quoted in Simon Maccoby, ed., *The English Radical Tradition, 1763–1914,* pp. 25–26.

33. Albert H. Smith, ed., *The Writings of Benjamin Franklin,* VI, pp. 348–349.

34. Peter Orlando Hutchinson, ed., *The Diary and Letters of His Excellency Thomas Hutchinson, Esq.,* I, pp. 251, 363.

A Dire Prediction

In his speech opening Parliament on November 30, 1774, the king assured his listeners that

> you may depend on My firm and stedfast Resolution to withstand every Attempt to weaken or impair the supreme Authority of this Legislature over all the Dominions on My Crown, the Maintenance of which I consider as essential to the Dignity, the Safety, and the Welfare of the *British* Empire, assuring myself that, while I act upon these Principles, I shall never fail to receive your Assistance and Support.[1] [italics in original]

In the House of Commons, Burke realized the implied threat of further punitive actions against America but argued that North's policies had backfired, America was united behind Massachusetts, and British commerce and industry were suffering in consequence. His motion opposing North's American policy, however, was outvoted by a margin of more than three to one.[2] Nevertheless, in December, Lord North agreed to supply information and form a committee to consult on colonial affairs, which he did on January 19, 1775.[3]

The debate in the House of Commons on the American question was precipitated by petitions by merchants from London, Bristol, Glasgow, Liverpool, and several other towns requesting a change in colonial policies because of the damage the Coercive Acts had done to their trade with America. In contrast, the traders and manufacturers of Birmingham petitioned against any relaxation of the Coercive Acts. Burke objected to this last petition as a "warlike, blood thirsty petition" not from persons involved in the trade with America, but it was taken into consideration with the others.[4] Burke then criticized North for adjourning Parliament just "to eat mince pies, and drink Christmas ale" at such a time of crisis and doubted his sincerity in forming the committee for American affairs. On January 26, he and Fox returned to the attack. Burke predicted that America could not be destroyed "without at the same time plunging a dagger into the vitals of Great Britain." Fox followed with an assertion that the Coercive Acts "were framed on false information, conceived in weakness and ignorance, and executed with negligence."[5]

On February 2, North presented a motion that a state of rebellion existed in Massachusetts abetted by the other colonies. Fox moved an amendment that would have attenuated the motion and Burke supported it, but North's original motion passed easily. Four days later, Burke and Wilkes (who had regained his parliamentary seat and was also Lord Mayor of London) warned against taking further punitive action against America. Wilkes spoke vividly of American financial support in past wars, their continued loyalty to Great Britain, and their ultimate "rise to independence, to power, to all greatness of the most renowned status" if the British government should persist in its present policy.[6]

On February 9, Fox accused North of planning to prevent New Englanders from fishing on the banks off Newfoundland. The next day, North proved him correct by not only presenting that bill but also moving to cut off New England's trade with Great Britain, Ireland, and the West Indies. Burke charged that this bill would "beggar" British merchants and manufacturers and wrote to a friend that it was a "most infamous Bill for famishing the four provinces of New England."[7] While debate on this bill was still pending, Lord North introduced a "conciliatory proposition" that exempted from parliamentary taxation any colony that voluntarily made a contribution satisfactory to the British government for military defense and support of its civil government and judicial system. Fox immediately declared that "No one in this country, who is sincerely for peace, will trust the speciousness of his expression, and the Americans will reject them with disdain." Burke, too, found the measure "calculated to increase the disorders and confusions in America." He claimed that as long as Parliament had the power to decide on the amounts of the colonial assessment and how it was to be used, it was just another form of taxation without representation and the colonies would never agree to it. Nevertheless, even though some members of the House felt that North's resolution was too lenient to America, it was approved on February 20 by a vote of more than three to one.[8]

In March, debates on the New England trade and fisheries bill resumed. Fox claimed that the bill was designed "to exasperate the colonies into open and direct rebellion." Burke asserted that the act would cause a famine in New England and economic failure in Great Britain. But once again the government's majority was better than three to one.[9] North then presented a similar bill that included the other American colonies. With its passage a foregone conclusion, debate on the bill was desultory, and neither Burke nor Fox was present when the bill was passed early in April by a majority of four to one.[10]

Earlier, on March 22, 1775, Burke had made his famous speech, *On Conciliation with America.* He opened by affirming that only the possibility of "an incurable alienation of our colonies" and the weakness of Lord North's conciliatory proposal impelled him to propose a more effective plan of conciliation. Before taking any rash steps, he asked his colleagues to take into consideration the large and ever-growing American population and the inestimable value of its trade with Great Britain. Then he pointed out that "a love of freedom" or "spirit of liberty" was the predominant characteristic of the American people. He gave six reasons for this phenomenon: (1) Americans are descendants of liberty-loving English citizens; (2) the colonial legislatures are "popular"; (3) most Americans are Dissenters; (4) slaveholders tend to be "by far the most proud and jealous of their freedom"; (5) Americans, even if not lawyers, are "smatterers in law"; and (6) "three thousand miles of ocean lie between you and them."[11]

This American "spirit of liberty" left Great Britain only three alternatives: "To change that spirit . . . by removing the causes; To prosecute it as criminal; Or to comply with it as necessary." Burke thought the first two alternatives "impractical," "inapplicable," or "in the highest degree inexpedient." Obviously, according to Burke, Great Britain must "conciliate and concede." His plan included the following components: (1) the surrender of Parliament's right to tax the colonies (he completely discounted the possibility of American representation in Parliament); (2) the return to the system of requisitions by the colonial legislatures (which, he contended had worked successfully until 1763); (3) the repeal of the Coercive Acts and certain acts of trade; and (4) the reform of the colonial judicial system by allowing judges to serve during good behavior (rather than at royal pleasure) and making the admiralty courts more accessible.[12]

Burke attempted to allay fears that British concession would only stimulate Americans to demand more privileges. He doubted whether "giving, by an act of free grace and indulgence, to two millions of my fellow citizens, some share of those rights which I have always been taught to value" would lead to the destruction of the empire. He contrasted his conciliatory plan with Lord North's, alleging that the latter's will not satisfy colonial objections that the proposed system of parliamentary taxation would be impossible to implement. Mine is "plain and simple," North's "full of perplexed and intricate mazes." Mine is "mild," North's "harsh." "Mine is what becomes the dignity of a ruling people; gratuitous, unconditional, and not held out as a matter of bargain and sale." Burke insisted his plan would raise an American revenue, North's, "not a shilling."[13]

Burke concluded dramatically:

> My hold of the colonies is in the close affection which grows from common names, from kindred blood, from similar privileges, and equal protection. These are ties which though light as air, are as strong as links of iron. Let the colonies always keep the idea of their civil rights associated with your government; they will cling and grapple to you; and no force under heaven will be of power to tear them from their allegiance. But let it be once understood that your government may be one thing, and their privilege another . . . that these two things may exist without any mutual relation; the cement is gone; the cohesion is loosened; and every thing hastens to decay and dissolution.[14]

Burke spoke for almost three hours and for the entire time "the attention of the House was riveted to him." It was the "ablest performance of the age." "It is thought this speech if not the best, was at least inferior to none, which Mr. Burke ever delivered." He never spoke "with more force and eloquence." These were some of the panegyrics that followed his oration. But Lord North had the votes; every one of Burke's proposals was defeated and his plan was dismissed by a vote of 270 to 78.[15]

In May, in his capacity of agent for the colony of New York, Burke attempted to win a hearing for a petition from that colony against some of the laws recently passed by Parliament. Burke argued the acceptance of a petition did not mean that Parliament approved of all its components and asserted that this was an ideal opportunity for "putting an end to the unhappy disputes with the colonies." North, however, condemned it as inadmissible because it denied parliamentary sovereignty over the colonies. Fox pointed out that New York was not denying Parliament's right to tax them but only the "exercise" of this right and felt that a refusal to hear the petition would only discourage American moderates from having any faith in British justice toward the colonies. Once again, North triumphed and the petition was never heard.[16]

John Wilkes also organized a petition campaign. In April 1775, he encouraged a group of aldermen and liverymen (members of London's guilds) to send a petition to the king requesting repeal of the Coercive Acts and the dismissal of the ministers responsible for them. The king received the petition but expressed "astonishment" at its sentiments and once again voiced approval of his ministers' policies. George III was so incensed at this petition that he had Wilkes informed that he would no longer receive petitions unless they were from the City of London in Common Council assembled. This was a change in procedure to which Wilkes objected but without success. In July 1775, the Common Council did send a petition requesting that conciliatory measures toward America be explored but, although it was heard, it too, was rejected (as were similar petitions in 1776 and 1778).[17]

Parliament had adjourned in May and was to reconvene in October. During that interim, the news of Lexington and Concord and Bunker Hill had arrived in Great Britain and, in August, the king had proclaimed the colonies to be in a state of rebellion. Burke also felt the need of a petition campaign to influence the upcoming session. He wrote Rockingham that "All direction of public humor and opinion must originate in a few." Burke realized that the war would almost automatically rally public support behind the government. Unless the opposition could find "support without Doors [outside Parliament]," its only viable option would be "to absent ourselves from Parliament." Rockingham had little confidence in public protests and preferred a parliamentary memorial to the king, but Burke insisted that if "something is not done before the meeting of Parliament, nothing which can be done afterwards, will avail in the smallest degree."[18]

Sadly, for the American cause, the Whigs would not cooperate with the Wilkites. In one letter to Rockingham, Burke wrote that a meeting called by Wilkes would only "throw disgrace upon all proceedings for pacification" and, in another, referred to his efforts "to keep the City [London], now and forever, out of the hands of the Wilkes's."[19] Burke had an embarrassing moment in connection with another petition, the Olive Branch Petition, sent by the Second Continental Congress to King George. Arthur Lee and many of his friends urged Burke to be present when it was delivered to Lord Dartmouth in order to reinforce his image as a defender of American liberties. Burke, however, felt that, as agent for New York, he could not participate because New York had not sent delegates to the Congress. In any case, he was positive that the king would refuse to entertain any petition from a group of rebels.[20]

In the royal address at the opening of Parliament in October 1775, the king pledged to put "a speedy End to these disorders [in America]" yet he was sending a commission to America so that when Americans "shall become sensible of their Error, I shall be ready to receive the Misled with Tenderness and Mercy."[21] The debate in the House of Commons was turbulent. Wilkes felt it necessary to protest against "an unjust, ruinous, felonious, and murderous war." He called upon the king to "sheath the sword . . . adopt some form of negotiation . . . and thereby restore peace and harmony to this distracted empire." Burke ridiculed North's earlier promises of subduing America and urged a speedy end to the war. Fox called North a "blundering pilot" and complimented Americans for resisting rather than "to submit to slavery." Still, the governmental policy was approved by a vote of more than two to one, although there was some dissatisfaction with the garrisoning of Gibraltar and Minorca with Hanoverian troops.[22]

Though always defeated, the opposition sniped at North whenever possible. When Barré inquired about the "numbers, state, and disposition" of the British army in America, he was offered figures as of the previous July. Fox and Burke immediately accused North of withholding information, the latter expressing the wish that Parliament were as well informed about the British army "as the continental congress."[23] When Oxford University sent an address to the king supporting his American policy, Burke "thundered out" that these "learned, religious men" should restrict their efforts to "pious prayers for the good of their country." Fox attacked an address from the Devonshire Militia as "unconstitutional," coming from a military group.[24] On November 16, however, Burke made another serious attempt to end the American war. He stated that this could be done in three ways: a war of conquest, a combination of war and conciliation, or through immediate concessions to America. He explained why he thought the first choice had "no probability of success" and would only embroil Great Britain in a European war.[25] Next, he discussed the second choice, the one favored by the ministry. "This armed negotiation for taxes," he claimed, "would therefore inevitably defeat its own purposes."[26] Finally, he advocated his own choice, "concessions previous to treaty." He placed the blame for the need of extensive concessions on North's mishandling of the problem and doubted whether he was competent to carry on the necessary negotiations. Burke did not advocate the repeal of the Declaratory Act (always a sensitive subject for him), or all the laws passed since 1763, but he did insist that the Coercive Acts be rescinded and that Parliament renounce its right to tax America. Only this plan could "put the standard of American liberty into the hands of the friends to British government." Once again, three and a half hours of oratory was rewarded with only 105 votes against the ministry's 210.[27]

Following his two-pronged policy of coercion and conciliation, North introduced two measures on November 20. One was a bill prohibiting all trade with the Thirteen Colonies and authorized the seizures of all American vessels; the other was a confirmation of the king's promise to appoint commissioners to make peace. In the debate on the bill, Fox called it "a declaration of perpetual war" against America and predicted it would ruin British manufacturers. The bill passed in December 1775, however, by a vote of 112 to 16.[28] Before the second bill was introduced, the Wilkites requested an investigation into "who the persons were that advised the present ruinous measures against America." Wilkes described the motion as crucial because Britain was "on the eve of an eternal, political separation from the western world." He cited the strength of America in men and arms and concluded that it "cannot be subdued." He felt that this motion might lead to merited impeachment of Lord North. Needless to say, this motion was defeated by an overwhelming vote of 163 to 10.[29]

The second proposal, the appointment of commissioners, received much less attention because it was to be a royal, rather than a parliamentary, commission. Even before it was formally announced, the Whigs tried to make sure that the commissioners were empowered to treat with any American governmental body "without enquiring into the manner in which they had been convened," while North assured his followers that Parliament's approval would be required on any agreement reached by the commissioners. In February 1776, David Hartley doubted the effectiveness of a commission that "had no power to offer redress of grievances" and could only grant pardons if Americans would agree to "unconditional submission." It was not until May 22, 1776, when adjournment was eminent (though the opposition had tried, but failed, to keep Parliament in session), that General Conway asked for a copy of the instructions given to Lord Richard Howe and his brother, General William Howe, who had been chosen to head the commission. He hoped that they included the renunciation of parliamentary taxing power over the colonies and the confirmation of colonial charters. North, however, was adamant; he refused the "communication of any instructions previous to their execution." Burke called North's response "nonsense," but once again the ministers were able to defeat Conway's motion and Parliament adjourned.[30] As Burke wrote, "Our session is over; and I hardly can believe, by the Tranquility of every thing about me, that we are a people who have just lost an Empire."[31]

The concern of Burke and his allies about the commission was well founded. Its instructions mandated it to insist on an American cease-fire, dissolution of the Continental Congress, reestablishment of legitimate colonial assemblies, acceptance of North's Conciliatory Proposal, and compensation for the Loyalists before making peace. In addition, the commission was not to sign a treaty with any colony that did not make a specific declaration of submission to parliamentary authority. In exchange, Lord Howe was authorized to grant pardons (with some exceptions), allow judges to serve during good behavior, and promise future discussion of colonial grievances (except the Quebec Act). These terms had been dictated by the hard-liners in North's cabinet; after the Declaration of Independence (and even before), the commission had no possible chance of success.[32]

In August, news of the Declaration of Independence reached Great Britain. Fox wrote Burke calling for a strategy meeting before the opening of Parliament, but Burke was discouraged by Howe's victories on Long Island and his occupation of New York City. Fox shared his distress but still believed that "some firm and vigorous step," rather than "secession" from Parliament, was the proper reaction.[33] However, no strategy decision was reached and, when Parliament reassembled on October 31, the king announced that further campaigns would be necessary before "the blessings of law and liberty" could be restored to the American colonies.[34] In a speech objecting to the royal address, Wilkes minimized the importance of Howe's victory on Long Island, blamed the declaration of American independence on "the unjust and sanguinary measures" of the ministry, and maintained that "It is impossible for this island to conquer and hold America." And if America were conquered, it would necessitate a large army to occupy it. Nevertheless, the royal address was overwhelmingly approved.[35]

A few days later, Parliament received a copy of a proclamation issued in America by Lord Howe in which he promised that the king would "concur in the revisal of all his acts by which his subjects there may think themselves aggrieved." Burke then seconded a motion to have the Commons discuss this "revisal" because he felt that Parliament should be involved. Lord North was put in an embarrassing position. He could not disavow Howe's offer, but he had no intention of allowing Parliament to be involved in the negotiating process. He therefore contended that the American declaration of independence had invalidated Howe's offer, although the proclamation was issued in September 1776. Burke responded that the seven-month delay in sending out the commissioners impelled Americans to declare their independence and now this declaration was being used as an excuse not to negotiate with them in good faith. North's rationale prevailed, however, and the motion was defeated.[36]

Many Whigs "seceded" from Parliament after this defeat. But during the Christmas recess, Burke busily planned strategy for the coming year. He believed that without French support, America would be forced to discuss peace terms with Great Britain. He hoped they might be willing to treat on the basis of his conciliatory proposals of November 1775. Burke temporarily thought of meeting with Benjamin Franklin but quickly dropped this idea. He, himself, was uncertain how to proceed; at one point, he suggested secession to Rockingham as "most advisable," at another point, he advised presenting a "succession of Measures" so that Whig attendance would remain constant. Unable to make a definite choice, the Rockinghamites delegated him to prepare *An Address to the King*, laying out their views on Anglo-American policy.[37]

Burke began his *Address* with an apology, but stated that "the situation into which the British Empire has been brought" made it necessary. He blamed the "disorders" in America on ministerial plans "laid in Error; pursued with obstinacy; and conducted without Wisdom." Their cardinal sin was "to dispose of the Property of a whole People without their consent." Burke claimed that all Americans (even the Loyalists) agreed that this was "subversive of all their rights." Burke affirmed that this unanimity, even if disputable, must be respected even if it conflicted with the rights of "*the Supreme Power*" [i.e., Parliament; italics in original]. He continued with a review of the ministerial measures, including the incitement of slave insurrections and Indian attacks, which drove Americans to war and independence.[38]

Burke then expounded the philosophy of the Whig opposition. We are opposed to "all attempts to render the Supremacy of one part of your Dominions inconsistent with the Liberty and safety of all the rest." A conquest of America would not only "utterly ruin our finances . . . It will become an apt, powerful, and certain Engine for the destruction of our Freedom here." Burke was very direct: "Your Throne cannot stand secure upon the principles of unconditional submission and passive obedience." As for Parliament, it, too, cannot be "a Protector of Liberty" to one part of the empire and "a friend of Despotism" in another. If Parliament had allowed the colonial assemblies to operate in their spheres, they would never have questioned Parliament's authority over them.[39]

Burke then alluded to the possibility of a Whig secession from Parliament. "The British Empire is in convulsions" but "we find ourselves wholly unable to oppose and unwilling to behold." However, if "but the smallest hope . . . appear, of a return to the . . . true policy of this Kingdom, We shall with Joy and readiness return to our attendance." And, he concluded, whatever happens, we will "have discharged our Consciences by the faithful representation to your Majesty."[40] Burke was afraid that the *Address* might lead to parliamentary censure or even prosecution of some of the Whigs for libel. Perhaps for this reason and/or the lack of expectation of public support, the *Address* was never presented to the king.[41]

Burke wrote another cogent but futile paper at this same time, entitled *Address to the Colonists*. In this document, he tried to dispel the unfortunate idea that there "no longer subsist between you and us any common and kindred principles, upon which we can possibly unite." He contended that "the largest and soundest part of this Kingdom, perseveres in the most perfect unity of sentiments, principles, and affections, with you." Even if America should be defeated, Burke promised that Britons would "put you voluntarily in possession of those very privileges, which you had in vain attempted to assert by arms." But he preferred, on the other hand, that America should remain independent rather than be in "Servitude" within the British empire.[42]

Burke reasserted his belief in an empire in which America would voluntarily pay its share of expenses and in which its charters would be inviolate. He expressed "shame and regret" for the use of foreign mercenaries, slaves, and Indians in the war. Yet, he still maintained that American liberty would be best served by remaining part of the British empire rather than under an "untried" form of government. Burke did not ask for "unconditional submission" but implied that under a different [Whig] administration, mutually satisfying terms could be speedily arranged. He also hinted that, although previously hoping that Parliament's authority over the colonies could be "limited by its own equity and discretion," events had convinced him that constitutional change was necessary in order to obtain "ratified security for your liberties and our quiet." Burke concluded with a call upon the colonies to act with discretion, remain part of the empire, and accept the congratulations of the "well wishers of the liberty and union of this Empire."[43]

This *Address* was never published or put to any use and the Rockingham group absented themselves from Parliament. This caused dissatisfaction particularly among Burke's constituents in Bristol and, in early April 1777, he was forced to write a defense of his actions (or inaction) in a *Letter to the Sheriffs of Bristol.*[44] Burke opened the *Letter* by discussing two acts that had passed during his absence from Parliament, one of which limited the right of habeas corpus for captured American seamen or persons accused of treason in America. He expressed his abhorrence of the act but pointed out that his presence in the House of Commons would not have prevented its passage.[45] Burke went on to generalize on the detrimental effects of the American war on English liberties, English manners, and the English economy. He insisted that only compromise could end the war and the opposition to it was not "encouragement to rebellion." Burke reasserted his belief in parliamentary supremacy but admitted his conversion to the belief that no "legislative rights can be safely exercised without regard to the general opinion of those who are to be governed." An imperial legislature must unify its empire but still respect the "liberty and safety" of its dominions.[46]

Burke then reviewed the history of British colonial administration, stressing particularly the growth in the powers of the colonial assemblies. He claimed it was only when "the colonies were too proud to submit, too strong to be forced, too enlightened not to see all the consequences which must arise from this system" that Parliament made the "fatal" mistake in attempting to tax the colonies. Though still defending the wisdom, in 1766, of passing the Declaratory Act, Burke believed that the events of the following decade made it necessary for Parliament to relinquish its powers of taxation over the colonies. It was better to part with a limb "to save the body." He was willing to do even more to end "a fruitless, hopeless, unnatural civil war." His opponents claimed this would have been tantamount to granting "independency, without a war" and, though Burke doubted that, he still felt it preferable to independency with a war.[47] Burke concluded with a defense of his own and his party's actions. He described the temper of the times as one in which "the least resistance to power appears more inexcusable in our eyes than the greatest abuses of authority." He blamed this on the American war and pledged himself to continue his fight for an "honorable and liberal accommodation" of the differences between Great Britain and its erstwhile colonies.[48] In a sense this letter, too, was unnecessary. By the middle of April, the Rockinghamites returned to Parliament to continue their opposition to ministerial policies.

Their first opportunity arrived when the king requested help in paying debts of over £600,000 on his civil list. The opposition claimed that much of this debt had been incurred through wastage and the bribery and corruption necessary to keep Lord North's government in power. Burke claimed that the demand "was full of indecency and impropriety" when all of Great Britain was saddled with excessive taxation. Nevertheless, the House of Commons agreed to discuss the request and on April 18 a member moved not only to pay the debt but to increase the royal allowance by £100,000 a year. During the course of the debate, Sawbridge minced no words in charging that the deficit had been caused by the "corrupting of both houses." The House erupted into "great confusion," which Burke attempted to calm by substituting the word "influence" for "corruption"—a term he thought somewhat "course and impolite." Yet he agreed that Sawbridge was essentially correct and that the present royal allowance, "if properly managed, was amply sufficient." After all the confusion, the House voted to increase the allowance.[49]

One more, almost humorous, event marked the passage of this bill. When announcing the passage of this bill to the king, the Speaker of the House referred to it as granting funds "great beyond your Majesty's highest wants." A few days later, a ministerial spokesman criticized the Speaker for implying that Parliament had been too generous. The Speaker was insulted and requested a vote of confidence from the House. This gave Burke the opportunity to write a motion (delivered by Fox because of Burke's hoarseness) declaring that the Speaker "did express . . . the zeal of this House for the support of the honour and dignity of the crown." The Speaker indicated that a defeat of this motion would force him to resign. The ministry was in no position to replace him as Speaker and was forced to support the motion to the amusement of the opposition.[50]

No question was too removed for Burke to bring up the American war. When a motion to vote £3,000 to the British Museum reached the floor, he requested that it be increased because when millions were granted "for slaying our brethren and fellow subjects in America," Parliament should be more generous in encouraging "the liberal and polite arts."[51] In May, during the debate on the budget, he warned that Great Britain had no hope of regaining American revenue or even American trade.[52] No other American, or related, business came up and Parliament recessed for the summer. During this recess, Burke tended to be pessimistic about America's ability to withstand British military pressure unless, and he was beginning to think it more likely, France and Spain would come to its aid. He was also pessimistic, as he wrote Fox, about "those whom we love and trust [the Rockinghamites] to do anything constructive about the situation" particularly considering the prowar state of British public opinion. Rockingham was more sanguine believing that "there is some dawn of light bring in upon the minds of the publick" but still preferring to wait for news of military results in America before deciding on strategy.[53]

When Parliament reconvened in November 1777, the king's speech expressed confidence in ultimate victory but felt it necessary to request additional funds for both the army and navy. The opposition instead recommended a cessation of hostilities and negotiations to settle outstanding differences. Wilkes made a speech in support of this motion, picturing a bloody, unsuccessful war that "must end in the ruin of our country." He dwelt at length on all these points, concluding with the hope that "guided by the principles of liberty and justice, that the blessings of peace and union may be restored, and permanently remain to the whole empire." Burke followed with a plea for Great Britain to offer proposals for peace before either side had a definite military advantage, so it could make them "with honour" and the colonists could accept them "without dishonour." Ministerial opposition defeated these suggestions decisively.[54]

Burke opposed the huge increase in the amount of money to be spent on the army and navy, the extension of the suspension of habeas corpus passed the previous year, and North's withholding of papers on the American situation.[55] He was, however, silent when Wilkes in December 1777, after the arrival of the news of Burgoyne's surrender, proposed the repeal of the Declaratory Act. Wilkes averred that this act, which authorized parliamentary taxation of America, was "the root of the evil, the confessed cause and origin of the American war," "the fountain from which not only waters of bitterness, but rivers of blood have flowed." Wilkes, as usual, covered all aspects of the war, including the use of Indian troops against the colonists, which was to be a constant source of concern to the opposition. In an appeal for Whig support, he excused them for passing the Declaratory Act on the ground that without it they could not have repealed the Stamp Act. Wilkes also announced that he planned to request the repeal of all American acts passed since 1763. Only in this way, he concluded, would Great Britain save itself and "regain our colonies." The Whigs did not respond to his appeal and his motion was defeated by a vote of 160 to 10.[56]

At this point, we may jump ahead to April 1778, when a motion was again made in the House to repeal the Declaratory Act. On this occasion, Burke observed that the act was "wise at the time it was made" but "in the present state of affairs, he thought it was time to give it up." However, North objected and the motion was not considered at the time.[57] As mentioned earlier, the Whigs were extremely sensitive to the employment of Indians against the colonists. In February, Burke requested information on this question, suggesting that their increased use was under consideration by the ministry. He stated that this policy would damage "our reputation, as a civilized people" and any hope of "reconciling the minds of the colonies to his Majesty's government." He pointed out that the Americans had never made any attempt to enlist them and that, though the British tried, they could not restrain Indian savagery. Burke also fulminated against the endeavors to incite slave insurrections. He closed by asking Parliament to censure these policies so it could not be accused of condoning practices "repugnant to all the feelings of humanity." North argued that these measures were "unavoidable" and the House agreed with him.[58]

Burgoyne's surrender and the rumors of an impending alliance between France and the United States forced Lord North in February 1778 to once again attempt peace negotiations with the United States. Parliament was to abandon its right of taxation and other terms were left open for negotiation. (Details of the commission's instruction are found in chapter 12.) Burke warned that the success or failure of the mission depended on the men chosen for it and hoped that a parliamentary committee would have a voice in their selection. This suggestion was not accepted.[59] The commission headed by the inexperienced earl of Carlisle did not embark for America until the middle of April. A few days before it left, the House of Commons entertained a motion to empower it to recognize American independence, if that were necessary to ensure peace. Burke had now come full circle.

> He thought it the duty of the Committee to prevent the further waste of treasure and expence of blood, by enlarging the terms of concession; and making the Americans, by an act of our legislature, what they had irrevocably, by the force of arms, made themselves a free people.[60]

The motion was not even brought to a vote. The Carlisle commission went to America and arrived home in December, after a half year of embarrassment, humiliation, and abject failure. During the interim, Burke kept up his incessant guerrilla warfare on the ministry. He objected to an expenditure for scalping knives, which he called "disgraceful for religion and humanity." When Wilkes moved to forbid private loans or gifts to the crown without the consent of Parliament, Burke supported him particularly when the money was to be used to raise troops. And he supported Hartley's motion made at the end of May 1778 to put an end to the American war (see chapter 13). Soon after, the session came to an end.[61]

After this date, Burke became less engaged in American affairs because of his involvement in attempts to reform the civil lists, improve Anglo-Irish relations, increase toleration for Catholics, and revise Britain's system of Indian governance. He was always concerned, however, with the treatment of American prisoners in Great Britain (which he described as "inhumane"). And, in 1781, he served as Benjamin Franklin's agent in securing the release of Henry Laurens of South Carolina, a revolutionary leader who had been captured at sea on his way to Holland and confined as a possible traitor in the Tower of London. Eventually, Laurens was released on bail and secured his freedom in exchange for that of Lord Cornwallis.[62]

But Burke had certainly been correct, if not actually overoptimistic, when he wrote Rockingham in 1775 that "I do not think that Weeks, or even Months, or years will bring the Monarch, the Ministers, or the people [to the necessity of] amendment or alteration of [North's] System."[63]

Notes

1. R.C. Simmons and P.D.G. Thomas, eds., *Proceedings and Debates of the British Parliaments Respecting North America, 1754–1783* (hereafter referred to as *Parliament Debates*), V, pp. 234–235.

2. Ibid., p. 242.

3. Ibid., pp. 261–266.

4. Ibid., pp. 287, 289, 300–302, 304, 321, 326–327.

5. Ibid., pp. 293, 313–314.

6. Ibid., pp. 347, 353, 360–361, 365–368, 380.

7. Ibid., pp. 407, 416; Thomas W. Copeland et al., eds., *The Correspondence of Edmund Burke* (hereafter referred to as *Burke Correspondence*), III, p. 131.

8. Simmons and Thomas, *Parliament Debates,* V, pp. 432–433, 445, 448–450.

9. Ibid., pp. 503–507, 513, 515.

10. Ibid., pp. 518–519; VI, pp. 10–11.

11. Ibid., V, pp. 599–609.

12. Ibid., pp. 610–625.

13. Ibid., pp. 626–630.

14. Ibid., p. 630.

15. Ibid., pp. 590–595, 597.

16. Ibid., VI, pp. 35–39; Copeland et al., *Burke Correspondence,* III, pp. 164–166.

17. James E. Bradley, *Popular Politics and the American Revolution in England: Petitions, the Crown, and Public Opinion,* pp. 43–49.

18. Copeland et al., *Burke Correspondence,* III, pp. 190–195, 205, 211, 214–216.

19. Ibid., pp. 210, 224.

20. Ibid., pp. 196–198, 227.

21. Simmons and Thomas, *Parliament Debates,* VI, pp. 69–70.

22. Ibid., pp. 97–98.

23. Ibid., pp. 117–118, 120, 128, 141, 157–158, 180–183.

24. Ibid., pp. 167–168, 260.

25. Ibid., pp. 260–262.

26. Ibid., pp. 262–264.

27. Ibid., pp. 264–267, 275; Copeland et al., Burke Correspondence, III, p. 254. This bill superseded the two bills passed earlier in the year to restrict American trade.

28. Simmons and Thomas, *Parliament Debates,* VI, pp. 278–279, 281, 344, 350.

29. Ibid., pp. 278, 291, 294–296, 302.

30. Ibid., pp. 193, 202, 406–407, 589–596.

31. Copeland et al., *Burke Correspondence,* III, p. 269.

32. Charles R. Ritcheson, *British Politics and the American Revolution,* pp. 205–208.

33. Copeland et al., *Burke Correspondence,* III, pp. 291, 293–294.

34. William Cobbett, ed., *Parliamentary History of England, from the Earliest Period to the Year 1803* (hereafter referred to as *Parliament History*), XVIII, col. 1367.

35. Ibid., cols. 1403, 1407, 1430–1431.

36. Ibid., cols 1434–1436, 1442–1444, 1448.

37. Copeland et al., *Burke Correspondence,* III, pp. 309–315.

38. Paul Langford, ed., *The Writings and Speeches of Edmund Burke* (hereafter referred to as *Burke's Speeches*), III, pp. 259–271.

39. Ibid., pp. 271–275.

40. Ibid., pp. 275–276.

41. Copeland et al., *Burke Correspondence,* III, pp. 312–313.

42. Langford, *Burke's Speeches,* III, pp. 277–279.

43. Ibid., pp. 279–286.

44. Copeland et al., *Burke Correspondence,* III, pp. 330, 332–334.

45. Langford, *Burke's Speeches,* III, pp. 289–299.

46. Ibid., pp. 299–319.

47. Ibid., pp. 319–324.

48. Ibid., pp. 324–330.

49. Cobbett, *Parliament History,* XIX, cols. 125, 151–152, 160.

50. Ibid., cols. 213, 224, 227–234; Copeland et al., *Burke Correspondence,* III, p. 339.

51. Cobbett, *Parliament History,* XIX, col. 192

52. Ibid., cols. 251–252.

53. Ibid., cols. 349, 368, 377, 381–385, 392–393, 399–402.

54. Ibid., cols. 354–355, 415, 417–427, 431, 442.

55. Ibid., cols. 458–459, 462–463, 465, 515–517, 547–548.

56. Ibid., cols. 563–576, 589.

57. Ibid., cols. 1010–1012; Langford, *Burke's Speeches,* III, p. 374.

58. Cobbett, *Parliament History,* XIX, cols. 694–699, 707–708.

59. Ibid., cols. 762–767, 778–789.

60. Ibid., cols. 1080, 1088; Langford, *Burke's Speeches,* III, pp. 375–376; Copeland et al., *Burke Correspondence,* III, p. 425.

61. Cobbett, *Parliament History,* XIX, cols. 971–972, 996–1009, 1223–1224, 1277.

62. Ibid., XXII, cols. 611–612, 853–862, 874–875; Copeland et al., *Burke Correspondence,* IV, pp. 383–397.

63. Ibid., III, p. 190.

8

The House of Lords

We have not, of late, been doing justice to the "friends" of America in the House of Lords. Chatham and Richmond we already know. Perhaps some background material on an already familiar name, Rockingham, will also prove enlightening. Charles Watson Wentworth, marquis of Rockingham, was born in 1730. At fifteen, he upset his family by running away to join the duke of Cumberland in his pursuit of the Young Pretender. Soon he returned to less strenuous pursuits, attended Cambridge, and made the obligatory grand tour of the Continent. Upon the death of his father in 1750, he assumed the title, served as Lord of the Bedchamber to both George II and George III, and supervised his extensive estates—his favorite activity. Like other country gentlemen, he dabbled in Whig politics but held no office until 1765 when, in the midst of a political vacuum, the duke of Cumberland's influence secured him the post of first minister. As noted in chapter 3, Rockingham's administration was brief but notable. For the next sixteen years (1766–1782), his signal accomplishment was to keep an opposition alive to the political juggernaut that kept Lord North in office for the last twelve of those years. Rockingham was certainly not a well man, a brilliant man, nor an energetic one (Burke had to supply these latter two qualities), but his imperturbability and facility for retaining the loyalty of disparate individuals enabled him to keep Whig principles alive and, eventually, if only briefly, to regain political power. As Burke later wrote at the base of Rockingham's mausoleum, he

> far exceeded all other statesmen in the art of drawing together without the seduction of self-interest, the concurrence and cooperation of various dispositions and abilities of men, who he assimilated to his character and associated in his labours.[1]

Rockingham spoke infrequently and usually briefly, leaving the oratory primarily to the duke of Richmond. In response to the speech from the throne in November 1774, the duke sponsored an objection that requested more information before any more punitive actions would be taken against America. He described the Coercive Acts already passed as "a System which has created the utmost confusion in the Colonies without any rational hope of Advantage to the Revenue, and with certain Detriment to the Commerce of the Mother Country" and which "may precipitate our Country into all the Calamities of a Civil War." Unfortunately, only eight other peers joined him in signing this protest.[2]

All during the last half of 1774, Chatham's correspondence showed his sincere sympathy with America. To Stephen Sayre, an American who had become one of the sheriffs of the City of London, he wrote, "millions must perish there [America] before the seeds of Freedom will cease to grow . . . and in the meantime, . . . England must sink herself, under the ruins of her own foolish and inhuman system of destruction." In another letter to Sayre, Chatham feared that "the bond of union between us and America will be cut off forever." And to both Sayre and Arthur Lee, he wrote, "it will be impossible for free men in England to wish to see three millions of Englishmen slaves in America." In the Sayre letter, Chatham expressed his satisfaction with the proceedings of the Continental Congress and expected a restoration of harmony between Great Britain and its colonies.[3]

Chatham also attempted a rapprochement with Rockingham. The two met early in January 1775, but Chatham's insistence that the Declaratory Bill must be repealed or, at least, amended to make clear that Parliament did not have the right to tax the colonies (an interpretation he had fought for during its passage in 1766—see chapter 3) greatly irritated Rockingham. Burke still advised Rockingham "if possible to fall in with him," although he did not feel that American affairs would be prominent in the upcoming parliamentary session.[4]

On January 20, 1775, Chatham offered a motion that General Gage should remove his troops from Boston as soon as "practicable." His speech defending the motion was delivered, by one account, "with the dignity of age, yet . . . the fire of youth." Chatham insisted that the troops were "a perpetual irritation" and a "bar to . . . all cordial reconcilement." Moreover, the Coercive Acts "must be repealed . . . you cannot enforce them." Otherwise, "His Majesty may indeed wear the crown; but the American jewel out of it will not be worth the wearing." He claimed that Americans only demanded their constitutional rights, not independence, and all Whigs should "run to embrace and support their brethren."[5]

Both Rockingham and Richmond spoke in favor of Chatham's motion, the former "with firmness."[6] On February 1, Chatham, after giving only one day's notice to Rockingham, presented a bill to the House of Lords "for settling the Troubles in America, and for asserting the supreme Legislative Authority, and superintending Power of Great Britain over the Colonies." He pictured Great Britain and America on the brink of warfare, from which "ruin and destruction must be the inevitable consequence to both parties." He reiterated his earlier argument that taxation and representation were inseparable but insisted that parliamentary supremacy must be maintained. When charged with rushing his bill through the House, Chatham replied, "we are told that America is in a state of actual rebellion"; speedy action must be taken. And finally, he charged the ministers with "weakness, temerity, despotism, ignorance, futility, negligence, blundering, and the most notorious servility, incapacity, and corruption." This bill would have abrogated Parliament's right to tax the colonies, authorized the Continental Congress to vote a colonial contribution, repealed the Coercive and other punitive acts, allowed colonial judges to serve for "good behavior," and guaranteed colonial charters. The duke of Richmond and a few other peers supported Chatham but his bill was rejected by a more than two-to-one margin.[7]

The duke of Richmond also spoke several times on February 7, during the debate on American affairs. He warned about possible French intervention and questioned the preparedness of the British navy. And when a bishop adamantly supported the American war, Richmond observed tartly that "he [Richmond] should not be surprised to see the lawn [clerical] sleeves . . . stained with the blood of their innocent and oppressed countrymen on the other side of the Atlantic."[8]

Both Rockingham and Richmond spoke against the bill to cut off New England's trade and fisheries and the later bill to interdict all American trade. Rockingham called the former bill "oppressive and tyrannical" and Richmond used the same terms to describe the latter bill.[9] The two also protested the royal address of October 1775. Rockingham merely stated that it was "big with the most portentous and ruinous consequences." Richmond was, as usual, more dramatic, accusing the ministry of "sacrificing the blood, treasure, commerce, and honour of this nation."[10] During the remainder of the session, Richmond undertook the tasks of opposing the hiring of Hessian mercenaries, inducing the House to accept the Olive Branch Petition of the Continental Congress, and pointing out the flaws in the instructions to the peace commissioner, Lord Howe.[11]

Although Richmond failed in all these attempts, both Richmond and Rockingham returned to the fray in the fall session of 1776. The colonies had already severed their ties with Great Britain and they bitterly attacked the bellicosity of the ministers, as contained in the royal address. Rockingham felt the colonies had no alternative to declaring their independence from Great Britain after "they were declared enemies." Richmond, in a longer address, berated the ministry for its use of "bribery and corruption" to impose its policies on Parliament. He recommended conciliation even if it meant "acknowledging them [the colonies] as so *many independent states*" [italics in original]. As can be seen from these remarks, Richmond was close to, if he had not already accepted, the idea of complete American independence.[12]

Although his supporters, Lord Camden and the earl of Shelburne, had been representing his views, the earl of Chatham had not been present in Parliament since 1775. Lord North, feeling that Chatham would live just "a little while longer" and that there was "nothing to fear from him," graciously asked the king to augment Chatham's pension. The king, less forgiving of his "abandoned" conduct, decided to wait until "decrepitude or death puts an end to him" and then give the pension to his son. But Chatham, though decrepit, was far from finished. In spite of past differences, he informed Rockingham of his imminent return to Parliament and of making another attempt to end the conflict with America. Burke was always resentful of Chatham, feeling that he had failed to cooperate, or had even sabotaged the Rockingham group's efforts to solve the American problem. He nevertheless requested Rockingham to hint to Chatham that any plan he offered must involve Parliament and must specifically deal with the problem of American taxation.[13]

At the end of May 1777, Chatham, wrapped in flannel to soothe his gout, limped into the House of Lords on a crutch. His voice was low but, as ever, he spoke dramatically. "If an end is not put to this war, there is an end to this country. America has carried you through four wars, and will now carry you to your death, if you don't take things [action] in time." After this prologue, he moved that the king be requested "to take the most speedy and effectual measures for putting a stop to such fatal hostilities" on the basis of "the removal of accumulated grievances." When accused of being vague, Chatham replied that the question of taxation and other American grievances must be resolved. When again asked for specifics, he demanded the repeal "of every oppressive act which your Lordships have passed since 1763." He warned that time was short, France would soon enter the war on the side of America, and British victory was impossible. Ninety-nine votes against twenty-eight defeated what the king called his "highly unreasonable" motion and a few days later the session came to an end.[14]

During the summer, Chatham's health improved and he wrote to his physician, "Could I be the fortunate instrument of healing the wounds of a distressed country. . . . I should have lived not in vain; but alas! I see no way of political salvation."[15] Fate, however, was against him. While riding, he was thrown from his horse and gout returned in full force. Yet, though again swathed in flannel like, as Burke put it, "an Aegyptian Mummy," Chatham felt silence would be "want of duty to the King, and utter insensibility to the public calamities."[16] He, therefore, contacted Rockingham who promised his group's support "in saving this country from utter ruin."[17]

Thus prepared in November 1777, Chatham responded to the address from the throne by claiming to be "old and weak" but still formulated a protracted indictment of ministerial policy. He reiterated "you cannot conquer America" and demanded to know who ordered "the tomahawk and scalping-knife" to be used against the colonists. Chatham proposed an "immediate cessation of hostilities, and the commencement of a treaty to restore peace and liberty to America, strength and happiness to England." Only this, he averred, might cause Americans to abjure independence and return to a "due constitutional dependency." When challenged that Americans would have used Indians if the British had not, and that the British army had also used them during the Seven Year's War, Chatham replied that Americans had pledged never to use Indians and that the French use of Indians in the previous war had made British use of them necessary.[18]

The duke of Richmond followed with a wide-ranging address in which he placed the responsibility for American independence on the constitutional deterioration of the British government. Although royal prerogative may have been weakened, "influence" has made the sovereign stronger than ever. His ministers, in their hunger for revenue to finance this system, attempted to extract a revenue from America. The result, as he had predicted from the start of the controversy, was a separation "forced by oppression." Richmond then reviewed the lack of British military success in America and castigated the "dreadful inhumanity" of using Indians and slaves and the atrocities perpetrated against "fellow-subjects." He also alluded to the threat of foreign invasion and British lack of preparedness. Richmond hoped that it might be possible "to unite America with England in some shape or other" but feared that Americans "will never be reconciled to hold any dependence on a nation from which they have received such unpardonable injuries." In this, he pointed out, he differed from Chatham, who, was certain that Americans would again accept British rule. Richmond, who, we have seen, had been willing even earlier to accept American independence, now stated that no "alliance with them as free states ought to be rejected. . . . I would sooner give up every claim to America, than continue an unjust and cruel civil war."[19]

Chatham's motion failed but the Chatham and Rockingham groups agreed that they must keep up the pressure on the government. It was very noticeable in the correspondence between the two men that no decisions were to be made before, as Rockingham wrote, "your Lordship would consider the proposition and give us your judgment." Rockingham was also reluctantly beginning to agree that the Declaratory Act had to be repealed. The decision was for motions to be made in both Houses of Parliament on December 2, 1777, for a debate on the "State of the Nation" to begin in February 1778.[20]

In December, Richmond opened his remarks by stating the inquiry was necessary whatever the military situation might be. (News of General Howe's victory over General Washington at Brandywine had reached London but so had rumors of Burgoyne's surrender at Saratoga.) He claimed that the existence of "a most unnatural civil war," the expenditure "of men and money" all to no avail required an inquiry into "how we came into this situation" and "what prospect there is of a happy end?" He also called for all necessary papers to be produced. When questioned if he were calling for information that "may not be properly and safely disclosed," Richmond made it clear that he only desired information that was "already known to our enemies." As arranged, Chatham rose to support the motion. He, as always, was concerned with British power in Europe, where he feared a resurgence of French aggressiveness. For once the opposition triumphed and the inquiry was scheduled for February.[21]

That same evening, news of Burgoyne's surrender was confirmed. Rockingham and Chatham again conferred and decided to have Chatham make a motion asking for copies of Burgoyne's orders and instructions. On December 5, Chatham made his motion, referred to the "public calamity," and expressed the need to find out how and why it had occurred. Chatham went on to criticize the conduct of the war and declared himself

> an avowed enemy to American independency. He was a Whig; and though he utterly from the heart abhorred the system of government endeavored to be carried into execution in America, he earnestly and zealously contended for a Whig government and a Whig connection between both countries founded in a constitutional dependence and subordination.[22]

This time the motion was not successful, though the papers were promised when General Burgoyne returned to Great Britain. Chatham then made a second motion to investigate the employment of Indians in Burgoyne's campaign but, in spite of lively support, it was also defeated.

The duke of Richmond fought vainly against the suspension of the right of habeas corpus for Americans and against the adjournment of Parliament at this critical juncture until January 20, 1778. Chatham, who had agreed to support the Rockinghamites, exclaimed that it was "not with less grief than astonishment" that he viewed adjournment at this time full of "awe, terror, and impending danger." Can we trust those "weak, ignorant, and mistaken" men "who brought these calamities upon us" to guard the nation's interests during the adjournment? They have "deluded" the king and the lords must "interpose" in order to "defend and support the throne." He painted a horrific picture of British military weakness and the impossibility of conquering America. Nor did he think that Americans would consider peace negotiations with the men who had attempted, "by cruel and devastating war, to enslave" them. And he concluded that before Parliament reconvened in January, the maker of the motion to adjourn "will have just cause to repent of his motion."[23]

Chatham was right on both counts. Franklin told an unofficial peace emissary of Lord North that Americans would never sign a peace treaty with men whose hands were "red, wet, and dripping with the Blood of my Countrymen."[24] His second warning referred to the danger of French intervention on behalf of America. And he was correct here too, for in December the French government agreed to sign a treaty with the United States, provided the United States would not conclude peace with Great Britain unless the latter recognized her independence. The treaty was signed in February but not announced in Great Britain till March.

These developments almost resulted in Chatham's return to political power. Lord North was well aware of his limitations. He had faithfully carried out royal policies even when he disagreed with them and the result was disastrous. By the beginning of 1778, he was convinced that he should step down and allow someone more qualified to conclude peace with America and to avert, even at this late date, a Franco-American alliance and war with France. As he wrote to the king at the end of January 1778, bringing in "some person [as chief minister] less pledged than himself might be of advantage to his Majesty's service." The king refused to consider this suggestion but North offered to resign in favor of Chatham whom he considered, of all the opposition, the person who would be of most service to his Majesty. Even Lord Bute, his old enemy, felt he should return to office. Only Horace Walpole, cynical as always, wrote, "everybody must have discovered that his [Chatham's] crutch is no magic wand, and if the lame leads the blind, it is not the way of shunning the ditch."[25]

By mid-March 1778, North was frantic; he claimed the "present ministry can not continue a fortnight as it is." He suggested that Chatham would be "more reasonable than Lord Rockingham's party, [and] he would be more attentive to the appearance of the dignity of the Crown, than the others." The king grudgingly agreed to accept Chatham, Shelburne, and Barré into the government but only if North remained at its head and he managed all the arrangements with Chatham so that the king would not have to meet with him. Chatham was unwilling to accept office on these terms; he promised to "attend to the wishes of his Majesty" but desired a personal interview with the king and a leading role in the reconstituted government. North urged the king to accept these terms but he refused to place into office "a set of men who certainly would make me a slave for the remainder of my days."[26]

North, for once, withstood the royal pressure. He insisted that "*new* men and *able* men" [italics in original] were needed to save the nation from "impending ruin." He cautioned the king that "sooner or later he [Chatham] or some other person in the opposition must be sent to, or this nation is undone." But he could not match the king in sheer stubbornness. The king replied

> no opposition in life shall make me stoop to Opposition. . . . I will rather risk my Crown than do what I think personally disgraceful. . . . it is impossible that the nation shall not stand by me, if they will not, they shall have another King.

The king reemphasized his willingness to accept opposition members to strengthen North's government but North assured him that Chatham "must be the head of any administration in which he acts."[27] The king was still not convinced but North importuned him to accept Chatham as chief minister before he formed a coalition government with the Rockingham group, which would make him even more unpalatable to the king. The king remained obdurate and all North could suggest was to name a new leader from among the king's supporters, though he continued to feel that a Chatham ministry was inevitable. This so irritated the king that he demanded that North answer three questions in writing:

- Can the ministry be strengthened by some opposition members?
- If not, will you continue to administer the government?
- If you will not continue, will you at least remain till the end of the parliamentary session?

To the first question, North answered that it could not be done if he were to remain chief minister; as to the second, he would prefer not to continue in office; and yes, he would remain to the end of the session.[28]

The king reluctantly acquiesced and North reciprocated by promising to remain in office until "his Majesty is able to arrange his servants in the manner most agreeable to himself." The king replied by "expressing his satisfaction" at North's selflessness. All question of Chatham's assuming office was aborted on April 7, 1778, when, as will be described later in this chapter, he suffered a stroke that was to end his life in little more than a month. The king was quick to ask North if Chatham's incapacity might not "encline You to continue at the head of my affairs." And North, devoted and submissive as ever, would remain in office for four more troubled years.[29]

The possibility of Chatham's reassuming the reins of government, slim at best, was further complicated by the split within the Whig opposition. Chatham and his followers adamantly refused to approve American independence while the Rockingham group, particularly the duke of Richmond, now felt its recognition inevitable. As Rockingham wrote to Chatham, "I conceive that America will never again assent to this country's having actual power within that continent"; he could not understand why Chatham could not admit that fact. Chatham replied that it was "no small concern to me, to find . . . that my judgments, on the fundamental of a treaty with America, differ so widely with those, whose persons and whose principles I so much respect."[30]

Chatham did not return to Parliament when it reconvened in January 1778. On February 2, as scheduled, the duke of Richmond opened the debate on the State of the Nation. He pointed out that all the papers the ministry had provided (though not all requested had been produced) clearly showed that "at no time were the affairs of this country in a more alarming and critical situation." He moved that no further troops from Great Britain, Ireland, Gibraltar, or Minorca be sent to America lest it leave Great Britain "in a most perilous, weak, and defenceless condition." He was frank in stating that his "grand object" was to end "on the most safe, honourable, and speedy means" the American war. The motion was defeated but the debate was adjourned until February 6, when the discussion centered on the damage to British commerce because of the war.[31]

On February 16, the lords debated the propriety of hearing a letter from General Horatio Gates, the conqueror of General Burgoyne. Gates, an Englishman who had formerly served in the British army, wrote to the earl of Thanet expressing the hope that a new administration, preferably headed by Chatham, would end hostilities, recognize American independence, and negotiate a commercial treaty between the two nations. Rockingham read the letter and Richmond felt it should serve as a basis for discussion, but the majority felt that the letter was "not only exceedingly improper, but grossly insulting." Richmond then continued his discussions of the deleterious effects of the war on the British economy but failed to convince his colleagues.[32]

The next major debate in the House of Lords occurred on March 5, 1778, and concerned Lord North's third conciliatory proposal (see chapter 12). Richmond immediately declared that he had "little more expectations of peace" from this bill than he had from its predecessors. He had no hope that America would deal with commissioners appointed "by those who had been the persecutors and oppressors of America!" The duke then read the grievances against Great Britain cited in the Declaration of Independence and dared the ministers to deny them. Next came his recommendations: withdraw British troops from America; negotiate a commercial treaty; and, if necessary, recognize American independence. Rockingham supported Richmond with a dire prediction that Great Britain would soon be unable "to make peace with the colonies, or defend ourselves against the attacks of our foreign enemies."[33]

A few days later, a royal message officially informed Parliament of the signing of the treaty between the United States and France. Rockingham asked, if the ministry knew of the impending treaty, why did they offer such a meager package of concessions to America, and if they did not know, it proved "their total incapacity." Only a recognition of American independence and a generous Anglo-American commercial treaty could save Great Britain from disaster. Richmond followed with the same advice and declared that "there was no necessity for us to commence a war [with France]" merely because of the signing of the Franco-American treaty. On March 23, he formally moved to withdraw all British military and naval forces from America. Richmond gave as his motive a desire for "a re-union with our revolted colonies" but, nevertheless, felt that "acknowledging her [America's] independency" might be a necessary precondition for such a reconciliation.[34]

Chatham had still not appeared in Parliament but his negative view of American independence was still to be reckoned with. On February 11, 1778, Viscount Mahon, Chatham's son-in-law, wrote him a lengthy letter outlining his conversations with the duke of Richmond. Lord Mahon reported that the duke felt "that there was never a time when so great a man as Lord Chatham was wanted as at present." But, Richmond then added, how chagrined he felt "that there *should be,* any kind of difference of opinion at such a critical and dangerous crisis" [italics in original]. Lord Mahon then asked Richmond whether he could blame Chatham for "attempting to prevent such a disgraceful and fatal dismemberment of this country?" The duke immediately wavered and promised to "give him every support in my power," if Chatham felt he could still retain the allegiance of the colonies. However, if he failed, Richmond promised to "put an end to this war, and procure peace" on whatever terms he could.[35]

Mahon complained that Richmond, himself, had recently advocated "a reunion between the two countries" but the duke reiterated that his primary objective was to end the war. Mahon felt that Richmond had the mistaken impression that Chatham believed the war should be prosecuted with increased vigor if America insisted on its independence. Mahon explained that the vigorous war advocated by Chatham was to be directed against France and any other European nation that might declare war on England. However, Mahon was not certain that Richmond was convinced and concluded "that seeming differences in sentiment did exist in more respects than one."[36]

The earl of Shelburne informed Chatham that Richmond intended to move for the removal of British troops from America and probably also to ask for recognition of American independence. He personally opposed the latter motion and hoped that Chatham might dissuade the duke from making it, lest such an obvious split between the Whigs could only encourage the ministers. The king was well aware of this difference of opinion and expected it to "greatly hurt Lord Rockingham's party." On April 5, Richmond, himself, sent a draft of his address to Chatham. He implored Chatham's support, claiming that he had tailored his plan "to accommodate it to the sentiments of all parts of Opposition" and particularly hoped it "would be most agreeable to your Lordship." Chatham, however, was not convinced. He expressed his regret "to find himself under so wide a difference with the duke of Richmond [on the issue of independence] that he despairs of bringing about successfully an honourable issue."[37]

In fact, Chatham felt so strongly on the issue that he dragged himself to the House of Lords on April 7, when Richmond was to introduce his proposed "Address to his Majesty." The duke opened by accusing the ministers of attempting "to enslave America" and warned that all attempts to subdue the colonies had proved futile and would ultimately "terminate in the ruin of Great Britain." Therefore, in order "to save the loss of more lives," he petitioned the king "to withdraw his fleets and armies from the thirteen revolted provinces." Chatham, who correctly interpreted this motion as "yielding up the sovereignty of America," arose to express his indignation. He had entered the House on crutches, leaning upon two friends. He looked pale and emaciated and one account, perhaps written after the event, described him as looking "like a dying man."[38]

Chatham alluded to his failing health, warned that this might be "the last time he should ever be able to enter its [the House of Lords] walls," but rejoiced "that I am still alive to lift up my voice against the dismemberment of this ancient and most noble monarchy!" He refused to countenance "an ignominious surrender of its rights and fairest possessions." He then concluded with a call for a war on France.[39] Richmond responded that he had "the highest veneration" for Chatham but did not believe that even he was "able to perform impossibilities." He compared Britain's power when Chatham first became chief minister during the Seven Years' War with its present power—much to the disadvantage of the latter. Richmond maintained that no one "more sincerely wishes that America would remain dependent on this country, than I do" but was convinced that it was "totally impracticable." Nothing remained to be done but withdraw the troops and replace the ministry.[40]

Chatham attempted to rise and answer Richmond, but after two or three attempts, fell into a faint and had to be carried out of the House. He was taken home but died on May 11, 1778. When news of his death reached the House of Commons, Colonel Barré moved, and the members voted, to erect a monument to him in Westminster Abbey. Later, a lump sum was given the family to settle his debts and an annuity to his heir. As Lord Camden, one of Chatham's supporters, reported to Lady Chatham, these bills were passed enthusiastically; Lord North approved them and Richmond, Fox, and Burke spoke in their favor. Chatham's supporters never knew that Burke's first reaction upon hearing of Chatham's collapse was that "he had spit his last Venom."[41]

Although lamenting Chatham's illness, Richmond reopened the debate on his motion on April 8. Shelburne, who assumed the leadership of Chatham's followers, stated categorically that "America was not lost, and that a war [with France] was inevitable." He worried about the fate of the Loyalists and of the nearby British possessions if Great Britain were to recognize American independence. He did agree, however, that a change of ministers was absolutely necessary. Richmond repeated his familiar arguments for American independence but the House voted against him decisively. The minority considered attempting to address the king anyway but never did. Burke was incensed at Shelburne, claiming that "such shuffling and prevarication was never known."[42]

Richmond did not speak again until the end of May, when he condemned Britain's lack of naval preparedness and favored the annuity for Chatham's heir, which had more difficulty passing in the House of Lords than in the House of Commons.[43] After the summer adjournment, neither Richmond nor Rockingham commented on the royal address of November 1778, which announced France's entry into the war. However, in early December, Rockingham took strong exception to the manifesto published by the Carlisle peace commission at the conclusion of its frustrating and almost farcical mission. He read portions of it, which threatened America with severe measures because of its alliance with France. Rockingham claimed that these threats were "totally repugnant to every principle of Christianity, morality, and good policy." He, therefore, moved (as had unsuccessfully been moved in the House of Commons) that the king formally disavow the manifesto. Although supported by the duke of Richmond and others, the motion met with the same fate in the House of Lords that it had in the House of Commons.[44]

Otherwise, the American war was not discussed in the House of Lords until June 17, 1779, when the king announced that Spain had also declared war on Great Britain. At that point, Richmond again unsuccessfully recommended the withdrawal of troops from America, and he and Rockingham warned that the present ministers were not capable of successfully defending Great Britain. Their advice was, as usual, not heeded and Parliament was adjourned from early June until late November 1779.[45] Once again, the two peers expressed displeasure at the royal address but were still outvoted eighty-two to forty-one.[46] No other debates on America took place in the Lords at this session of Parliament, and neither Rockingham nor Richmond reacted to the royal address when it reconvened in October 1780. Only the announcement in January 1781 that Holland had recognized American independence and that a state of war existed between Great Britain and Holland rekindled a spark of opposition but it soon died down.[47] The only other references to the American war during the remainder of the year were in response to the royal address in November. Richmond particularly resented the statement that the ambition of Britain's enemies was prolonging the war; he placed the blame entirely on the king's ministers.[48]

It took the news of General Cornwallis's surrender at Yorktown to bring the American question again before the House of Lords. In February 1782, the duke of Chandos, a longtime supporter of the ministry, made the motion for an inquiry into how the army had become prisoners of "the United States of America." A lively debate ensued on whether these words were equivalent to recognizing American independence. The makers of the motion denied the implication but asserted that the official articles of surrender contained the term. The duke of Richmond ridiculed the entire discussion by explaining that after the surrender by Cornwallis, "all idea of the [non] recognition of America was now past consideration." Nevertheless, the term "United States of America" was deleted from the motion.[49]

During the debate, even the duke of Chandos was very clear that the cabinet was ultimately to be blamed for the lack of a sufficient naval force to protect Cornwallis's army. Richmond agreed with him and demanded the resignation of Lord Sandwich, the First Lord of the Admiralty. The ministry escaped on this occasion but on March 20, 1782, Lord North announced amid a wave of skepticism that the king had finally agreed to a new administration. The House of Lords met on March 22 and Shelburne, who had intended to make a motion for the removal of the ministers, announced that it was no longer necessary and that he looked forward to new ministers who would have "the confidence of the people, save the empire from destruction, and rescue the character of the nation from contempt."[50]

Lord North had been preparing the king for this contingency ever since General Conway's motion to end the American war had been approved on February 28, 1782, by a majority of nineteen votes. That same day, North suggested that at least some members of the opposition be taken into the ministry. Negotiations began with the duke of Grafton but he declined. It soon became obvious that either Rockingham or Shelburne was the only viable choice, but Rockingham laid down certain demands including the recognition of American independence, which the king found unacceptable. On March 19, North assured the king that "the fate of the present Ministry is absolutely and irrevocably decided" and that he [the king] could yield without loss of honor "to the opinion and wishes of the House of Commons" and select either Rockingham or Shelburne as his chief minister. The king's churlish reply to his faithful minister was to warn him, "if You resign before I have decided what I will do, You will certainly for ever forfeit my regard." North could only abjectly beg the king to allow him to resign rather than be "forever stigmatized" as having been ousted from office by a vote in the House of Commons.[51]

One of the outgoing ministers then approached Shelburne, whom North thought more pliable than Rockingham, but he was only willing to serve under Rockingham. Finally, the king capitulated and on March 27 accepted Rockingham as his chief minister and Richmond as master general of the Ordinance.[52] Rockingham had been in opposition for sixteen interminable years, but his return to office was terminated in a little more than three months by his untimely death on July 1, 1782. And on that sad note, we shall terminate this chapter and return to our "friends" outside of Parliament.

Notes

1. George Thomas, Earl of Albemarle, *Memoirs of the Marquis of Rockingham and His Contemporaries,* II, p. 245. Hereafter referred to as *Rockingham Memoirs.* The most recent useful work on Rockingham is Ross J.S. Hoffman, *The Marquis: A Study of Lord Rockingham, 1730–1782.*

2. R.C. Simmons and P.D.G. Thomas, eds., *Proceedings and Debates of the British Parliaments Respecting North America, 1754–1783* (hereafter referred to as *Parliament Debates*), V, p. 237.

3. William Stanhope Taylor and Captain John Henry Pringle, eds., *Correspondence of William Pitt, Earl of Chatham* (hereafter referred to as *Pitt Correspondence*), IV, pp. 359–361, 368; Richard Henry Lee, *The Life of Arthur Lee, LLD,* II, p. 212.

4. Thomas W. Copeland et al., eds., *The Correspondence of Edmund Burke* (hereafter referred to as *Burke Correspondence*), III, pp. 30, 89–92.

5. Simmons and Thomas, *Parliament Debates,* V, pp. 268–271, 273–274.

6. Ibid., pp. 274–275.

7. Ibid., pp. 329–330, 333–336; John Almon, ed., *Anecdotes of the Life of the Right Honorable William Pitt, Earl of Chatham* (hereafter referred to as *Pitt Anecdotes*), II, pp. 412–422; G. Thomas, *Rockingham Memoirs,* II, pp. 269–270.

8. Simmons and Thomas, *Parliament Debates,* V, pp. 393, 396–398, 400.

9. Ibid., pp. 527, 533–534, 537–538, 550–551, 587; VI, pp. 359–361, 363–364, 369, 372.

10. Ibid., pp. 77, 83–84.

11. Ibid., pp. 152–153, 185–186, 189–190, 220–223, 429–433, 474–477.

12. William Cobbett, ed., *Parliamentary History of England, from the Earliest Period to the Year 1803* (hereafter referred to as *Parliament History*), XXVIII, cols. 1369–1370, 1376–1380.

13. Sir John Fortescue, ed., *The Correspondence of King George the Third from 1760 to December, 1783,* III, nos. 1691–1692; Copeland et al., *Burke Correspondence,* III, p. 343; G. Thomas, *Rockingham Memoirs,* II, pp. 324–325.

14. Cobbett, *Parliament History,* XIX, cols. 316–320, 343–344, 352; Fortescue, *Correspondence of King George III,* III, no. 2006.

15. Taylor and Pringle, *Pitt Correspondence,* IV, p. 444.

16. Copeland et al., *Burke Correspondence,* III, p. 400; Taylor and Pringle, *Pitt Correspondence,* IV, p. 449.

17. Ibid., pp. 450–456.

18. Cobbett, *Parliament History,* XIX, cols. 360–375, 386–387, 409–411.

19. Ibid., cols. 397–410.

20. Taylor and Pringle, *Pitt Correspondence,* IV, p. 457–464; Copeland et al., *Burke Correspondence,* III, pp. 398–399, 405.

21. Cobbett, *Parliament History,* XIX, cols. 472–478, 481–482, 485.

22. Taylor and Pringle, *Pitt Correspondence,* IV, p. 470–471; Cobbett, *Parliament History,* XIX, cols. 485–491, 507–512.

23. Cobbett, *Parliament History,* cols. 560–562, 592–602.

24. Albert H. Smyth, ed., *The Writings of Benjamin Franklin,* VII, p. 101.

25. Fortescue, *Correspondence of King George III,* IV, nos. 2179, 2182, 2193, 2207; Taylor and Pringle, *Pitt Correspondence,* IV, pp. 485, 493–495, 511–512, 515; Walpole quoted in G. Thomas, *Rockingham Memoirs,* II, p. 349; Lord John Russell, ed., *Memorials and Correspondence of Charles James Fox,* I, pp. 169, 179–187.

26. Fortescue, *Correspondence of King George III,* IV, nos. 2119–2226.

27. Ibid., nos. 2228, 2230, 2232, 2234–2235.

28. Ibid., nos. 2237, 2239–2241, 2245–2247, 2255–2257.

29. Ibid., nos. 2258–2260, 2262, 2266–2267, 2281, 2284.

30. Taylor and Pringle, *Pitt Correspondence,* IV, p.480–484, 489–499.

31. Cobbett, *Parliament History,* XIX, cols. 650–659, 663, 672, 708–718.

32. Ibid., cols. 730–736, 742–751, 754–758.

33.Ibid., cols. 839–844, 856–858.

34. Ibid., cols. 912–914, 918–922, 958–962.

35. Cobbett, *Pitt Correspondence,* pp. 492–499.

36. Ibid., pp. 499–502; A. Francis Steuart, ed., *The Last Journals of Horace Walpole During the Reign of George II from 1771–1778,* II, pp. 92–93.

37. *Pitt Correspondence,* pp. 513–514, 516–518; *Correspondence of King George III,* IV, no. 2184.

38. Cobbett, *Parliament History,* XIX, cols. 1012–1021, 1030.

39. Ibid., cols. 1022–1026.

40. Ibid., cols. 1027–1029.

41. Ibid., cols. 1224–1255; Taylor and Pringle, *Pitt Correspondence,* IV, pp. 524–528; Copeland et al., *Burke Correspondence,* III, p. 427.

42. Cobbett, *Parliament History,* XIX, cols. 1032–1059; Copeland et al., *Burke Correspondence,* III, p. 427.

43. Cobbett, *Parliament History,* XIX, cols. 1145–1150, 1160–1161, 1236–1237, 1249, 1253–1254.

44. Ibid., XX, cols. 1–8, 17–21, 43.

45. Ibid., cols. 877–879, 892, 969–975, 978–989, 996–997, 999–1001, 1019.

46. Ibid., cols. 1027–1035, 1068–1078, 1080–1081, 1092.

47. Ibid., XXI, cols. 960–967, 994–995, 1009–1012, 1015–1019, 1021–1023.

48. Ibid., XXII, cols. 650–653.

49. Ibid., cols. 984–989.

50. Ibid., cols. 990–991, 997–999, 1214–1234.

51. Ibid., col. 1085; Fortescue, *Correspondence of King George III,* V, nos. 3535, 3537, 3542, 3547, 3551, 3553, 3555–3557, 3563–3565, 3567–3568.

52. Ibid., nos. 3566, 3569, 3571, 3575–3577, 3581–3582, 3589–3590, 3592–3593; G. Thomas, *Rockingham Memoirs,* II, pp. 324–325; II, pp. 446–447.

9

Richard Price: Apostle of Liberty

On October 6, 1778, the Continental Congress passed a resolution asking that Dr. Price

> be informed that it is the desire of Congress to consider him a citizen of the United States; and to receive his assistance in regulating their finances; that if he shall think it expedient to remove, with his family, to America and afford such assistance, a generous provision shall be made for requiting his services.

This resolution was sent to Dr. Price together with a cordial letter from Benjamin Franklin, John Adams, and Arthur Lee.[1] Who was this Dr. Price whose services to the cause of the American Revolution were deemed important enough to grant him citizenship and an invitation to come to the United States? The recipient of this honor was an English dissenting clergyman who had written several works favorable to the American Revolution and whose studies on the English national debt had made him one of the leading experts on government finance of his time.

The son of a Presbyterian minister, Richard Price was born on February 23, 1723, in Wales. He completed his education at a dissenting academy in London and was ordained a minister at the age of twenty-one. In 1756, both his patron and an uncle died and their legacies made him financially independent. He married the following year and settled down to become a successful minister to a London congregation.[2]

Price was not destined to limit his talents to preaching. In 1758, he published his first book, *A Review of the Principal Questions and Difficulties in Morals.* Nine years later, he followed it with a published version of his sermons, which won him the respect of Lord Shelburne and a Doctor of Divinity degree from Marischal College, Aberdeen, Scotland. However, Price's main claim to fame, during the 1760s and early 1770s, was gained through his studies of mathematical probability, life expectancy, and the national debt. These studies won him election as a Fellow of the Royal Society and were read in the North American colonies as well as in England. Price was not content to be a theoretical moralist and mathematician, he was also deeply interested in practical problems. Price not only fought for the removal of the legal disabilities suffered by Dissenters but felt that English political life in general was seriously in need of reform. This led him to join his friends in gatherings of the "Honest Whigs."

No question agitated him more than the deepening crisis between Great Britain and its Thirteen Colonies in America. Price received first-hand accounts of events in Massachusetts from his friend, Charles Chauncey, the minister of the First Church in Boston; the Reverend Ezra Stiles; John Winthrop, the professor of mathematics at Harvard; and William Gordon, an English clergyman who resided in America from 1770 to 1786. Price was also kept informed by Lord Shelburne of the aims and tactics of the Whig opposition in Parliament.

As early as 1772, Chauncey warned him that in America "the alternative now seems to be submission to Slavery, or an exertion of ourselves to be delivered from it." Price responded that civil and religious liberty were so endangered in Great Britain that "America is the country to which most of the friends of liberty in this nation are now looking; and it may be in some future period the country to which they will be all flying." He therefore urged Americans to "resist . . . every attempt to reduce them to a State of civil or spiritual slavery." Chauncey and Winthrop informed him of the united colonial reaction against the Coercive Acts, the effectiveness of non-importation, and the military preparations that were going forward.[3]

Price encouraged both the Americans and the Whig parliamentarians in their opposition to North's colonial policy. In February 1775, he congratulated Lord Chatham on his (failed) attempts to persuade Parliament to relinquish its right to tax the colonies and to remove the troops from Boston. Price added that North's measures were "not only unjust but wild in the highest degree" and doomed to failure.[4] That same month, he wrote Chauncey,

> they [the Americans] have, in my opinion, infinitely the advantage in this dispute. If they continue firm and unanimous it must have a happy issue, nothing being more certain than that the consequence of the present coercive measures must in a year or two be so felt in this kingdom as to rout the present despotic ministry, and to bring in new men who will establish the rights and liberties of the colonies on a plan of equity, dignity and permanence. In such circumstance, if the Americans relax or suffer themselves to be intimidated or divided, they will indeed deserve to be slaves. For my own part, were I in America I would go barefoot; I would cover myself with

skins and endure any inconveniences sooner than give up the vast stake
now depending; and I should be encouraged in this by knowing that my
difficulties would be temporary, and that I was engaged in a last struggle
for liberty, which perseverance would certainly crown with success. I
speak with earnestness, because thoroughly convinced that the authority
claimed by this country over the Colonies is a despotism which would
leave them none of the rights of freemen, and also I consider America as
a future asylum for the friends of liberty here, which it would be a dreadful calamity to lose. By the government which our ministers *endeavour* to
establish in New England, and that which they have established in Canada, we see what sort of government they wish for in this country; and as
far as they can succeed in America, their way will be paved for success
here. Indeed the influence of the crown has already in effect subverted
liberty here; and should this influence be able to establish itself in America, and gain an accession of strength from thence, our fate would be
sealed, and all security for the sacred blessing of liberty would be
destroy'd in every part of the British dominions. These are sentiments
that dwell much upon my heart, and I am often repeating them[5] [italics in
original].

Later, in this same letter, Price informed Chauncey of Chatham's attempt
at conciliation, the passage of the declaration that Massachusetts was in a
state of rebellion, the imminent passage of the bill to restrict the trade and
fishing privileges of New England, and, "to the amazement of everybody,"
the offer of Parliament to yield its right of taxation over any colony that
would voluntarily tax itself for the common defense. Price hoped fervently
that no colony would fall into this trap, whose purpose was "to produce
differences among the Colonies."[6]

Letters from Ezra Stiles and John Winthrop early in April 1775 reassured
Price that Americans were standing firm and that the process of forming
provisional governments and organized military forces was well advanced.[7]
And in the spring of 1775, before the news of Lexington and Concord
reached England, Price wrote to Josiah Quincy, Jr., that the prevalent British opinion was that "either the Americans will not fight, or if they should
they are a mere rabble who will be easily subdued by a disciplined army."
Price expected fighting to break out and expressed his hope that the American people would soon "have wiped off these aspersions from their characters; and proved to the confusion of their vile slanderers that they deserve to
be *free* by showing themselves brave"[8] [italics in original]. He also reminded Quincy that both houses of Parliament still contained sincere
friends of America.[8]

A letter from William Lee to Quincy, also written just prior to the fighting at Lexington and Concord, passed on information on British troop
movements, which he had obtained from Price.[9] However, by the time

Price's next letter was sent to America (December 1775), he had already received reports of the battles at Lexington and Concord and Bunker Hill; he felt he had to be more circumspect. He was hesitant to comment on political affairs because "it is not possible to know into what hands any letters may fall or what use may be made of them." He vaguely referred to some information he had sent to Chauncey by word of mouth, sent regards to his other American friends, pleaded for news from America, and assured his friends that "I continue to think as I always did."[10]

Price's thoughts on the conflict between Great Britain and the colonies were made known to the entire world in February 1776, in a pamphlet entitled *Observations on the Nature of Civil Liberty, The Principles of Government, and the Justice and Policy of the War with America.* As Horace Walpole, the great diarist of the period, reported, it "made a great sensation" and the Common Council of London expressed its approbation of the pamphlet by granting him the "Freedom of the City in a Gold Box." A thousand copies were sold within two days of its publication and, before the year was out, it had run through fourteen English editions of over sixty thousand copies. The *Observations* was, of course, widely circulated in America and was even printed in French, Dutch, and German editions.[11]

In the *Observations,* Price was attempting to convince his compatriots that America's fight for its liberties was a fight for English liberties as well. The Observations opened with the question of whether the Americans were correct in their contention that Great Britain was attempting to rob them of their liberty. To answer this question, Price felt it necessary to analyze the nature of liberty in general and civil liberty in particular. The first two sections of the pamphlet dealt with these problems. Price divided liberty into physical (self-determination), moral (following one's own sense of right and wrong), religious (worshiping as one pleases), and civil (self-government) liberties. The absence of the first three liberties was defined as servitude and the absence of the fourth, equivalent to slavery.[12]

Price believed that civil liberty, "in its most perfect degree," could only exist in states small enough to have all citizens participate directly and personally in political affairs. However, he was willing to concede that a large and/or populous nation could still enjoy civil liberty through a system of representative government, in which members were elected to a popular assembly for short terms by universal suffrage and held strictly accountable to the electorate. As long as it was clearly understood that sovereignty was lodged with the people and that the popular assembly had "a negative on all public measures together with the sole power of imposing taxes and originating supplies," Price even felt that the addition of a "Hereditary Council and Supreme Executive Magistrate" (i.e., a House of Lords and king) might contribute "vigor, union and dispatch" to a government "without infringing liberty."[13]

The third section of the *Observations* dealt with the question of colonialism. Price felt that any colony was automatically in a state of slavery because it was "subject to the legislature of another country, in which it has no voice." Because of the geographical distance and disparity of interests between any mother country and its colonies, he felt this to be potentially the most absolute and most degrading form of slavery. This was true even when the colony had its own legislature because, in case of conflict between it and the imperial government, the imperial government would utilize all the power at its command, including military force, to assert its authority. Price pointed to the events in Massachusetts during 1774–1775 to prove this point.[14]

Price refused to admit that the people of a colony lost the right to their civil liberty because of any compact with, or any favors originally received from, the home country, much less through any right of conquest. He felt that a federal empire was a possibility only if each portion of the empire had complete control of its own "taxation and internal legislation" and if the power of the imperial legislature (made up of representatives from each portion of the empire) was limited to "common concerns of the Empire."[15]

Having concluded with this theoretical background, Price devoted the final five sections of the *Observations* to a detailed study of the moral, constitutional, and practical implications of the official British policy toward the Thirteen Colonies. Price could find no justice or constitutional sanction in this policy at all. Had not the colonists themselves "converted a wilderness into fruitful and pleasant fields," had not their "trade with us been for many years one of the chief sources of our national wealth and power," and had not they "fought by our side, and contributed much to our success in the wars against France?"[16]

It was inconceivable to Price that any group of English citizens would settle new lands if it were supposed that "the people from whom they withdrew, should forever be masters of their property, and have power to subject them to any modes of government they pleased." Nor could he accept the argument that because English people accepted virtual representation, or the authority of a notoriously unrepresentative Parliament, that Americans should do the same. As Price concluded, the fundamental principle of our government is "The right of a people to give or grant their own money" and the British government had no more right to violate it in the colonies than at home.[17]

Price felt that the British policy toward its colonies was motivated by a sheer lust for power "from which no advantages can possibly be derived."

He portrayed the Thirteen Colonies as loyal, extremely valuable, even self-sacrificing members of the British empire until 1763, when Parliament began passing the series of acts that resulted in a "horrid civil war" with potentially disastrous results for English commerce, manufacturing, and its entire financial structure. As Price ghoulishly summed up the prospect:

> The Empire dismembered, the blood of thousands shed in an unrighteous quarrel; our strength exhausted; our merchants breaking, our manufacturers starving, our debts increasing, the revenue sinking, the funds tottering, and all the miseries of a public bankruptcy impending. . . . At such a crisis should our natural enemies eager for our ruin, seize the opportunity. . . . The apprehension is too distressing.[18]

From such a prospect, Price felt that "Prudence, no less than true Honour requires us to retract." He felt that the present British policy was dishonorable as well as impolitic and should be reversed voluntarily rather than under duress. He was convinced that Great Britain, "an old state, great indeed, but inflated and irreligious; enervated by luxury; encumbered by debts; and hanging by a thread," had no possibility of winning a war against its colonies, "rising states in the vigor of youth, inspired by the noblest of all passions, the passion for being free, and animated by piety."[19] Price concluded his *Observations* with a summary of a proposal from Lord Shelburne (a follower of Chatham and his eventual successor) for reconciliation, which included the suspension of hostilities, the repeal of the Coercive Acts, and Parliament's renunciation of the right to tax (but still to regulate the trade of) the colonies.[20]

As might be expected, Price's *Observations* was not allowed to go unchallenged. Price complained of "a torrent of opposition and abuse" from about forty pamphlets, some sponsored by the government, others written by sincere opponents of his arguments such as John Wesley and Edmund Burke, who attempted to refute his arguments. Most of these writers argued that Americans, like most English, had been virtually represented in Parliament and that it was only a perverse desire for independence that had led them to challenge the authority of that body.[21]

In 1777, to answer these critics, Price issued *Additional Observations on the Nature and Value of Civil Liberty, and the War with America.* This volume, combined with the original *Observations* and additional material on financial implications of the American War, was republished in 1778 as *Two Tracts on Civil Liberty, The War with America, and the Debts and Finances of the Kingdom.* In the preface to this volume, Price made his purpose and feelings quite clear.

> I cannot expect any other than a tragical and deplorable issue to this contest. But let events turn out as they will, I shall always reflect with satisfaction, that I have . . . bore my testimony with deep felt conviction against a war which must . . . shock the feelings and the reason of every considerate person.[22]

Price began the volume by reiterating his views on the nature and value of self-government. Next, he attacked the fiscal policy of the government and mocked its claims that the American war had not damaged England's economy. He rhetorically queried the government, "If without America we can be in a state so flourishing, a war to reduce America must be totally inexcusable. . . . Why not let America alone if we can subsist without it?"[23] Actually, Price completely rejected the government's optimistic financial estimates and devoted much of the volume to refuting them. The most interesting segment of the volume, however, is Price's summary of the causes and consequences of the American Revolution. He denied that the colonists had always wanted their independence, claiming that it was the British government's lack of prudence and moderation that had pushed them reluctantly into revolt. Price had lost virtually all hope that conciliatory measures might still induce the colonies to remain part of the British empire. He was positive that the use of force would be counterproductive and would only speed them into an alliance with France. It is obvious that only Price's fears for the military security and economic welfare of his own country deterred him from openly celebrating what he prophetically described as "that disruption of the new from the old world which will begin a new era in the annals of mankind; and produce a revolution more important, perhaps, than any that has happened in human affairs."[24]

It was this volume that led to the invitation of Price to live and work in the United States. With it came a fulsome letter from Arthur Lee.

> It is the voice of wisdom which calls you to the noblest of all works: the assisting to form a Government which means to make the principles of equal justice and the general rights the chief object of its attention. Generations yet unborn will bless the Contributors to this inestimable work, and among them I trust the name of Dr. Price will hold a distinguished place.[25]

Price was flattered by this offer but formally declined it on grounds of lack of qualifications and the fact that he was "so connected in this country and also advancing so fast in the evening of life that he cannot think of a removal." However, he requested Franklin to assure Congress that he "feels the warmest gratitude for the notice taken of him, and that he looks to the American States as now the hope and likely soon to become the refuge of mankind."[26] As he later wrote to Arthur Lee, the offer had given him "the highest pleasure and I shall always reckon it [the offer] among the first honors of my life" and "abundant amends" for the criticism directed toward him by his countrymen.[27] Price had written in the preface to his *Two Tracts* that, with its publication, he planned to "withdraw from politics,"[28] and for the next several years he wrote nothing directly on American affairs. Perhaps the abuse he received for his earlier efforts contributed to this silence. Also, he seemed to have felt that he could achieve nothing more for the American cause by merely reiterating his already well-known views. Both these interpretations were borne out by a 1777 letter from Price to Arthur Lee, in which he again alluded to the "torrent of opposition and abuse" he had suffered and then added that "having endeavoured to promote the cause of liberty and justice . . . I have taken my leave of politics."[29]

Nevertheless, Price continued to correspond with Benjamin Franklin (who was in France) throughout the war, sometimes conveying to him information that might be helpful to the American cause, though writing Winthrop that "I am becoming a person so marked and obnoxious that prudence requires me to be very cautious."[30] Many of the letters, however, were purely social: "The Society of honest Whigs which you used to honor with your company, are soon to renew their meetings for the winter; and you will undoubtedly be one of the first subjects of our conversation" is a sentiment he reiterated. Franklin replied in the same tenor several times: "I never think of the Hours I so happily spent in that company [the Honest Whigs] without regretting that they are never to be repeated."[31] Nor did Price cease his criticism of the British government, particularly in a strong sermon that he delivered in February 1779. He described America as a "distant country, once united to us, where every inhabitant has in his house . . . a book on law and government, to enable him to understand his civil rights, a musket to enable him to defend these rights, and a Bible to enable him to practice his religion." How, Price argued, can such a nation be conquered by Great Britain, where "Public and private virtue has been for some time declining" and profligacy prevails in "the court, the camp and the senate." He painted a somber picture of contemporary Great Britain: "A third of our empire is lost . . . we see powerful enemies continuing against us, our commerce languishing, and our debts and taxes . . . likely soon to crush us." All Price could hope was that, with divine help, Great Britain might "avert the storm or, if it must break, may its fury be mitigated."[32]

In another sermon Price preached in February 1781, he reiterated his belief that the corruption of British society and government was responsible for the problems facing the nation. By this date, it was clear that the war in America was lost and Price felt justified in taking credit for his pro-American stance. As he remarked, "I can, in particular, reflect with pleasure on the part I have taken in that dispute with the colonies . . . to which we owe all our present difficulties." He reminded his congregation that he had predicted the American alliance with France, the European coalition against Great Britain, and the inevitable loss of the colonies. He again expressed his personal satisfaction with his efforts in the American cause and concluded, "had they [the ministers] been influenced by it this kingdom, instead of being on the brink of ruin, would now have been enjoying its former prosperity."[33]

After all the abuse he had taken, Price was certainly entitled to a little complacency. He had opposed the Coercive Acts and all the punitive measures taken in 1775 and 1776. As soon as he heard of the treaty signed by the United States and France (February 1778), he wrote Lord Shelburne beseeching him to attempt to organize a new government that would "recognize the independence of the Americans." Only this measure, he believed, could prevent a war with France and ultimately ensure a commercial and cultural (but not a political) rapprochement between the United States and Great Britain. Price realized that recognition might be painful but felt it preferable to "the humiliation which will attend a public Bankruptcy, and perhaps, our becoming a Province to France."[34]

He worried constantly about America. In May 1778, he wrote Franklin hoping that the rumors he heard about divisiveness and defeatism in America were false and was happy to hear from Chauncey that the opposite was true.[35] He condemned the alleged cruelties of Britain's Indian allies, though welcoming the fact that they made any hope of reconciliation between the two nations impossible.[36] And Price joined other British humanitarians in attempting to alleviate the deplorable conditions under which American prisoners of war were suffering.

But Price's contributions to American independence had still not ended. In 1780, he coauthored an anonymous pamphlet entitled *Facts: Addressed to the Landholders, Stockholders, Merchants, Farmers, Manufacturers, Tradesmen, Proprietors of Every Description, and Generally to all the Subjects of Great Britain, and Ireland,* which appeared on the English scene. The major author of the pamphlet was John Horne Tooke, but two chapters were contributed by Price. The purpose of the pamphlet was to expose the damage done to all sectors of the English economy by the policies of the government. In his chapters on the "Expence of the War" and "Remarks on Lord North's Method of raising Money by Loans," Price clearly showed that the huge cost of the war was being financed for the most part by ruinous taxation and extravagant loans. As he summed it up:

Industry is cramped, Commerce Starves, and Land falls . . . Complaints of distress are general. The spirits of men are soured, and many disposed to break out into open resistance. These evils will increase whilst the war continues: and whether we are invaded or not, must at last terminate in a dreadful convulsion.[37]

The pamphlet contributed significantly to the fall of Lord North's government in 1782 and the resulting peace treaty with the United States. As soon as Shelburne came to power in 1782, Price implored him to "acknowledge the independence of America." He still hoped that an independent America would "enter an alliance with us, and they will rejoyce in a family compact which will give us greater advantages than can be derived from any dominion over them." He also advised against requiring the Congress of the United States (rather than the states) to compensate the Loyalists, fearing that it might undermine the peace negotiations.[38] Fortunately, the British government did not insist on this point and the preliminary treaty of peace was approved late in November 1782. The final treaty was ratified only in September 1783, after the overthrow of the Shelburne ministry by the Fox–North coalition.

Americans were appreciative of Price's efforts on their behalf. In 1781, Yale College awarded him and George Washington, honorary Doctor of Laws degrees.[39] Later, the American Academy of Arts and Sciences in Boston as well as the American Philosophical Society of Philadelphia, elected him a Fellow. Price reciprocated these honors by donating scientific apparatus to Yale and books to both Harvard and Dartmouth colleges. He also kept up a lively correspondence on religious, scientific, and financial matters with his many American friends.[40] He wrote Benjamin Rush of Pennsylvania that the new nation must form a federal union, which "shall give due energy to the decisions of the delegation [Congress of the Confederation] that forms the union without encroaching too much on the liberty and independence of the confederated states." In a succeeding letter, Price predicted that if this were successfully accomplished, the American Revolution "may prove to be an introduction to times of more light and liberty and virtue than have been yet known." If not, as he wrote to another correspondent, the American Revolution "which might have proved a blessing to them [the Americans] and to the world may prove to be a curse."[41]

Finally, in 1784, Price informed Franklin that though not "qualified" and not expecting his advice "will carry much weight," yet "to satisfy my own mind," he had a "last offering of my good will" to make to the American cause.[42] He was much concerned about the future of the United States, whose weak government, he feared, was even less prepared to solve the peacetime problems of the nation than it had been to fight a war. In addition, as he wrote in a letter to Joseph Willard, president of Harvard,

> I am however very much mortify'd by accounts which have been sent me of the state of manners in some of the United States. There is, I am informed, among them an avarice, a rage for foreign fineries, an excess of jealousy, etc, etc, which are likely to do them the greatest injury, and to disappoint the hopes of the friends of liberty.[43]

Franklin encouraged the project and, in 1784, a small volume of advice, entitled *Observation on the Importance of the American Revolution,* appeared. The book began by congratulating the American people on winning their independence and expressing the hope that people in England and the entire world might emulate their love of liberty.[44] In the following sections of the book, Price exhorted the new nation to foster full civil and religious liberty (not merely toleration); encourage education that would "teach how to think, rather than what to think"; avoid extremes of wealth and poverty by a sound fiscal and commercial policy, as well as the abolition of primogeniture and titles of nobility; and withdraw from European entanglements lest they "expose themselves to the danger of being involved in its quarrels."[45]

In a few brief but deeply prophetic comments, Price discussed the inherent dangers to the American people of any long-term continuance of slavery. The slave trade he described as "cruel, wicked, and diabolical" and he warned his readers that

> nothing can excuse the United States if it [the abolition of slavery] is not done with as much speed and at the same time with as much effect as their particular circumstances and situation will allow. . . Till they have done this it will not appear they deserve the liberty for which they have been contending.[46]

But Price's gravest concern was the weakness of the central government under the Articles of Confederation. He felt that the American people need have no fear of external attack but that they were in serious danger of "fighting with one another."And in cases of conflict between the states or between a state and the central government, the powers of the Congress of the Confederation were obviously inadequate. Price urged an immediate grant of military and financial powers to the central government. Otherwise he feared that

> The fairest experiment ever tried in human affairs will miscarry and that a Revolution which had revived the hopes of good men and promised an opening to better times, will become a discouragement to all future efforts in favor of liberty and prove only an opening to a new scene of human degeneracy and misery.[47]

Price sent this pamphlet only to his American friends. (Later, it was reprinted in Great Britain.) In the letters that accompanied it, he excused his presumption on the grounds of good intentions and requested their reaction.[48] Franklin thought the pamphlet "excellent . . . and will do us a great deal of Good," although he felt that the reports of American problems to be the results of the "imaginations and wishes of English newswriters and their employers."[49] John Adams also welcomed Price's advice particularly on religious freedom.[50] Washington received it "with the highest gratification" and agreed with Price's fears about the weakness of Congress.[51] Henry Laurens of South Carolina, an old friend of Price's, approved of the general tenor of the pamphlet but disagreed with Price's antislavery stand. Laurens believed that slavery might eventually be abolished but blamed its inception and growth on Great Britain. Laurens's reaction greatly discouraged Price about the future of liberty in America.[52]

The fullest response to the pamphlet came from Thomas Jefferson. In one letter, he explained the status of slavery in America and at least partially reassured Price that the persistence of slavery would not corrupt American democracy. In another letter to Price, Jefferson described the pamphlet as "wise and just" and expected it to "produce much good" in the United States. Jefferson also reassured Price that "the want of power in the federal head was early perceived . . . and a spirit to enlarge the powers of Congress was becoming general," although he feared that actual hostilities between two or more states might be necessary before the central government would be given all the power it required.[53]

Shays's Rebellion must have made Jefferson's words seem prophetic to Price. Early in 1787, he wrote Willard hoping that "convulsions in your state [Massachusetts] . . . have been quieted" and that Americans would learn from the upheaval the necessity of "frugality" and "strengthening their federal government."[54] Shortly after, he wrote Arthur Lee that he regretted that relations between England and its former colonies were not better, but felt that some of the blame for this must be shared by the United States because, its "Congress being a mere shadow," the British government had no one with which to deal.[55]

It is tantalizing but futile to speculate what, if any, influence Price's call for a stronger federal government exerted. We know he was disappointed with the failure of the Annapolis Convention in September 1786 and with a proposal to divide America into three regional confederations. He was, however, extremely satisfied by the passage of Virginia's Statute of Religious Liberty, which he described as a "happy omen of the benefit to mankind that may arise from the American Revolution."[56] Obviously, then, Price welcomed the convening of the Constitutional Convention, in which he felt "the collected wisdom and weight of so many of the first men in America" would solve the problem.[57] Benjamin Rush wrote him encouraging letters about the proceedings of the Convention but, as Price wrote Willard in October, he was still "waiting impatiently for an account of the result of the deliberations" because if "a wise and efficient plan of federal government be there [the United States] established, we shall here know where to go when calamities come."[58] Nor was he disappointed in the new constitution. He expressed hope that it would be speedily adopted because, as he wrote to Lee in 1788, "I must own to you that the new federal constitution in its principal articles meets my ideas."[59] In October 1787, Price wrote Jefferson expressing his happiness at the adoption of the Constitution and his confidence that whatever defects it might have will be removed by "time and experience."[60] And at the end of the year, he wrote Franklin, "I rejoyce to find that the federal constitution has been adopted by the states. This confirms me in the hope that a state of things is commencing there more favourable to human rights, than any that has yet been known in this world."[61] Price must also have rejoiced at the inauguration of Washington, whose name he had prophesied at the time they received their Yale degrees would "always shine among the first in the annals of the world."[62]

It is worthy of note, however, that in the same sermon Price preached in 1787, in which he declared "that every friend of the human race must wish success" to the U.S. Constitution, he was careful to distance himself from a charge of being a republican.

> I cannot help taking this opportunity to remove a very groundless suspicion with respect to myself by adding that so far am I from preferring a government purely republican, that I look upon our own constitution as better adapted than any other to this country.[63]

Thus ends Price's connection with the American Revolution. His remaining years were spent in abortive attempts at parliamentary reform and more successful planning for the reduction of Britain's national debt. But another revolution soon attracted his attention. Not surprisingly, Price was one of the leading British defenders of the French Revolution and it was his writings that helped lead to Burke's rejoinder, *Reflections on the Revolution in France*. What Price's views on the later developments of the French Revolution might have been will never be known. For, on April 18, 1791, he died. It was the French who dubbed Price "the Apostle of Liberty" but, as Joseph Priestly said of him in the sermon delivered shortly after Prince's death, his finest moments came during the American Revolution when he was "the first, the loudest, and the most incessant in his cries against that most cruel, unjust and impolitic war."[64]

Notes

1. Charles Francis Adams, ed., *The Works of John Adams,* VII, p. 71.

2. The best modern accounts of Price's life and thought may be found in Carl B. Cone, *Torchbearer of Freedom;* Roland Thomas, *Richard Price: Philosopher and Apostle of Liberty;* and D.O. Thomas, *The Honest Mind: The Thought and Work of Richard Price.*

3. W. Bernard Peach and D.O. Thomas, eds., *The Correspondence of Richard Price,* I, pp. 143, 164, 166, 170–173, 175–177, 181–185. Hereafter referred to as *Price Correspondence.*

4. Ibid., pp. 186–187.

5. Ibid., pp. 188–189.

6. Ibid., pp. 189–191.

7. Ibid., pp. 198–204.

8. Ibid., pp. 206–207.

9. Mark Anthony DeWolfe Howe, ed., "English Journal of Josiah Quincy, Jr., 1774–1775" *Massachusetts Historical Society Proceedings* L, p. 494.

10. Peach and Thomas, *Price Correspondence,* I, pp. 208–212, 215–221, 225–229, 234–235.

11. A. Francis Steuart, ed., *The Last Journals of Horace Walpole During the Reign of George III from 1771–1783,* I, p. 529; Peach and Thomas, *Price Correspondence,* I, pp. 243–244, 246–248.

12. Richard Price, *Observations on the Nature of Civil Liberty, the Principles of Government, and the Justice and Policy of the War with America,* pp. 1–5.

13. Ibid., pp. 6–12.

14. Ibid., pp. 19–24.

15. Ibid., pp. 24–28.

16. Ibid., pp. 34–40.

17. Ibid., pp. 40–43, 49–50.

18. Ibid., pp. 50–87.

19. Ibid., pp. 87–89, 91–98.

20. Peach and Thomas, *Price Correspondence,* I, pp. 237–240.

21. Ibid., pp. 246, 248; Cone, *Torchbearer,* pp. 82–83.

22. Richard Price, *Two Tracts on Civil Liberty, the War with America, and the Debts and Finances of the Kingdom,* pp. viii–ix. Hereafter referred to as *Two Tracts.*

23. Ibid., p. 71.

24. Ibid., pp. 72–89.

25. Ibid., pp. 30–31.

26. Francis Wharton, ed., *The Revolutionary Diplomatic Correspondence of the United States,* II, p. 474.

27. Ibid., III, p. 27.

28. Price, *Two Tracts,* p. xvi.

29. Peach and Thomas, *Price Correspondence,* I, pp. 258, 270.

30. Ibid., pp. 257, 259. Cf. Howe, "English Journal of Josiah Quincy, Jr.," *Massachusetts Historical Society Proceedings,* L, p. 494, and Charles Isham, ed., "The [Silas] Deane Papers," I, pp. 486, 496.

31. Peach and Thomas, *Price Correspondence,* II, pp. 53, 57, 82, 114, 193.

32. Bernard W. Peach, ed., *Richard Price and the Ethical Foundations of the American Revolution,* pp. 280–281, 283, 285.

33. D.O. Thomas, ed., *Political Writings: Richard Price,* pp. 92–93.

34. Peach and Thomas, *Price Correspondence,* I, pp. 273–275.

35. Ibid., II, pp. 19–20, 39–40.

36. Ibid., pp. 51–52.

37. John Horne Tooke and Richard Price, *Facts: Addressed to the Landholders, Stockholders, Merchants, Farmers, Manufacturers, Tradesmen, Proprietors of Every Description and generally to all The Subjects of Great Britain and Ireland,* 4th ed., pp. 14–21, 102–111.

38. Peach and Thomas, *Price Correspondence,* II, pp. 116, 150–156.

39. Ibid., pp. 195–196.

40. Cone, *Torchbearer,* pp. 104–106.

41. Peach and Thomas, *Price Correspondence,* II, pp. 162, 185, 199.

42. Ibid., pp. 215, 218.

43. Ibid., p. 225.

44. Richard Price, *Observations on the Importance of the American Revolution and the Means of Making It a Benefit to the World,* pp. 1–2.

45. Ibid., pp. 20–76.

46. Ibid., pp. 83–84.

47. Ibid., pp. 14, 19, 85.

48. Peach and Thomas, *Price Correspondence,* II, pp. 232, 234–235.

49. Ibid., pp. 223, 225.

50. Ibid., pp. 271–272.

51. Ibid., pp. 324–325.

52. Ibid., pp. 263–265, 290–291, 293–294.

53. Ibid., pp. 298–299, 261–262, 313.

54. Ibid., III, p. 113.

55. Richard Henry Lee, ed., *The Life of Arthur Lee, LLD,* II, p. 352.

56. Peach and Thomas, *Price Correspondence,* III, pp. 22, 30, 44, 57, 76.

57. Ibid., p. 145.

58. Ibid., pp. 132, 139, 151.

59. Ibid., pp. 164, 170.

60. Ibid., pp. 182–183.

61. Ibid., p. 194.

62. Ibid., II, p. 196.

63. D.O. Thomas, *Political Writings,* pp. 161, 164–165.

64. Joseph Priestly, *A Discourse On the Occasion of the Death of Dr. Price,* p. 13.

10

The Single Legal Victim of the American Revolution

The trial fittingly commenced on the fourth of July. The year was 1777 and the defendant, "a wicked, malicious, seditious, and ill-disposed person," was charged with attempting to

> stir up and excite discontents and seditions among his majesty's subjects and to alienate and withdraw the affection, fidelity, and allegiance of his said majesty, and to insinuate and cause it to be believed that divers of his majesty's innocent and deserving subjects had been inhumanly murdered by his said majesty's troops in the province, colony, or plantation of the Massachusetts Bay in New England, in America belonging to the crown of Great Britain, and unlawfully and wickedly to seduce and encourage his majesty's subjects in the said province, colony, or plantation, to resist and oppose his majesty's government. . . . [1]

No, the defendant was not some unfortunate American patriot captured by the British army and brought to trial for treason. Rather it was our old "friend," John Horne Tooke "late of London, Clerk" who was charged with "false, wicked, scandalous, malicious, and seditious libel of and concerning his said majesty's government and the employment of his troops."[2] What precisely were his misdeeds to have called forth such a scathing indictment?

Tooke's organization, the Society for Constitutional Information (founded as a rival of the Wilkite-dominated Society for the Supporters of the Bill of Rights), had continued the fight for American rights. It was at a meeting of this group that Tooke moved that a subscription of £100 be raised for

> the relief of the widows, orphans, and aged parents of our beloved American fellow-subjects, who, faithful to the character of *Englishmen* preferring death to slavery, were, for that reason only, inhumanly murdered by the King's troops at or near Lexington and Concord, in the province of Massachusetts, on the 19th of last April[3] [italics in original].

The motion passed and the money was raised and ultimately transmitted to Benjamin Franklin on behalf of the intended recipients. An account of the transaction was printed over Tooke's name in several newspapers. At this time, the government took no action against him or any of the other participants in the affair, perhaps because the Americans were not yet officially in a state of rebellion. However, after that situation changed, three printers were fined £100 each for having published the article. And, as noted, on July 4, 1777, Tooke himself was brought to trial in the Court of King's Bench on a charge of seditious libel.[4]

Tooke's longtime antagonist, Lord Mansfield, presided at the trial, and Tooke seized every opportunity to provoke him. The prosecution was conducted by the attorney general, soon to be known as Lord Thurlow, whom Tooke also badgered. Tooke acted on his own behalf. He assumed the offensive almost at once by objecting to the selection of one juror on procedural grounds. Next, Tooke demanded a guarantee that, if the defense examined no witnesses, the defendant would have the "last word" at the hearing and the attorney general would be forbidden to reply. When Mansfield refused this request, he informed Tooke that he had a "remedy," an appeal to a higher court. Tooke termed this a harsh remedy, reminding Mansfield that, although a higher court had eventually overturned his ruling against him in the libel suit brought by Onslow, it had nevertheless cost him a large amount of money in legal fees.

Thurlow outlined the case against Tooke. He claimed that Tooke had deliberately planned "to defy the laws and justice of the country" by publishing as outrageous a statement as possible in order to challenge the government to prosecute him or else admit the bankruptcy of its American policy and/or the ineffectuality of the law of libel. Thurlow then presented two newspaper publishers who testified that the articles were in Tooke's handwriting and that he had paid the costs of their publication.[5]

In his cross-examination of one of these witnesses, Tooke brought out that he had always admitted his authorship of, and responsibility for, the article. He also established the point that the publishers had been under the threat of prosecution for printing his article for almost two years, but no steps had been taken against them until January 1777. It was only then, in order to protect themselves, that they had taken advantage of the permission Tooke had given them in advance and testified to his authorship of the article. Tooke also unsuccessfully attempted to elicit admissions from the witnesses that governmental pressure had been applied to their publishing activities on other occasions.

The prosecution then rested its case and Tooke commenced his formal defense. He opened his address to the jury by commenting that he much preferred to place his life in their hands rather than rely on the uncertain mercy of the judge and expressed the hope "that the verdict which you shall give; may be really your own . . . and not the judge's."[6] Tooke then compared the recent treatment of prisoners accused of libel to those accused of murder, sodomy, treason, or violation of anti-Catholic laws, and charged that the former were often treated more harshly than any of the latter.

Tooke took vigorous exception to the fact that he was being tried by a special jury upon information brought against him by the attorney general, rather than the more usual course of indictment by a grand jury and trial before an ordinary jury. He pointed out that the office of attorney general was a purely political one and that he was obliged to follow the policy of the ministry then in power. As Tooke noted, "Put in then another minister and the attorney-general thinks me an honest man, but if there comes a different minister and a different attorney-general 'O put him out of the world, he is not fit for human society, shut him up like a mad dog."[7] Tooke also pointed out that the court officials had more power in the selection of a special jury than in that of an ordinary jury; moreover, special jurors tended to be more affluent than ordinary jurors and because of their economic interests they were more accepting than most English citizens of the administration's policy toward America. He also bitterly attacked the two years' delay in his prosecution, accusing the authorities of moving against him after he returned to the study of law and began to oppose the then-current interpretation of libel. In summary, Tooke claimed that Thurlow's procedures gave the Crown "an unjust, an illegal, a wicked and oppressive advantage."[8]

Tooke was convinced that he was being tried for his political opinions. He accused the ministry and its majority in the House of Commons of being "the most corrupt assembly of men that ever existed on the face of the earth."[9] He felt that the government was determined to "take whatever little money out of my pocket I may have there, and to imprison me, and so exclude me from that society of which I have rendered myself unworthy."[10] Tooke claimed that he was selected to be made an example of from a large field of opponents of the government's policy, because he was an outspoken opponent of the king's party and had lost the support and sympathy of the Whigs and reformers, after his split with Wilkes and the disclosure of his disinterest in the Church. The truth of Tooke's allegation was at least symbolically confirmed by a friendly visit paid by Wilkes to Lord Mansfield during the trial.

Having attempted to establish the political motivation of his trial, Tooke then called attention to the fact that the bloodshed at Lexington and Concord took place before the American colonists were officially declared to be in rebellion. But, he continued, even if they had been rebels, they should have been dealt with according to the law rather than attacked by soldiers. He also maintained that he was not the original author of the charge of murder against the British troops. It was made by Benjamin Franklin in articles dated May 30–31, 1775, repeated by Arthur Lee, whose brother William was then residing in London, and echoed in numerous other articles after that date.

Tooke admitted that he accused the troops of murder but denied that any such accusation could be equated with libel against the government. Many accusations had been made against individual soldiers in the past; Wilkes, now Lord Mansfield's friend, had done so, and he himself had done so in the William Allen case mentioned earlier, but never had a libel charge been brought against the accuser. Tooke antedated the legal theory of the Nuremburg trials, by averring that a claim that the soldiers were acting under their officers' orders "could be no defense for their actions."[11] He recounted the mild punishment of the Master of Stair, the advisor of King William who was responsible for the massacre of the McDonald clan by English troops at Glencoe in 1692.

Tooke went on to picture the Americans as

> sleeping quietly in their beds ... roused at the dead of the night, with an alarm that a numerous body of the King's troops ... were marching toward them by surprise in an hostile manner. Rather than flee, or submit, they hastily armed as well as they could, they collected together as they might ... determined not to attack, but to defend themselves from lawless insult, or to sell their lives as dearly as they could.[12]

Next, he read into the record an account of the battles of Lexington and Concord by a British officer who participated in the engagements, which might be interpreted as stamping the British troops as aggressors. Tooke claimed that the troops were encouraged to attack the colonists by the law passed by Parliament, which granted them a right to trial in England for any crimes they might commit in America.

Tooke then completed his address to the jury and began to call his witnesses. He first attempted to question the attorney general. However, Mansfield insisted that the attorney general had the right to refuse to answer questions put to him and Thurlow took advantage of this ruling to ignore Tooke's questions concerning the manner of timing of the charge brought against him. Tooke then called General Gage, who in 1775 was commander in chief of the royal troops in America, and Lord George Germaine, the secretary of state in charge of American affairs, but neither was available.

Tooke next attempted to prove that the newspaper article's description of the raising of the subscriptions for the widows and orphans of Americans killed at Lexington and Concord was true and not a mythical episode concocted by him to stir up political passions. Two witnesses testified to the voting of the subscription and its delivery to Benjamin Franklin. And, finally, Tooke called Edward Gould, an American who added his personal recollections of events leading to the battles of Lexington and Concord.

Lord Thurlow then recapitulated the prosecution's case, asserting that Tooke's accusation of murder against the troops was false and that, even if true, a newspaper article was not the proper vehicle for such a charge. He denied any sinister motives in the method, or the timing, of Tooke's trial and asked for a verdict against him. Lord Mansfield concluded the case by instructing the jury that no doubt existed about Tooke's authorship of the article and that their verdict must depend on their opinion of whether the battle of Lexington and Concord could be defined as "murder" on the part of the royal troops. If it could not, as Mansfield strongly implied, then the article must be considered as "an arraignment of the government."[13]

The jury took an hour and a half to reach its verdict. It is, of course, impossible to reconstruct with any certitude what determined their decision. It is highly probable that no group of jurors in the year 1777, no matter how much they might, or might not, have disagreed with British policy toward America, could have subscribed to Tooke's charge of murder. Nor could the jury have been favorably impressed by Tooke's assertion that the entire episode "was the most deliberate act of my life; I will never cease repeating the charge I have made" even if I have to "go to prison for life."[14] In any case, the verdict was guilty.

The court then adjourned until November 19, 1777. At that time, Tooke claimed that the information filed against him did not contain sufficient detail to formally charge him with a crime, but Lord Mansfield disagreed. On November 24, Thurlow designated Tooke as a flouter of the law and an encourager of rebellion and urged a severe penalty including a fine, imprisonment, and even the pillory. Mr. Justine Ashton, Mansfield's colleague on the bench, then sentenced Tooke to twelve months in prison and a fine of £200. He was furthermore to post a bond of £800 (£400 from himself and £200 each from two guarantors) to insure his good behavior for three years after the end of his imprisonment. Tooke did not object to the first part of the sentence but showed his disagreement with the good behavior bond by warning the judges that perhaps they should imprison him for three years because he still viewed his support of America "as the most meritorious action of my life."[15]

Tooke, after unsuccessfully appealing his sentence to the House of Lords, was committed to the King's Bench prison but was allowed to live in a small house just outside its walls. During his incarceration, he completed his legal studies and applied for admission to the bar. But, once more, his political enemies objected, and his application was refused on the ground that he had once been a clergyman. At the expiration of his prison term, Tooke did post the necessary securities for good behavior. However, in the following year, 1780, he published, jointly with Dr. Richard Price, a pamphlet entitled *Facts addressed to the Landholders, Stockholders, Merchants, Farmers, Manufacturers, Tradesmen, Proprietors of Every Description, and Generally to All the Subjects of Great Britain and Ireland.* The purpose of the pamphlet was to illustrate the waste and corruption occasioned by the American war.

The authors of the pamphlets estimated that the war would add £13,000,000 to the national debt and had already done serious damage to English commerce, manufacturing, and agriculture. They also detailed the huge increases in the allowance granted the king and the cost of maintaining and supplying the army and navy as compared with earlier wars. The pamphlet concluded with the warning that the

> corrupt influence of the crown is risen to such a height that it will not be sufficient merely to *clip* the wings with which it mounted, they must be *seared* to prevent their putting forth again. We are now arrived at a period when either corruption must be thoroughly purged from the Senate, or the nation is finally and irrevocably undone.[16] [italics in original]

Although Lord Shelburne, the Whig leader, at first encouraged the composition of this pamphlet, he later attempted to discourage its publication. Nevertheless, it was widely circulated, went through several editions, and contributed to the fall of Lord North's ministry. Interestingly enough, there seems to have been no attempt to prosecute Tooke (or Price) for libel, or for what might have been construed as a violation of the former's bond for "good behavior."

The close of the Revolutionary War ended the necessity of Tooke's support of the American cause. Although he was later to meet Thomas Jefferson and Joel Barlow, by that date, Tooke's energies were turned to philosophy and philology. In 1794, during the hysteria caused by the French Revolution, Tooke, along with several other radical reformers, was tried on a charge of treason. On this occasion, Tooke wisely utilized the services of legal counsel. His trial lasted six days but the jury required only eight minutes to bring in a verdict of "not guilty."[17]

The remainder of Tooke's life was relatively peaceful. In 1801, after several unsuccessful efforts, he was elected to the House of Commons as a representative of Old Sarum, one of the rotten boroughs that he had for so long fought to eradicate. However, his victory was destined to be ephemeral. Once again his opponents used his former profession against him. A bill was passed barring any cleric from holding a seat in the House of Commons. Even though he had long since left holy orders, Tooke was included in that category. He was allowed to complete his term but was deemed ineligible for reelection.[18]

Tooke then returned to his home at Wimbledon where he continued his philosophical studies and entertained numerous friends. Death came to him on March 8, 1812. One hundred and seven years later, a tablet in honor of his contributions to the cause of the American Revolution was placed near his grave by the New England Society of Brooklyn, New York. Certainly, this recognition was due the man who, as Tooke described himself, "Merely for attempting to prevent the final dismemberment of the empire . . . became . . . the single legal victim during the contest and the single instance of proscription after it."[19]

Notes

1. T.B. Howell, ed., *A Complete Collection of State Trials and Proceedings for High Crimes and Other Crimes and Misdemeanors from the Earliest Period to the Present Time*, XX, pp. 652–654.

2. Ibid.

3. Alexander Stephens, *Memoirs of John Horne Tooke*, I, p. 435.

4. Howell, *Complete Collection*, XX, pp. 652–789, is the basic source for Tooke's trial. A pro-Tooke account is found in Stephens, *Memoirs*, I, pp. 448–477.

5. Howell, *Complete Collection*, pp. 669–670.

6. Ibid., pp. 675–676.

7. Ibid., p. 695.

8. Ibid., p. 682.

9. Ibid., p. 696.

10. Ibid., p. 684.

11. Ibid., p. 726.

12. Ibid., p. 737.

13. Ibid., p. 761.

14. Ibid., pp. 685, 702, 710.

15. Ibid., p. 789. Tooke appealed this decision but it was affirmed.

16. John Horne Tooke and Richard Price, *Facts Addressed to the Landholders, Stockholders, Merchants, Farmers, Manufacturers, Tradesmen, Proprietors of Every Description, and Generally to All the Subjects of Great Britain and Ireland*, 4th ed., p. 115.

17. Stephens, *Memoirs*, II, pp. 126–150.

18. Ibid., pp. 236–260.

19. John Horne Tooke, *The Diversions of Purley*, part I, p. 1.

11

Dean Tucker: He Told Them So!

We have already discussed Dean Tucker's views on America. The outbreak of hostilities at Lexington and Concord was to him only a corroboration of his contention that the colonies should be granted immediate independence. Never optimistic about converting either Lord North or the opposition to this strategy, he placed his hope in the "landed interest," the independent members of Parliament. His next pamphlet, therefore, was addressed to this group. Tucker reminded them that events were forcing them to make a choice between three alternatives:

- Parliament's plan to coerce the colonies;
- Burke's plan of volunteer contributions from America; or
- Tucker's plan of granting the colonies their independence.

He asked them to judge these alternatives on the basis of practicality, expense involved, the probability of solving the problem permanently, and their effects on the English form of government.[1]

Tucker made no attempt to judge Parliament's coercion policy partly, as he said, "out of respect to the August body" but primarily because he was certain of its ultimate failure.[2] As to Burke's plan, Tucker claimed that it was impractical and no solution of the problem because Americans would continue to attempt to limit or ignore Parliament's authority; it was expensive because it would still saddle Great Britain with the costs of colonial administration and protection; and it was constitutionally dangerous to accept the colonists' contention that they were subject to the king alone, rather than to the king and Parliament. Tucker felt that his own plan would solve the problem simply, inexpensively, and with no risk to the British constitution or economy.[3]

Most of the remainder of the pamphlet was devoted to the probable effects of American independence on British trade. Tucker once again contended that their own self-interest dictated that Americans would still trade with Great Britain, but even if that trade should decline, he cited statistics indicating that the American trade was of diminishing importance to the British economy. He capped his argument by pointing out that, in spite of the fact that the colonists had been practicing nonimportation and nonexportation since 1774, English "trade was never brisker in most Articles."[4]

Tucker added a postscript to the pamphlet, in which he apologized halfheartedly to Benjamin Franklin for accusing him of soliciting a position as a stamp tax collector for himself (actually it was for a friend). Next, he attempted to give the reasons why Parliament did not (except for a post tax) lay any internal taxes on the Irish people while it did on the Americans (because Ireland was not a financial burden on England). And, finally, he included a "general muster" of the two divisions in English society, one of which he felt was attempting to subvert the English constitution ("Wilkesites," Republicans, parliamentary reformers, political "outs," and adventurers) and the other could be counted on to support the constitution (the nobility, the gentry, merchants, manufacturers, investors in government securities, lawyers, the Anglican and some of the dissenting clergy, members of Parliament, and the king himself). As Tucker concluded, it was obvious with which division any "constitutional Patriot," "honest Englishman" and "loyal Subject," or any "prudent Man" would wish to affiliate.[5]

Obviously, Tucker's views were not welcome even by other "friends" of America. One of these, the eloquent Edmund Burke, wounded Tucker, or at least Tucker's vanity, most severely. In his speech *On American Taxation* of April 1774, Burke, apparently stung by references in Tucker's writings to "mock-Patriots" who had encouraged American resistance to parliamentary authority for their selfish political purposes, referred to him as "vermin" and accused him of attempting to ingratiate himself with the king and the ministry in order to become a bishop.[6] It is difficult to see why Burke thought that Tucker's ideas would please the king or his ministers. In any case, the insult rankled and when Burke made his famous speech, *On Conciliation with America,* in March 1775, Tucker welcomed the opportunity to obtain revenge. He addressed a *Letter* to Burke, which opened with a few acidulous remarks promising to analyze Burke's speech "with more Decency and good Manners" than Burke showed to others, but finding it difficult because "you [Burke] excel in the Art of ambiguous expressions."[7] Burke had suggested that six factors had contributed to the "Spirit of Liberty" found in America (see chapter 7). Tucker insisted that these same six factors made it much more sensible to free the colonies rather than attempt (futilely, according to Tucker) to conciliate them. Tucker also used Burke's arguments about the great increase in the colo-

nial population and the vast expansion of western settlements as proof of
the impossibility of any successful conciliation.[8]

Tucker denied Burke's basic premise that America had always cooperated with Great Britain prior to 1763. He gave examples of opposition to
the Navigation Acts as far back as 1696, refusal to vote military requisitions
during the French and Indian War, trading with the enemy during the war,
and the failure of Americans to pay their debts to English merchants.[9]
Tucker then pointed out the flaws in Lord North's plan of conciliation,
though ironically entreating Burke not to tell him lest he "deny me a Bish-
opric which you say I am aiming at."[10] And, in conclusion, Tucker face-
tiously imagined Burke as head of a government financed by "free gifts and
voluntary donations," with everyone "joyfully pouring forth *their free will
Offerings* . . . in the *exuberant Plenty* of rich Luxuriance"[11] [italics in origi-
nal]. Burke had to admit in a letter to a political associate that "There is wit
at the end of the Pamphlet and it made me laugh heartily. The rest did not
alter any of my opinions."[12]

By 1776, Tucker became serious again. He had already presented all
possible arguments to buttress his point of view, but he still felt it necessary
to issue an additional tract in order to refute the many objections that had
been raised to his plan. In the preface to this new volume, Tucker carried on
his running feuds with Burke and Franklin, claimed the Whigs had incited
the Americans to rebellion by repealing the Stamp Act and then passing the
Declaratory Act, and lashed out at Richard Price for his defense of colonial
rights. Then, in a brief introduction, he reiterated his plan for American
independence.[13]

The rest of the tract was devoted to meeting fourteen objections to his
plan. Objection 1 centered on the difficultly of collecting the debts owed by
Americans, if they were to be independent. Tucker answered this by claiming that the withholding of payment was being used by Americans merely
as a political weapon and, once it was no longer necessary, the Americans
would pay their debts in order to reestablish commercial relations with
Great Britain.[14] Objection 2 was the concern lest the new American nation
attempt to conquer the British West Indies. Tucker doubted whether the
United States had the strength, or the desire, to acquire the West Indies and,
true to his economic theories, felt that even if they were lost, Great Britain
would be able to acquire sugar and other products grown in the West Indies
more cheaply on the open market.[15]

Objections 3 and 4 dealt with the possibility that the new American
nation might become a commercial rival of Great Britain. Tucker once
again predicted that when Americans won their independence, they would
turn their attention westward and continue to trade as before with Great

Britain because it would still be to their advantage.[16] This also partially answered Objections 5, 6, and 7, which posed the problem of where England would obtain naval supplies, rice and tobacco, and provisions for the West Indies. Tucker's additional answer to these objections was again that other nations might sell them to Great Britain at even lower prices than the colonies had charged.[17]

Objections 8 and 9 were concerned with possible damage to British manufacturing and its merchant marine because of the loss of the colonies. Tucker answered these objections by stating that lack of capital and natural resources would prevent American factories from competing with British industry, particularly when the flow of English workers to the colonies would be cut off when they were no longer part of the empire. As to the merchant marine, he predicted that it would continue to grow as British trade increased all over the world.[18]

Objection 10 was a suggestion that some type of legal union with America would be preferable to splitting with them entirely because, as Objections 11 and 12 stated, the loss of the colonies would weaken the English constitution and possibly lead to the loss of Ireland. Tucker refused to accept the validity of any of these objections. He believed that even if the colonies were to be placed in a status somewhat similar to Hanover, in which they recognized the authority of the king but not that of Parliament, they would insist on all the privileges of union with Great Britain but would still refuse to accept the accompanying duties and responsibilities.

Tucker viewed the Irish and American situations as quite different. A union between England and Ireland would be, in his opinion, of benefit to both nations and a definite deterrent to any movement for Irish independence. And lastly, he claimed that American independence would only strengthen the English constitution because it would bring a halt to the efforts of those English citizens who were only supporting the American cause in order to subvert the British form of government.[19]

Tucker also had a simple solution to Objection 13—how could the Loyalists be compensated if America were to be granted its independence? Just use the money that would have had to be spent to coerce the colonists to assist the Loyalists. He also thought that large numbers of Loyalists in the middle colonies might make it just possible for Great Britain to hold this territory and set up a puppet state in which all American Loyalists could reside.[20]

Tucker was deeply concerned about the possibility of surmounting Objection 14: "Who will dare to move in either House of Parliament for the Separation?" But even here, he hoped that events would soon convince some "Real Patriots," "Men of unbiased Principles," to make the attempt.[21]

Having thus completed this all-embracing refutation, Tucker closed his tract with an attack on Locke and those English politicians whom he blamed for the American Revolution, a pledge that he would not seek or accept clerical preferment (Burke's accusation still rankled), and a warning that the initial British military successes were bound to be ephemeral and did not weaken his arguments in the least.[22]

Tucker had subtitled this pamphlet *The Concluding Tract of the Dean of Glocester* and for five years, until 1781, he kept his word. During that period, however, he did write a brief pamphlet and a longer *Treatise Concerning Civil Government* controverting the ideas of John Locke and his followers, Price and Priestley, whom he blamed, at least in part, for the American Revolution and the desire for parliamentary reform in England. In the course of this latter work, Tucker parenthetically repeated many of the points he had made in his earlier writings. He welcomed the separation of the Thirteen Colonies and only wished that they had done it fifty years earlier and that the West Indies would join them. Colonies, to Tucker, were "the Authors of our present Misfortunes; and they will involve us still greater, if we shall obstinately persist in retaining these remote, unmanageable Possessions."[23]

Later that same year, Tucker wrote a pamphlet entitled *Cui Bono?* This volume took the form of a series of letters to the recently dismissed French finance minister, Jacques Necker, in which Tucker attempted to show the futility and the mutual disadvantages of the war between England and France. Basing his arguments on strictly economic grounds, he showed that victory for either nation would be disastrous for both.

In his fifth letter, Tucker discussed the possible consequences of a British victory over the colonies. He saw the British war aims in this conflict as: (1) recovery of the American trade, (2) convincing the Americans to pay their share of governmental expenses, and (3) maintenance of British power and glory. As to the first, he felt that the American trade was never lost. The second he believed was hopeless because if the Americans had been recalcitrant before the war when they were prosperous, they would certainly be even less cooperative if defeated and bankrupt. As to the third, he claimed that colonies conferred no real benefits upon the home country and that British glory had been proudly preserved by the courage of its soldiers and sailors. Even if the colonies were to surrender unconditionally, Tucker wrote, it would be in our "*Interest* not to accept of such a present"[24] [italics in original].

In the sixth and seventh letters, Tucker predicted that England might be able to retain the three southernmost colonies as a refuge for the Loyalists and that the United States would be eternally plagued by discord, high taxes, and economic problems. However, just before completing the pamphlet, he received news of Cornwallis's surrender at Yorktown. Tucker's reaction was characteristic.

> To congratulate my Country on being defeated is contrary to that Decency which is due to the Public and yet, if this defeat should terminate in total Separation from America, it would be one of the happiest events that hath ever happened to Great Britain.[25]

After 1781, Tucker lived and wrote (primarily on the importance of union between England and Ireland) until 1799, but the years 1782–1783, when it was clear to all that American independence was just a matter of time, may well have been the high point of his career. It was in 1782 that the *Gentlemen's Magazine,* which, like most other periodicals, had initially ridiculed Tucker's proposal, apologized to him with the statement that if his advice had been followed, although America would still have been independent, it would have been "our ally and friend, and many thousands of lives and millions of money would have been saved to both nations."[26]

Even before the news about Yorktown arrived, Tucker had written in *Cui Bono?* that he expected that people would one day say, "What a Pity that the Dean of Glocester's Advice had not been more attended to."[27] And by 1783, when he addressed a tract entitled *Four Letters on important National Subjects* to the earl of Shelburne, he felt that his unpopular position had been completely vindicated and that he could state with assurance:

> I have the Satisfaction to believe that there is not a Man in Great Britain, but is inwardly convinced, that it would have been happy for us, had the advice I gave [on America], been taken many years ago.[28]

And who was there to gainsay him!

Notes

1. Josiah Tucker, *An Humble Address and Earnest Appeal to the Landed Interest of Great Britain and Ireland Respecting Our Present Disputes with the Rebellious Colonies,* pp. 3–6, 19–20.

2. Ibid., p. 6.

3. Ibid., pp. 21–42.

4. Ibid., pp. 44–75.

5. Ibid., pp. 76–93. For the accusation against Franklin, see Robert Livingstone Schuyler, ed., *Josiah Tucker: A Selection from His Economic and Political Writings,* p. 351 (not in later editions).

6. Paul Langford, ed., *The Writings and Speeches of Edmund Burke,* II, p. 446.

7. Josiah Tucker, *A Letter to Edmund Burke, Esq.; Member of Parliament for the City of Bristol, and Agent for the Colony of New York in answer to His Printed Speech said to be spoken in the House of Commons on the twenty-second of March, 1775,* 2d ed., as found in Schuyler, *Josiah Tucker,* p. 375.

8. Ibid., pp. 377–393.

9. Ibid., pp. 395–398.

10. Ibid., p. 398.

11. Ibid., pp. 400–401.

12. Thomas W. Copeland et al., eds., *The Correspondence of Edmund Burke,* III, p. 180.

13. Josiah Tucker, *A Series of Answers to Certain Popular Objections Against Separating from the Rebellious Colonies, and Discarding Them Entirely,* pp. IX, XIV, XV.

14. Ibid., pp. 15–17.

15. Ibid., pp. 18–22.

16. Ibid., pp. 23–31.

17. Ibid., pp. 32–40.

18. Ibid., pp. 41–52.

19. Ibid., pp. 53–78.

20. Ibid., pp. 79–83.

21. Ibid., pp. 84–86.

22. Ibid., pp. 86–108.

23. Josiah Tucker, *A Treatise Concerning Civil Government in Three Parts,* as found in Schuyler, *Josiah Tucker,* pp. 437 (footnote), 445, 460 (footnote), 493, 515 (footnote), 532.

24. Josiah Tucker, *Cui Bono? Or an Inquiry What Benefits Can Arise either to the English or the Americans, the French, the Spaniards, or Dutch, from their Greatest Victories, or Successes in the Present War?* 2d ed., pp. 70–87.

25. Ibid., pp. 91–140.

26. As quoted in Solomon Lutnick, *The American Revolution and the British Press, 1775–1783,* p. 195.

27. Tucker, *Cui Bono,* p. 138.

28. Josiah Tucker, *Four Letters on important National Subjects, Addressed to the Right Honorable the Earl of Shelburne,* pp. 5–6.

Governor Pownall Fights to the Finish

We have already recounted Thomas Pownall's plan for a British "commonwealth" and his attempts to explain the colonial situation and point of view to his fellow members of the House of Commons. As we shall see in this chapter, his lack of success did not deter him from continuing, if not intensifying, his efforts.

Pownall's shift to the ministerial side may account for his silence when petitions requesting repeal of the Coercive Acts and other questions relating to the colonies were discussed during January and February 1775. He explained his reluctance to speak as the result of a promise he made during the 1774 debates, "as to opinions, I shall never more trouble the House with mine on the subject [of America]," though he remained ready to supply information if requested.[1] He broke his vow of silence, however, to support Lord North's proposal to conciliate the colonies by a tentative surrender of Parliament's power to tax them, if they would tax themselves. He thought the proposal "a fair and just preliminary that must lead to peace."[2]

Pownall approved of North's proposal as a "preliminary," because it appeared to him to be a first step toward the realization of the guidelines he had suggested in the 1774 edition of *The Administration of the British Colonies*. In a second volume, which he added to the work at that time, Pownall conceded that American representation in Parliament was no longer, if it ever had been, acceptable to either party in the dispute and that the only alternative to a return to the status quo prior to 1763 (which he opposed) was an "American union" into which the colonies would unite but still remain a dominion of the British empire.[3]

In the speech supporting North's proposal, Pownall stressed that it must be followed by a "compact" between Great Britain and its North American colonies to give them *"once for all,* such a constitution as is fit for such dependent communities within the empire" [italics in original]. Otherwise

Great Britain would only be able to hold the colonies "*by the tenure of a war,* that will cost more than they are worth, and finally ruin both"[4] [italics in original].

In March 1775, during the debate to cut off New England's trade, Pownall again supported Lord North. He assured the House that the allegations that the bill would cause famine and starvation were "groundless." Then he again relapsed into silence until November, when a debate was held on military expenses. He recognized that a state of war between Great Britain and its colonies was already *de facto* in existence but felt that his dominion plan might still result in a peace "on safe and honorable terms." Lord North, however, evinced no interest in the plan and Burke ridiculed it openly.[5] Pownall, in turn, attacked Burke's plan of conciliation, which was debated later that month. He felt it was motivated by party politics and was a short-sighted, piece-meal solution, which would be unacceptable in America and hazardous for Great Britain. Pownall also opposed Burke when he requested an accounting of the royal quit rents collected in North America.[6]

Otherwise, except for some comments on a Nova Scotia requisitions bill, Pownall did not speak in Parliament until December 1777. By that time, the American victory at Saratoga confirmed his conviction that neither North nor the Whigs would or could bring about a reconciliation with the colonies. In a debate on Charles James Fox's motion to consider the State of the Nation, particularly in regard to the war in America, Pownall burst out bitterly that his advice had been ignored for the past ten years with the result that

> the Americans never will return again to their subjection to the government of this country . . . you are no longer sovereigns over America, but the United States are an independent, sovereign people—until you are prepared to treat with them as such; it is of no consequence at all, what schemes or plans of conciliation this side of the house or that, may adopt.

He went on to suggest formal recognition of American independence, abandonment of Great Britain's mercantilistic policies, and negotiation of as favorable a commercial treaty with the United States as it was able to obtain.[7] However, Pownall's words on this, as on previous occasions, went unheeded.

Nevertheless, in February 1778, during a debate on Burke's motion to investigate the use of Indians against Americans, Pownall made an impassioned speech against the practice. However, he was realistic enough to recognize that "No war can be carried out in that country [America] in which the Indians will not mix." He therefore volunteered to serve as a commissioner to negotiate an agreement between Great Britain and the

United States, in which both would pledge to forgo the use of Indian allies. Pownall hoped that such an agreement might eventually lead to a permanent peace settlement between the two nations.[8] On this occasion, his proposal met with a generally favorable response in the House of Commons but the government refused to take it seriously.

Pownall had not spoken of a peace proposal merely on his own initiative. It was a result of overtures made to him by the American commissioners in France (Benjamin Franklin, Arthur Lee, and Silas Deane) in September 1777, when they felt that substantial French aid to the United States was not to be forthcoming. He made this revelation in March 1778 in the debate in the House of Commons, following the receipt of the news of the Franco-American alliance. He read from an August 1777 memorandum from the American commissioners to the French court, warning that only a Franco-American treaty could "prevent the colonists from being shortly reconciled to Great Britain." However, the French government failed to respond and it was then that the commissioners contacted Pownall, expressing willingness, if American independence were recognized, to sign a treaty of reconciliation with Great Britain in which "they [the Americans] would do everything to save the honor of their parent country." Pownall communicated this proposal to the ministry, which found the recognition of American independence "inadmissible."[9]

Pownall castigated Lord North for his shortsightedness but felt that amicable Anglo-American relations could still be restored if American independence were recognized. He requested that the 1778 peace commission headed by the earl of Carlisle, which North had already established, be authorized to recognize this independence and negotiate a commercial and military treaty between Great Britain and the United States. Ironically, North had finally come around to the dominion solution, which Pownall had continually advocated for over a decade. The Carlisle commission was empowered to: (1) surrender the right of parliamentary taxation, (2) suspend all acts concerning America since 1763, (3) recognize the American Congress (as long as it did not infringe on parliamentary sovereignty), (4) grant American representation in Parliament, (5) assist America in retiring its public debt, (6) make all civil offices in America elective, (7) allow any future customs service to be composed only of Americans, (8) and arrange an armistice. The British government was to retain for itself the power to regulate trade, manage coinage, and supervise military, naval, and foreign affairs.[10]

Pownall (and the Rockinghamites, reluctantly) approved of the instructions given to the commission but warned that unless his amendment were adopted, its mission "will be a mockery, and end in disgrace" and the United

States would demand "Canada, Nova Scotia, and the Newfoundland fishery" in compensation for wartime damages. Peace with America, he added, would also facilitate the redeployment of ships and men to meet a French threat to the West Indies or elsewhere. And finally, he concluded with an appeal to the North government to advise the king to place Lord Chatham once again at the head of the government—"in that moment we should have peace in America and should lower the haughty crest of France."[11]

The government was still unwilling to accept Pownall's logic and the Carlisle commission proved to be a fiasco. No wonder then that nothing more was heard from him until June 1779 and then only to urge an increase in the size of the militia in order to meet the threat of French invasion.[12] In April 1780, he spoke in favor of John Dunning's resolution "that the influence of the crown has increased, is increasing, and ought to be diminished."[13] Then, in May, he at first opposed a plan of General Conway (who had long been a supporter of America) to surrender Parliament's right of taxation over the colonies, annul all the Coercive Acts and laws unduly restricting American trade, alter or repeal the Quebec Act, and once again send commissioners to America. Pownall felt it was similar to, and just as pointless as, the instructions given the Carlisle commission but, after General Conway assured him that the Declaratory Act was one of the laws to be repealed, he reluctantly agreed to support it as a possible step toward peace.[14]

Conway's proposal was defeated, but later that month Pownall advanced his own bill to "empower his Majesty to make peace, truce, or convention with America." The rationale for his proposal was that two parties exited in America: a pro-English faction, and a pro-French faction and that the former group predominated at that moment. He, therefore, believed that "proper conduct on our part might lead to a speedy and happy conciliation" and urged Parliament to empower the king to send envoys to America to conclude a treaty, which would be "convenient and necessary for the honor and welfare of his majesty and his people." The House was poorly attended at that moment and his proposal was defeated by a vote of 113 to 52.[15]

This setback ended Pownall's parliamentary career. Realizing that he lacked support from any party, he refused to run again. However, this did not signal the end of his support for the American cause. He returned to writing and, in 1780, composed *A Memorial Most Humbly Addressed to the Sovereigns of Europe, on the Present State of Affairs between the Old and New World*. Pownall did not sign this work but pretended that it was written by a man recently deceased, who had "determined him to quit Europe, and to settle in America" but who, because of the American Revolution, had instead settled in the Azores.[16]

Pownall revealed his own frustrations by having the author bemoan the fact that he had been correct in his analysis of American affairs but completely unable to persuade others of his views. His basic thesis was that "North America is *de facto* an independent power *which has taken its equal station with other powers,* and must be so *de jure.*" He urged the leaders of Europe to accept this fact so that "the lives of thousands may be spared; the happiness of millions may be secured; and the peace of the whole world preserved." Otherwise, he predicted dire consequences.[17]

Pownall painted an enthusiastic picture of the freedom, size, potential population, strength, and riches of the United States and compared them to the decadence of the Old World. He completely ruled out the possibility that Great Britain or any other European nation could ever again control it either politically or economically. On the contrary, he predicted that the United States would become the premier commercial and naval power of the world. Pownall argued that the sooner all the European nations realized these facts, abandoned their mercantilist principles, and negotiated free trade agreements with the new nation, the sooner they would share in its growth and prosperity.

Pownall hoped that this "communion of nations," this commercial system, could be developed peacefully through a system of treaties rather than come about only after a long series of disastrous wars between the European powers. He felt that the formation of an Atlantic "Council of Commerce" would help regulate commercial rivalry and might even serve as an arbitrator in case of conflicts. All this Pownall insisted was the only intelligent response to the de facto independence of the United States.[18]

The *Memorial* proved to be an influential document. A capsule edition of 1781, which summarized its main argument in more lucid style, was widely read. John Adams, although disapproving of some of Pownall's thoughts and not certain that he was a "friend of America," still believed it might "be of service to our [the American] cause" and had it translated into French.[19] By this time, Cornwallis had surrendered at Yorktown and it was obvious that American independence had been won. Nevertheless, the king still ignored two additional *Memorials* sent to him by Pownall on how peace might be negotiated with the Untied States before it became inextricably tied to France. However, in 1782 North resigned and peace negotiations began. Yet, ironically, it was a coalition government jointly headed by North and Charles James Fox that finally signed the definitive peace treaty with the United States in 1783.

Even then, Pownall continued his interest in the new nation. In 1783, he wrote to James Bowdoin, a friend in Massachusetts, requesting him to extend Pownall's congratulations to the people of the United States on their independence and announcing his intentions of settling in the United States, "where I can be best at ease for the remainder of my daies." His only concern was that English citizens might not yet be welcome in their former colonies. Pownall also promised to donate land that he owned in Maine to Harvard College, in order to establish a professorship in political science.[20]

Bowdoin transmitted Pownall's congratulations to the Massachusetts legislature and assured him that, if he settled in the United States, he would be welcomed by all. The only unhappy piece of news he had to transmit was that Pownall's land had been sold for nonpayment of taxes during the war. Pownall replied that he hoped that the land might still be reclaimed; that he intended to bequeath his books to Harvard; and that he would appreciate receiving a commission from the state of Massachusetts as major or lieutenant-general so that, as he said, "I may appear in Europe in my American rank, which I will be proud of, and will not dishonor."[21]

By the time Pownall's land was redeemed from its new owner and the tax arrears paid, it brought very little revenue to Harvard College. Pownall never received his commission. As Bowdoin wrote, the granting of such a commission "would be inconsistent with good policy" and "might involve the state in disagreeable consequences."[22] Nor did Pownall fulfill his intention of settling in the United States. And no record exists that his library was ever received by Harvard.

But Pownall did make another contribution to the welfare of the new nation. In 1783, he published *A Memorial to the Sovereigns of America.* In the preface to this volume, he sarcastically warned that "its homespun reasonings will be unintelligible to British Statesmen" who are still fatuous enough to believe that the United States would still consider some form of union with Great Britain. He then continued by congratulating the American people on their newly won freedom and apologizing for his temerity in attempting to advise them. Nevertheless, he ventured to offer them a few suggestions. Pownall asserted that the future of the new nation depended in large measure on the strength of its constitution. Up until 1783, the American people had accepted their form of government because they were involved in a struggle for their independence. Now that independence was won, their dedication to the liberty of the individual must not be allowed to degenerate into "the libidinous passion of Licence." But Pownall was confident that the people of the United States were too mature politically and too fortunate in their social and economic system to fall into this error.[23]

Pownall, although lauding the Articles of Confederation, did not hesitate to criticize its lack of an adequate executive branch. He felt that "a distinct branch of Magistracy for Administration" was an absolute necessity for effective government. Pownall suggested a dual executive with a short term of office. With this addition, he felt that its present constitution would enable the United States to grow into a prosperous and powerful nation that would teach the world "Political Truths . . . to render men more free and happy under Government." Interestingly enough, in the body of this memorial, Pownall also made a plea for the abolition of imprisonment for debt, which he called "not relevant to the ends of distributive Justice and contrary to every idea of the advantages which the community is supposed to derive from every individual." He also expressed a hope that the United States would abolish slavery. Pownall felt that their gratitude at winning their own freedom might impel Americans to "extend this blessing to their fellow creatures."[24]

In *Three Memorials* (1784), which included the *Memorial to the Sovereigns of Europe* and the two *Memorials* he had sent to the king early in 1782, Pownall added a long preface reviewing his own role in the struggle and the errors of the British government, which he severely censured for precipitating, mismanaging, and then prolonging the conflict. One wishes to know what Pownall's reaction was to the Constitutional Convention and to the government it created but the records fail to enlighten us. One may only assume from his *Memorial to the Sovereigns of America* that he preferred it to the Articles of Confederation.

Pownall's last years were spent as a country gentleman and antiquarian. He eschewed politics but did take an interest in reform of the corn laws. He was also sympathetic to Latin American independence and gave much support to Francisco de Miranda. Pownall's last written work, *A Memorial Addressed to the Sovereigns of Europe and the Atlantic* (1803), recommended a commercial and military alliance between Great Britain and the United States, which would liberate Latin America and lead to the creation of an Atlantic federation.[25] Two years later, in 1805, Pownall died at the age of eighty-three. He always felt himself a prophet without honor. True, his concepts of a British commonwealth and an Atlantic community of nations were perhaps ahead of their time. Today, however, we can recognize Pownall as a true and enlightened "friend" of peace and liberty.

Notes

1. R.C. Simmons and P.D.G. Thomas, eds., *Proceedings and Debates of the British Parliaments Respecting North America, 1754–1783* (hereafter referred to as *Parliament Debates*), IV, pp. 277–278.

2. Ibid., V, pp. 441,444.

3. Thomas Pownall, *The Administration of the British Colonies,* 5th ed., II, pp. 86–87.

4. Simmons and Thomas, *Parliament Debates,* V, p. 443.

5. Ibid., p. 514; VI, pp. 212, 214.

6. Ibid., pp. 269–272, 287–288.

7. William Cobbett, ed., *Parliamentary History of England from the Earliest Period to the Year 1803,* XIX, cols. 526–528. Hereafter referred to as *Parliament History.*

8. Ibid., cols. 701–705.

9. Ibid., cols. 930–935.

10. Samuel Eliot Morison, ed., *Sources and Documents Illustrating the American Revolution, 1764–1788, and the Formation of the Federal Constitution,* 2d ed., pp. 186–203.

11. Cobbett, *Parliament History,* XIX, cols. 939–944.

12. Ibid., XX, cols. 956–959.

13. Ibid., XXI, cols. 347, 365–366.

14. Ibid., cols. 582–583, 588–591.

15. Ibid., col. 627; Francis Wharton, ed., *The Revolutionary Diplomatic Correspondence of the United States,* III, pp. 779–780.

16. Thomas Pownall, *A Memorial Most Humbly Addressed to the Sovereigns of Europe, on the Present State of Affairs between the Old and New World,* pp. i-ii.

17. Ibid., pp. v-vi, 4–6.

18. Ibid., p. 115.

19. Charles Francis Adams, ed., *The Works of John Adams,* VII, pp. 248, 332–333, 339; IX, p. 509.

20. Charles C. Smith, ed., "The Bowdoin and Temple Papers," *Collections of the Massachusetts Historical Society,* VI, pp. 3–6.

21. Ibid., pp. 21–23, 26–27, 30–33.

22. Ibid., pp. 38–40.

23. Thomas Pownall, *A Memorial Addressed to the Sovereigns of America,* pp. iii-iv, 35.

24. Ibid., pp. 109, 123, 136, 158.

25. Thomas Pownall, preface to *A Memorial Addressed to the Sovereigns of Europe and the Atlantic.*

David Hartley: Amateur Diplomat

The treaty of Paris finally ending the conflict between Great Britain and thirteen of its former colonies in North America was not signed at the royal palace of Versailles. More fittingly, it was endorsed at the Paris residence of David Hartley, an Englishman who, perhaps more than any of his compatriots, was responsible for the conclusion of hostilities between the two combatants.

David Hartley is difficult to characterize. He was born in 1731 and educated at private schools and Oxford. Like his distinguished father, David Hartley, Sr., David was interested in medicine and philosophy. But the son also had an interest in, and aptitude for, science. He was responsible for the invention of a process for making buildings fire proof or at least fire resistant, which helped him financially and won him the respect of many outstanding personages not the least of whom were the king and Lord North.[1] However, like Benjamin Franklin, his American friend whose career in so many ways paralleled and intertwined with his own, Hartley was drawn into politics. His proclivities aligned him with the Whigs and those who felt the necessity for parliamentary reform. Hartley authored several pamphlets criticizing Lord Bute and George Grenville, among others, but his major contribution to the American cause was made as a member of the House of Commons representing Kingston-upon-Hull. Hartley took his seat in November 1774, just as American affairs were approaching a crisis. Earlier in the year, the Coercive Acts had been passed to punish the people of Boston for their Tea Party.

We have no account of Hartley's first remarks in Parliament. The records merely reported that on December 5, "Mr. Hartley (a new member) entered fully into the contents of the [king's] Speech and Address and urged strongly the necessity of the proposed Amendment" (which implied disapproval of the ministerial policy toward America).[2] A few days later, in the course of a preliminary discussion of American affairs, Hartley claimed that the Americans had been willing to provide for their own support, and urged at least a temporary suspension of the Coercive Acts "in order to see if the colonists still continued to be of the same way of thinking."[3]

Hartley next spoke on December 20, when he chided the ministers for adjourning Parliament until the middle of January 1775, while the situation in America was so serious and the people of Boston, as well as the British troops stationed there, were in danger of starvation as a result of the British blockade of the port. He, himself, expressed willingness to "sit on Christmas Day" to alleviate the situation.[4] Nevertheless, the recess was taken and Hartley had to wait until February 1775 to question the sending of additional troops to America. Later that month, he described Lord North's offer to waive parliamentary taxation, if the colonies taxed themselves as "attended with menaces and threats, therefore not a lenient or conciliatory measure, but only thrown out as such for a pretext." (See chapter 7.) In March, he requested that the act proposed by Lord North to restrain the trade, commerce, and fisheries of New England should explicitly state that it did not prohibit the importation of "fuel, meal, corn, flour, or other victual" from the other colonies into New England. Otherwise, Hartley warned, the act would be viewed by Americans as an attempt to starve the people of Boston and they would have no alternative but armed resistance. He also predicted that British merchants and manufacturers would suffer as a result of this bill. When North presented a similar bill cutting off the trade of the other colonies, Hartley characterized it as an attempt to "Drive the whole continent of America into despair."[5]

On March 27, 1775, Hartley presented his own plan to conciliate the colonies. It was based on his earlier contention that the colonists had been perfectly agreeable to underwriting their political and military needs as long as they were voted by their own colonial legislatures rather than by Parliament. Hartley also pointed out that Great Britain contributed very little to the development of the colonies. The colonists themselves cultivated the land, built towns, subdued the Indians, and cooperated in the wars against France. Hartley, therefore, proposed that the king, in consultation with Parliament, send letters of requisition to each colony requesting its legislature to vote sufficient money for the maintenance of an adequate military and naval force to defend its frontiers and its commerce. He felt that this plan avoided the implied threat embodied in North's conciliatory proposition and would be welcomed by the colonists. In the interim, Hartley recommended the suspension of the three punitive measures against America passed at the last session of Parliament. Hartley concluded with a personal plea to Lord North:

> The eyes of all this country, and America too, are turned toward the noble lord
> . . . to receive his final determination, as to the measures which are to decide
> the safety or ruin of this empire. The ways of peace are still before him.[6]

One of North's followers derisively styled Hartley's speech as a "tedious panegyric" more suitable to be delivered in "an American Congress than in a British House of Parliament." Lord North disapproved of it strongly, and it did not even come to a vote.[7]

Hartley was not surprised at his defeat and continued the struggle. He warned that ministerial policy could only result in an armed uprising in which the colonies would be supported by France and Spain. He also predicted that their policies would reduce the revenue produced by the colonies and would ultimately result in vast military expenses, which would have to be borne by the English taxpayer, particularly the landowner. "Why," he queried, "are ministers so obstinately bent to plunge the nation into inextricable perplexities and boundless expence?"[8]

Hartley was also one of the earliest opponents of slavery. He attempted to combine his interest in the welfare of slaves with his desire to avoid a breach between Great Britain and its colonies. On several occasions, he suggested that if Parliament felt it necessary, as North indicated, to assert the authority over the colonies, it should pass a law requiring all slaves to be tried by a jury in criminal cases. Hartley believed that by accepting this law, the colonies would prove their recognition of parliamentary jurisdiction over them and that all laws regarding the colonies, including the Coercive Acts, could then be repealed. He also reiterated his belief that Parliament should return to a requisition system to raise a revenue from the colonies. Hartley viewed this strategy not only as a conciliatory measure but as "the first step to correct a vice [slavery], which has spread through the continent of North America, contrary to the laws of God and man, and to the fundamental principles of the British constitution." He did not advocate immediate, but rather gradual, abolition. But he was perceptive enough to realize that "those who seek justice and liberty for themselves [must] give that justice and liberty to their fellow creatures."[9] Hartley also attacked the African slave trade and was a member of an abolitionist society.[10]

Hartley had presented his plan of conciliation with America on December 7, 1775, in response to a petition from the members of the Continental Congress declaring their loyalty and desire to be reconciled to Great Britain. Hartley claimed that this petition proved the colonists' willingness to honor requisitions upon their colonial assemblies and to make reasonable concessions in order to restore peace. However, Lord North referred to the "unreasonableness of the motion" and this was sufficient to ensure its defeat by a vote of 123 to 21.[11]

Two weeks later, Hartley made an impassioned speech in which he prophetically admonished his colleagues about the disastrous effects that must result from the repressive measures being aimed at the colonies. "Your land force has been disgraced . . . who . . . shall be responsible if the navy of this country should be brought to disgrace and defeat." He predicted the difficulties that would face any British attempts at military conquests of America. And he concluded his speech with:

> The fate of America is cast. You may bruise its heel, but you cannot crush its head. It will revive again. The new world is before them. Liberty is theirs. They have possession of a free government, their birthright and inheritance, derived to them from their parent state, which the hand of violence cannot wrest from them. If you will cast them off, my last wish to them; may they go and prosper.[12]

In February 1776, a debate concerning the projected use of German mercenaries in the conflict gave Hartley another opportunity to inveigh against the government's policies, which "have so madly driven them [the Americans] on to unavoidable resistance." Then, he again warned of the "hazard of public bankruptcy" if the war were to continue or expand. And the use of foreign troops would be "the most disgraceful, the most unjust and unnatural, and big with the most fateful consequences, of any measure that has been, or could be adopted." He warned that as soon as German troops were utilized by Britain, the colonists would also avail themselves of foreign aid and "all possibility of reconciliation and return to our former connexion is totally cut off."[13]

The sincerity of these sentiments is attested to by a letter written by Hartley to Benjamin Franklin in the same month. In this missive, Harley berated the "treacherous Administration" for the "incessant injuries" that it was inflicting upon "our unhappy fellow subjects in America." Yet he implored Franklin to continue to do everything possible to "soften animosities and to put off the evil day when the people of America might become so disillusioned with the people of Great Britain that the colonists might take some rash step that would forever separate them." Hartley assured Franklin that it was "want of power," not "want of will," that prevented the English people from seeing that justice was done to America.[14]

Hartley also attacked the military budget when North presented it to the House of Commons in March 1776, expressing astonishment at "the confidence with which ministers asked, and the ready compliance of Parliament to every requisition, without either examining the nature of the services for which the money was given, or afterwards enquiring into the expenditure."[15] Again on April 1, during the discussion of naval expenditures,

Hartley warned that Parliament was being asked to give the ministry a virtual blank check to pay the expenses of the American war. Hartley, therefore, made nine motions all aimed at forcing North to tender official estimates of the cost of the war up until March 1776 and for the twelve months following. He hoped that the revelation of the enormous expenses involved (Hartley estimated them at £10–12 million) would cause Parliament to attempt a reconciliation with the colonies rather than bankrupt the nation. For this purpose, he had drawn up a petition to be presented by the House of Commons to the king requesting him to send commissioners to America who could offer to them (the Americans) some specific line of national obedience, instead of unconditional submission, and to give them assurance of redress to all their reasonable complaints of grievances, together with a full security of all their constitutional rights. This petition also urged the king to place the American colonies on the same footing as Ireland in respect to taxation (Ireland was taxed by its own representatives). Lord North, however, maintained that it was impossible to estimate the costs of the war and all of Hartley's motions were voted down.[16]

In May, Hartley spoke in favor of a similar motion by Sawbridge to grant the American colonies the same degree of control over their finances as Ireland. When this suggestion was again rejected, Hartley explained, "We have bid an everlasting farewell to America."[17] Nor was he any more successful in his attempt to hold Parliament in session through the summer of 1776, in order to be prepared to meet any new developments in the crisis between the mother country and the colonies.[18] Parliament was, therefore, out of session when the Continental Congress voted to declare American independence from Great Britain.

Hartley did not speak in the House of Commons again until May 1777, when Lord North presented his budget. Once again Hartley painted a depressing picture of the effect of the war on all classes of English citizens. He pointed out that a reconciliation based on a return to the pre-1763 era, which would have been possible prior to July 1776, was now out of the question. Hartley realized that he was too far ahead of parliamentary opinion, but he still recommended that Great Britain suspend hostilities and voluntarily "bestow upon the colonies an entire freedom of their legislative powers within themselves, hoping thereby to lay a foundation for a perpetual and indissoluble bond of affection and alliance."[19]

Hartley fought hard to convince his colleagues that a cessation of hostilities and an alliance between Great Britain and the United States was the only realistic solution to the quarrel between the mother country and its colonies. In December 1777, he once again recounted the cost in men and money of the American war. He repeated his proposal of the previous May and moved that "it is unbecoming the wisdom and prudence of Parliament, to proceed any further in the support of this fruitless, expensive and destructive war." However, once again, North spoke against it and his motion was "negatived without a division."[20]

Hartley repeated his motion in substantially the same form in April and May 1778. By this time, France had agreed to aid the United States and he had hoped that the ministry might recognize the necessity of the wisdom of his recommendations for recognition of American independence and the negotiation of an alliance between the United States and Great Britain. However, the motion was never brought to a vote because its proponents feared they were still in a minority.[21] The truth of this contention was borne out by the vote on Hartley's motion not to prorogue Parliament. This motion, which also included the recommendations that American independence be recognized, free trade be established between the two nations, and their respective nationals be permitted to hold dual citizenship, was defeated after heated debate by a vote of 105 to 53.[22]

Not only did Hartley fight for peace but he also did his best to mitigate the horrors of war. In October 1777, Franklin answered Hartley's letter of February 1776. Franklin claimed that the breach between the two nations was already irreparable. However, he did beseech Hartley to do whatever he could to alleviate the conditions of American prisoners of war who were held in British prisons without proper provisions or winter clothing. Apparently, this letter never reached Hartley because Franklin sent him another similar letter by messenger in December 1777.[23] Hartley attempted to convince Lord North to have both Great Britain and the United States appoint official commissioners to deal with the problem but failing this helped solicit private funds to meet the prisoners' needs.

Franklin, however, was interested in more than improving conditions for American prisoners in Great Britain. He was eager to secure their release by exchanging them for English prisoners held by the United States. He again entreated Hartley's aid and received his full cooperation. The negotiations for this exchange were long and discouraging. It was not until March 1779 that actual exchange began. Even then, many difficulties arose that required all of Hartley's patience and resourcefulness to resolve. As Franklin wrote, "This exchange is the more remarkable, as our people were all committed for high treason."[24]

The negotiations over the exchange of prisoners placed Hartley in contact with both the American commissioners in France and with the British ministers. He took full advantage of these contacts to attempt to secure a cessation of hostilities between the two nations. In February 1778, Franklin hinted that if "wise and honest men"—among whom he included Hartley—

were to come to Paris, Great Britain "might not only obtain peace with America, but prevent a war with France."[25] Lord North seemed to have no objection to such an unofficial undertaking and, in April, Hartley departed for Paris.

Little is known of the details of Hartley's visit. He met with the American commissioners and the Count de Vergennes, the French minister of foreign affairs, and apparently discussed British recognition of American independence in return for an alliance and a grant of special commercial privileges for Great Britain. Hartley also made it clear that Great Britain had no intention of surrendering Halifax, Nova Scotia, or any part of Canada (all territories that the American peace commissioners were hoping to annex to the United States), but might consider ceding them Florida.

Hartley seemed to blind himself to the fact that the United States had entered into a treaty with France. He assumed that the commissioners were in a position to act without any reference, or deference, to their French ally. He was also handicapped by the fact that he had no official credentials. Franklin recognized his good, if misguided, intentions, but John Adams considered him a spy and sensed, correctly, that the Englishman hoped to detach the United States from its French alliance. Adams also considered, unfairly, that Hartley's opposition to the ministry "was the only basis for his friendship to America." Vergennes viewed Hartley's purpose as merely to "sow distrust" between the United States and France. Hartley's mission was therefore a complete failure, but it did not deter him from further efforts in another direction.[26]

Unsuccessful in Parliament and in Paris, Hartley took his case to the people. In four *Letters on the American War,* written to his constituents in the town of Kingston-upon-Hull during September and October 1778, he reviewed the entire course of the controversy. Hartley's first *Letter* described events from November 1774 to June 1777. He castigated Lord North for always being tardy in offering any reasonable compromise to the American colonists and, thus, losing them completely.[27]

In his second *Letter,* Hartley recounted the parliamentary maneuvers of the period between November 1777 and June 1778. This *Letter* is important for Hartley's explanation of the ministerial policy toward America. He viewed it as a carefully laid plot to "establish an influential dominion, to be exercised at the pleasure of the crown, and to acquire from America an independent revenue at the disposition of the crown, uncontrolled and not accountable to Parliament." Hartley argued that it was this sinister plot to obtain revenue that could be spent solely at the discretion of the king that explained Lord North's refusal to offer a realistic compromise to the American colonies, because any such compromise would only afford a revenue that would be controlled by Parliament. As proof of his contention, Hartley offered as evidence the fiscal situation in the province of Quebec, where the revenue had fallen completely under royal control.[28]

In his third *Letter,* Hartley attempted to refute the charges that the Whigs had first encouraged the colonists to revolt and then interfered with the prosecution of the war against them. To meet the first charge, he quoted from several colonial protests made during the years 1764 and 1765 against the power of Parliament to tax the colonies, which was long before Pitt first challenged the right in Parliament in 1766. As to the second charge, Hartley laid the full blame for the failure of the American war on the ministry, whose complete control of Parliament made it possible for it to pass all its own measures and defeat all those suggested by the opposition.[29]

Hartley's final *Letter* was devoted to an appeal for peace and reconciliation between the United States and Great Britain. He recalled all the attempts of the colonists to resolve their difficulties with their mother country peacefully and insisted that the two nations could still have an "alliance founded upon mutual affection, common interest, and common consent," if Great Britain would recognize America's independence. Unfortunately, however, he believed that Lord North still planned to continue the struggle in order to establish the crown at the head of all the executive and federal powers of the whole continent of America, independent of and uncontrolled by Parliament. Only if the members of Parliament realized the danger to the nation and removed North from power could the country be saved.[30] Franklin wrote Hartley expressing his agreement with the tenor of these *Letters,* taking exception only to Hartley's hope that the United States would soon desert its French alliance.[31] John Adams also expressed his resentment at Hartley's desire to split the United States from France and for a federal union between Great Britain and the United States, even though he described him as "more for peace than any man in the kingdom [Great Britain]."[32] And Horace Walpole, in the final entry in his *Journal* for the year 1778, called Hartley's *Letters* "a justification of the colonies; it shows that they were forced into rebellion by the most cruel treatment, and that nothing but passive submission to despotism would content the Crown."[33]

When Parliament reconvened in 1779, the actions of the ministry bore out Hartley's allegations. In spite of his clear implication that the American commissioners were obviously willing to negotiate with authorized representatives of Great Britain, Lord North remained obdurate. In March, Hartley warned that Spain would soon join the alliance against Great Britain and urged a speedy peace with America. In June, he seconded a motion to that effect. Later that month, he offered his own peace plan based on a ten-year truce. And in December, he appealed to the country gentlemen, the independent members of Parliament who in the past had "rescued their country in moments of danger," to force a reversal of the government's American policy. As before, all his recommendations to initiate peace negotiations were defeated, often without debate.[34] As the harsh realist John Adams wrote early in 1780:

> Mr. Hartley's motions and speeches have never . . . been much attended to; from whence I conclude, if the present great leaders, even the opposition in the House [of Commons] were seriously disposed to do anything towards a pacification which we could attend to, they would not suffer Mr. Hartley to have the honor of making the motion.[35]

Yet Hartley was not completely without effectiveness. He had North's tacit consent to correspond with Franklin in regard to a truce of some five to seven years, on the basis of each side holding the territory then under its control. Franklin was willing to consider the proposition if the truce were extended to twenty-one years and France were included, but the British government felt these terms were unacceptable and refused to negotiate further at that time.[36]

Even though Parliament still had over a year to run, Lord North called for new elections in the fall of 1780. Hartley correctly viewed these elections as an attempt by North to secure parliamentary approval for a continuation of the war. As part of his bid for reelection, Hartley wrote an *Address to the Committee of the County of York* in which he bitterly attacked the ministerial war policy. He vividly pictured the vast outlay of money spent on the war and the financial damage it had done to all classes of English citizens, except those members of Parliament who enjoyed lucrative government contracts. Hartley urged his constituents to elect members of Parliament who would vote to end the war and regain American friendship and trade before Great Britain found itself completely isolated militarily and ruined economically.[37]

Though the ministry did not make the expected gains, Hartley's constituents were not as yet ready to grant independence to the United States and resented Hartley's close association with Franklin and other Americans. Hartley, therefore, lost his seat and did not return to the House of Commons until 1782. Yet in June 1780, prior to the election, he once again introduced a bill to reopen negotiations with the United States and immediately declare a ten-year cessation of hostilities. He reported the bill's failure to Franklin and Adams, with the promise that he would remain "devoted to the restoration of peace upon honorable terms."[38] Fortunately, his half brother Winchcombe Henry Hartley, who shared his views on America, retained his seat. On May 30, 1781, he presented a motion to "restore Peace with America." The ministry tried to shut off debate on the motion but failed. A lively discussion in which Burke spoke bitterly against the ministers ensued and the motion was defeated—but by the relatively narrow margin of 106 to 72. Winchcombe Henry Hartley also supported Fox's motion to end the war later that year.[39]

Although David Hartley returned to the House of Commons in 1782 and again spoke on the American issue on several occasions, his greatest contribution to the cause of peace was made largely behind the scenes.[40] He maintained contact with Lord North and Franklin and, in June 1781, was once again on the verge of traveling to Paris to attempt to lay the groundwork for discussions between the two nations. However, both Franklin and Vergennes agreed that the trip would be fruitless unless Hartley came as an official emissary; the project was aborted.[41]

Nevertheless, Hartley was still not discouraged. In January 1782, he wrote Franklin about the possibility of a separate peace between the United States and Great Britain to which France would not object. Hartley pointed out that it was "the unfortunate union of common cause between America and France which has for the past three years turned aside the wish of the people of England for peace." He hoped that France would not continue to involve the United States in a "war of European resentments and jealousies beyond her original views and engagement." He added that North was willing to enter negotiations for a ten-year truce if the British government was not required to begin by formally recognizing the independence of the United States.[42]

Franklin apparently misunderstood Hartley to mean that the United States was to sign a separate peace without consulting France. This he vehemently refused to do. He also refused to sign a treaty that did not recognize the independence of the United States. Hartley immediately responded that he had no intention of requesting the United States to sign a treaty without the consent of France. However, he did not (and probably could not) discuss the problem of recognizing American independence but did, in a later letter, assure Franklin that the ministers had "good dispositions toward peace."[43]

By this time the ministers were well aware that the political situation virtually dictated that they be well disposed to peace. On February 22, 1782, General Conway's motion to end the war had been defeated by a single vote—194 to 193.[44] (See chapter 14.) Earlier in February, Hartley had prepared a memo for Lord North, which he entitled a "Breviate." This document embodied substantially the same suggestions that Hartley had made to Franklin: a separate peace between Great Britain and the United

States made with the consent of France, which would provide for an indefinite truce without specific recognition of American independence.[45]

However, Lord North still refused to commit the ministry to these terms, and before the end of March it was replaced by a Whig ministry headed by Lord Rockingham. Hartley's ambition was finally to be realized; he was to take an active role in peace negotiations with the United States. But that story requires its own chapter.

Notes

1. The most thorough study of Hartley is by George H. Guttridge, *David Hartley M.P.—An Advocate of Conciliation, 1774–1783.*
2. R.C. Simmons and P.D.G. Thomas, eds., *Proceedings and Debates of the British Parliaments Respecting North America, 1754–1783* (hereafter referred to as *Parliament Debates*), V, p. 241.
3. Ibid., pp. 248–256.
4. Ibid., pp. 257–258, 260, 261.
5. Ibid., pp. 429, 474, 511–513, 519.
6. Ibid., pp. 638–649.
7. Ibid., pp. 638, 649–650.
8. Ibid., VI, pp. 29, 237–238, 241–242.
9. Ibid., pp. 169–170, 332–337, 570–572.
10. William Cobbett, ed., *Parliamentary History of England, from the Earliest Period to the Year 1803* (hereafter referred to as *Parliament History*), XIX, cols. 315–316.
11. Simmons and Thomas, *Parliament Debates,* VI, p. 339.
12. Ibid., pp. 383–384.
13. Ibid., pp. 405–408.
14. Albert H. Smyth, ed., *The Writings of Benjamin Franklin* (hereafter referred to as *Franklin Writings*), VI, pp. 441–443.
15. Simmons and Thomas, *Parliament Debates,* VI, pp. 454–455, 460–462.
16. Ibid., pp. 494–500.
17. Ibid., pp. 570–572.
18. Ibid., p. 598.
19. Cobbett, *Parliament History,* XIX, cols. 253–262.
20. Ibid., cols. 549–560.
21. Ibid., cols. 1068–1080, 1204–1207.
22. Ibid., cols. 1207–1223.
23. Smyth, *Franklin Writings,* VII, pp. 68–72, 75.
24. Ibid., pp. 232–233, 267–268, 320; VIII, pp. 1–3, 6–7, 111.
25. Ibid., VII, p. 109.
26. Ibid., pp. 105–106, 115, 142–144, 146, 153; Charles Francis Adams, ed., *The Works of John Adams* (hereafter referred to as *J. Adams Works*), III, pp. 136–137, 150–151, 185; and B.F. Stevens, ed., *Facsimiles of Manuscripts in European Archives Relating to America, 1773–1783,* XXII, pp. 1917, 1919.
27. David Hartley, *Letters on the American War,* 6th ed., pp. 1–44.
28. Ibid., pp. 55–56, 61–66.
29. Ibid., pp. 69–91.
30. Ibid., pp. 120, 123–125.

31. Smyth, *Franklin Writings*, VII, pp. 220, 225–229.

32. Francis Wharton, ed., *The Revolutionary Diplomatic Correspondence of the United States*, III, p. 569.

33. A. Francis Steuart, ed., *The Last Journals of Horace Walpole During the Reign of George III from 1771–1783*, I, p. 529.

34. Cobbett, *Parliament History*, XX, cols. 272–280, 838, 901–915, 1185–1191, 1196–1197.

35. Adams, *J. Adams Works*, VII, pp. 148, 164–165, 226, 253.

36. Smyth, *Franklin Writings*, VII, pp. 234, 305–311.

37. David Hartley, *An Address to the Committee of the County of York on the State of Public Affairs*.

38. Cobbett, *Parliament History*, XXI, col. 171; Adams, *J. Adams Works*, VII, pp. 227–228; Wharton, *Diplomatic Correspondence*, III, pp. 670–671, 837–838, 864–865.

39. Cobbett, *Parliament History*, XXII, cols. 336–337, 480–481.

40. Ibid., XXIII, cols. 135, 319–320, 563, 640, 727.

41. Wharton, *Diplomatic Correspondence*, IV, pp. 522, 527–528.

42. Ibid., V, pp. 80–84, 294–295, 303–304.

43. Ibid., pp. 112–114, 127–130, 144, 207–208; Smyth, *Franklin Writings*, VIII, pp. 381–383, 427–428.

44. Cobbett, *Parliament History*, XXII, col. 1048.

45. Wharton, *Diplomatic Correspondence*, V, pp. 386–392.

Charles James Fox:
The Life of the Party

In November 1776, the king wrote Lord North:

> I have learnt . . . that Charles Fox . . . should set out for Paris and not return
> till after the recess: I think therefore You cannot do better than bring as
> much forward [while he is absent] as real business is never so well consid-
> ered as when the Attention of the House is not taken up by noisy declama-
> tions.[1]

This quotation illustrates the extent to which, by 1776, Charles James Fox
had assumed the leadership of the Whig opposition to the American war.
By this time, he clearly realized that the American cause and the struggle of
Parliament to free itself from royal domination were inextricably linked. As
he wrote to his political associate, Lord Ossory, America's defeat would
"give the completest triumph to Toryism that it ever had."[2] His rise to
leadership is more remarkable because in 1774, when he began criticizing
ministerial conduct of American affairs, he spoke more as an individual
than as a member of any political party or group. Then, during 1775, he
unofficially joined the Rockingham Whigs (he did not formally affiliate
until 1779) and, as we read in chapter 7, loyally supported Edmund Burke,
whose speech *On Conciliation with America* he enthusiastically seconded.

He introduced a motion when Parliament assembled in February 1776,
requesting a committee "to enquire into the Causes of the ill Success of his
Majesty's Arms in North America." In what the *London Chronicle* called
"one of his most able and best directed speeches," Fox disclaimed any
desire to reopen constitutional questions and focused on the Coercive Acts,
their application, and their consequences. He alleged that "there had been
mismanagement and misconduct somewhere" and insisted that it was cru-

cial to pinpoint the blame. The debate lasted eleven hours but, at its conclusion, the majority accepted North's contention that such an inquiry must wait for "the proper season."[3]

Fox and North continued their duel for the rest of the session. Early in March, Fox challenged North to resign because he had been part of the administration that had authorized Hillsborough to promise the colonies that Parliament would not tax them (see chapter 3) but had now reversed that policy. Later that month, Fox (and Burke) eulogized the American general Richard Montgomery (who had distinguished himself on the British side during the French and Indian War) upon his death while attempting to capture Quebec. North retorted that he might have been brave, able, humane, and generous, he was still "only a . . . rebel." Fox rejoined that "all the great assertors of liberty" had at one time "been called *rebels*"[4] [italics in original]. In April, he tried to provoke North by accusing him of being inconsistent in allowing the public into the House to hear the debates at certain times but not at others and spoke against the use of Hessian troops against the colonists.[5] In May, he seconded General Conway's motion that Parliament be apprised of the terms that the Howe brothers were authorized to treat with the Americans. In his remarks, Fox mocked North's statement that the Howes would "sound out the [American] people" about taxation and declared that this would make them "spies not . . . commissioners."[6] Lord North defeated this motion and all other opposition motions during the first year of the war, which, on the whole, was militarily successful for the British armies in America.

The Declaration of Independence only complicated matters for the Whig opposition. Their need of a new strategy was obvious. As Fox wrote Burke in August, "the declaration of independency seems to be an event which we ought surely not to pass over in silence" and requested a meeting of party leaders.[7] Rockingham and Burke felt that the secession of the Whigs from Parliament would be the most effective protest that could be made at the time, particularly since General Howe had just won what seemed to be a decisive victory on Long Island. Fox disagreed vociferously. To Burke he wrote, "a Secession is totally unadvisable, and that nothing but some very firm and vigourous step will be at all *becoming*" [italics in original]. And he wrote to Rockingham in a similar vein, stating that the Whigs must "make it a point of honor . . . to support the American pretensions in adversity as much as we did in their prosperity."[8]

The Whigs followed Fox's advice and attended in full force when Parliament met again in October 1776. Fox delivered so "masterly" a speech, in the words of the historian Edward Gibbon, or such a "noble performance," as described by Edmund Burke, that no one from the ministerial benches dared to reply.[9] In this address, he compared the Declaration of Independence to the Glorious Revolution in England, warned of foreign intervention on the side of America, and claimed that a conquered America would be a burden rather than an asset. And in closing, Fox cautioned that a military conquest of America might be "very unfavorable to the liberties of this country [Great Britain]." For this reason, he exclaimed that if forced to make a choice between "conquering or abandoning America . . . I am for abandoning America." The ministers, however, though unable to reply to Fox, were still able to win the vote by a margin of almost three to one.[10] A few days later, news reached Great Britain that the Howe commission, upon being rebuffed by the United States Congress, had promised in the king's name to "concur in the reversal of all his acts by which his subjects there [in America] may think themselves aggrieved." When questioned about this document, Lord North temporized, then deferred it to Lord George Germaine, the successor of Dartmouth as secretary of state for the American colonies, who acknowledged its authenticity.[11] Fox and the Whigs expressed their resentment at this insult to parliamentary authority but welcomed the development and requested that a motion be passed confirming it.[12] The ministry, however, claimed that such a motion would undercut the authority of the commissioners and complicate their mission and defeated it by a vote of 109 to 47. Following this defeat, the Rockinghamites followed their initial strategy and declined to attend sessions of Parliament dealing with the American question.[13]

Fox spent a few relaxing weeks in Paris but, unlike most of his Whig colleagues, was present when Parliament reassembled in January 1777. One of the first bills brought forward by the government was designed to suspend the right of habeas corpus for those accused of treason in America or on the high seas. Fox pointed out that such a bill would not only limit American freedom but lead to the "spreading of the same system of [arbitrary] government into this country." In spite of his objections the bill passed with only slight modifications."[14]

Fox's stand, however, apparently convinced his Whig colleagues that secession from Parliament was counterproductive and in April they resumed attendance. The occasion of their return was the vote on the civil list by which Parliament was asked to pay over £600,000 of the king's debts. In his futile opposition to the bill, Fox blamed North but his actual target was royal manipulation of the House of Commons. As he summarized, "Corruption and patronage had overspread the Land."[15] And in May, he opposed Lord North's budget, which was predicated upon increased efforts to retain the Thirteen Colonies. Fox asserted that "our force was not equal to conquest" and that "sensible men, the noble Lord's own friends, are grown sick of war."[16] Nevertheless, as usual, ministerial forces triumphed.

Undiscouraged, Fox returned to the attack in November 1777, when Parliament reconvened after the summer recess. "The idea of conquering America was absurd and . . . absolutely impossible."[17] As early as February 1777, he had warned that "we were on the eve of a war with France," which would soon come to the aid of the United States and make American independence inevitable.[18] Still unknown to him and his compatriots the stage for French intervention had already been set with the October surrender of General Burgoyne to American forces at Saratoga.

Even before Parliament reconvened, Fox undertook to reenergize the Rockingham group. Although given somewhat reluctantly, the encouragement of the earl of Chatham helped them to decide that, in December, Fox in the House of Commons and the duke of Richmond in the House of Lords would move that on February 2, 1778, each House should meet as a committee of the whole to consider the "State of the Nation," by which was meant the status of the American war. Even though Fox admitted "we have not yet got one vote this year," he believed that "the *opinion* of the majority of the House is now with us" and that this would eventually translate into "*votes*" [italics in original]. His optimism was soon to be intensified by the arrival of the preliminary reports of Burgoyne's surrender.[19]

On December 2, Fox made his motion specifying the need to discuss the financial cost of the war, the casualties caused by the war, the effects of the war on British commerce, the present status of the war, and the progress of peace negotiations. North agreed to the motion in principle but objected to producing papers that might prove "inconvenient or hurtful to the country," by which he meant particularly the instructions given the peace commissioners. Fox countered that the House of Lords had already agreed to a similar motion to his made by the duke of Richmond and, therefore, secrecy was impossible. Nevertheless, Fox's motion was defeated.[20]

Official news of Burgoyne's surrender arrived that evening and debate ensued on the following day. Fox (and others) challenged Lord George Germaine to furnish an official explanation of the report. Germaine reluctantly replied, calling the surrender "a most unfortunate affair." Fox emotionally called for an inquiry, defended General Burgoyne, and called Germaine "a blunderer" who was "solely responsible" for the disaster. But still, the House of Commons refused to authorize such an inquiry.[21] By this time, Fox was grudgingly beginning to accept the idea of American independence.

> We ought to give America perfect security on the subject of taxation and her charters. I would treat with them . . . on the very topic whether they should

be independent or not; but my wish is that America may remain dependent on this country. I am no friend to the independence of America; nevertheless if no better terms can be had, I would treat with them as allies. They might be good and useful allies, nor do I feel the consequence of their independence.[22]

During the months of December and January, North and Fox continued to cross swords. When North objected to John Wilkes's motion to repeal the Declaratory Act, Fox sarcastically queried whether the loss of one army had not made Great Britain "unsuccessful enough" to attempt to conciliate with America. In the debate whether to adjourn Parliament until January 20, Fox seized the opportunity to again predict the entrance of France into the war and to inform North, in very unparliamentary language, that America "would never listen to any treaty" coming from a "man whom they suspected, detested, and despised." When Parliament did reconvene, he compared the present government's actions toward America to those of King James II in England and again requested the papers necessary for an investigation of the Burgoyne fiasco (though he later temporarily withdrew it because of Lord North's absence from the session). A few days later, his motion was approved after Lord North himself seconded it in order to assuage the feelings of General Burgoyne.[23]

All these were merely preliminary skirmishes to what was expected to be a major debate on February 2, 1778. Fox opened with a two-hour-and-forty-minute speech, which scathingly reviewed British policy toward America since 1774. He summarized by stating

> the war is impracticable, and that no good will come from force only; that the lives that have been lost, and the treasures that have been wasted, have been wasted to no purpose; that it is high time we should look to our own situation and not leave ourselves defenseless upon an idea of strengthening the army in America.

He then moved that no more troops "be sent out of the kingdom." To everyone's surprise, when he sat down, not a single member of the majority party attempted to answer him. Instead, they moved the previous question (a parliamentary technicality) and defeated his motion by a vote of 259 to 165, a vote so close that Walpole called it "a surprising minority, that much alarmed the Administration." Fox termed it "a very good division compared with the past but a very bad one . . . considering the circumstances of the country" (because it meant the continuation of the North ministry.)[24]

The report of Fox's speech in the *Parliamentary History* is incomplete. Notes taken on it by Alexander Wedderburn, solicitor general in the North ministry, indicate that Fox also recommended the independence of the United States and that commercial relations between the two nations be reopened.[25] However, the motion not to withdraw any more troops from England was what put the government in a dilemma. To agree with it was to admit the bankruptcy of their American policy; to disagree with it was to weaken their defenses against a possible French attack. It was a painful choice but the government preferred to gamble on the latter. North, however, was so uncomfortable with the decision that he offered to resign. The king refused his resignation but did allow him to attempt to strengthen his government by adding to it such opposition figures as Chatham, Shelburne, Fox, and Barré. However, this plan failed because the king refused to modify his American policy to any significant degree.[26]

Meanwhile, the duel between Fox and North continued. Fox spoke against the use of Indians to fight the colonists. He estimated that twenty thousand British lives had already been lost and at least £25 million spent on the war, "all to no manner of purpose."[27] In February 1778, North had managed to persuade the king to allow him to send another group of commissioners to America, this time with assurances that Parliament would abandon its right to tax the colonies and annul the Coercive and other punitive acts against the colonies. The commissioners were authorized to treat with the American Congress and were not to insist on the renunciation of American independence, at least until they arrived at a satisfactory agreement. He concurred with Fox (though not crediting him) that conciliation was necessary to prevent "the effusion of blood, and the immoderate expence" that further fighting would entail.[28] Fox replied for the opposition: It could not disagree with North's proposals as it had been advocating these same policies for three years, but only wished they had been made earlier because—and here he dropped a bombshell—the United States and France had just signed an alliance. According to Horace Walpole (who had passed the information to Fox just before the session began), Lord North was thunderstruck but he nevertheless told Parliament that "it was possible, nay too probable."[29]

During the debate on North's conciliatory proposals, Fox objected to an amendment that would have placed the power to name the commissioners in Parliament rather than the king. He felt that any commissioner appointed by the ministry would be more likely "to irritate, rather than to appease America." And, for the first time in years, Fox found himself on the winning side of a vote. In later discussions, Fox reiterated his support of the bill but still felt that its chance for success was minuscule; however, "as the prize was so great, as that of a peace with a dependant America, it was worth the trial."[30]

During March, April, and May of 1778, Fox continued his efforts to topple the ministry. In a March discussion of the Franco-American treaty, he accused it of "supiness, folly, and ignorance." He moved that Lord George Germaine be censured because either his "ignorance or negligence" caused the loss of Burgoyne's army. He was so upset by the failure of his motion that he "declared that he would not make another motion; and taking the resolution of censure out of his pocket, tore it in pieces." By April, Fox came to the considered conclusion that the British peace commissioners should recognize the independence of the United States. He felt this would end the American war, avoid conflict with France and Spain, and "secure a larger share of the commerce of the Americas" than if they remained colonies. In addition, it would also put a halt to the "predominancy" of the executive branch over the legislative, which he viewed as "dangerous to our constitutional existence."[31]

In May, when Parliament was asked to vote additional funds for military and naval purpose, Fox asked rhetorically who could trust this government "with the expenditure of a single shilling?" He also criticized the government's inefficiency in preparing for possible French attack. In the inquiry into Burgoyne's surrender, he continually attempted to place the blame on the ministry rather than on the general. At the end of May, when Hartley made his dual motion (see chapter 13) to end the war and keep Parliament in session, Fox reminded his colleagues that the last long recess at Christmas left Parliament out of session at a critical time, when treaty negotiations between the United States and France were underway. He also took the opportunity to criticize the ministry's lackadaisical military and naval preparations.[32]

Nevertheless, Parliament did not reassemble until the end of November. The Whig opposition still had not decided upon any definite plan of action. Should American independence be recognized or should efforts toward conciliation without independence continue? Although for the former, Fox believed that the independent members of the House of Commons were "not ripe" for such an extreme measure. His strategy, as exemplified by his remarks throughout the new session of Parliament, was to act as if withdrawal of British forces from North America were taken for granted and concentration on preparations for war with France, and possibly Spain, were to receive top priority. Burke supported him, "avowing the independency of America . . . was now become a matter of necessity."[33]

Another difference of opinion among the Whigs concerned the wisdom of accepting office as part of a coalition government or waiting until they were strong enough to form a government of their own. Although Fox would have preferred a Whig government, he knew that the king would, at best, accept a coalition government and felt that the best interests of the nation dictated that he and other colleagues accept offices in such a government. Rockingham and Burke disagreed; Fox felt that continued opposition was fruitless and it would be shameful if "its [Great Britain's] best men . . . deprive it of the best assistance it can have." In any case, the king would not consider the possibility of American independence and again all attempts to form a coalition government failed.[34]

From the beginning of the session, Fox promised to "use all my exertions to remove the present ministry," even if he should be accused of doing it only in order to win office for himself. His advice was "for withdrawing your forces from America entirely [and] attack France." He continued to harass the ministry at every turn, until he found a cause célèbre.[35] In July 1778, the British and French fleets fought an indecisive sea battle. The government tried to place the blame for this lack of success on Admiral Augustus Keppel, a distant relative of Fox's, but a court martial completely exonerated him. The Whigs then went on the offensive and, in March 1779, Fox proposed a motion of censure on the Admiralty for sending Keppel out with a fleet of twenty ships, when they knew or should have known that the French fleet numbered at least thirty ships. He blamed Lord Sandwich, the First Lord of the Admiralty, for "greatly hazarding the safety of the king-dom" and demanded his removal. Fox's accusations were supported by evidence from Keppel himself, and Lord North was only able to defeat the motion (by a vote of 204 to 170) by making it clear that a censure of Sandwich would be a vote of "no confidence" in the entire cabinet.[36]

Fox was so encouraged by the closeness of this vote that he tried three more times to pass censure motions, but each time the government forces were better prepared and he was finally defeated in April by a resounding vote of 221 to 118.[37] Fox had never been a proponent of parliamentary reform but these events opened his eyes to the "political machine," to use modern terminology, which the king had constructed and could only be demolished by substantial changes in the organization of the House of Commons. Thus, in March 1779, he voted to make holders of governmental contracts ineligible to sit in the House and he supported Burke's reform bill of February 1780, which would have stripped the king of much of his patronage.[38]

Meanwhile, Great Britain's military situation had become increasingly perilous. Fox, abetted by Burke, continued to be critical of the ministry's military policy. He stated that "it was impossible to subdue America, or reduce her to allegiance by force of arms; to what end, then, should we continue our chief military force across the Atlantic when it was so much wanted at home?"[39] His words acquired more weight when, later in June 1779, Spain declared war on Great Britain. However, the Whigs, if only to allay possible charges of disloyalty, rallied to support the measures taken to defend the nation against possible attack, although Fox continued to express their lack of confidence in the ministry.[40] In the fall of 1779, Lord North again expressed a desire to resign. Fox thought, "there is now a possibility of saving the country" but the king would not release North. By this time, Fox, though disappointed that the king persisted in maintaining North in power, came to realize that it would be fatal to join a coalition with the virtually discredited ministry.

> What! enter into an alliance with those very ministers who had betrayed their country; who had prostituted the public strength, who had prostituted the public wealth, who had prostituted what was still more valuable, the glory of the nation! The idea was too monstrous to be admitted for a moment.[41]

Fortunately for Great Britain, France and Spain did not press their naval advantage and, when Parliament reconvened in November 1779, Fox began his attack on the ministry by noting that the address from the throne neglected to even mention the American war. "Was it too trifling a subject to . . . have the least notice taken of it?" Next, he took the almost unprecedented step of indirectly challenging George III himself. He reminded the king that Charles I lost his life and James II his throne because of "wicked ministers" and accused the present ministers of being "ten times more wicked and ignorant than those were." Fox went to the extent of predicting that, unless the ministry was turned out, "the people would inevitably take up arms, and the first characters in the kingdom would be seen in their ranks."[42]

Fox's remarks on this occasion were made in response to a speech defending the administration by William Adam, who had formerly voted with the opposition. Adam felt so personally insulted by Fox's criticism of him that he challenged him to a duel in which Fox was slightly wounded.[43] His wound did not keep him away from Parliament long. On December 6, in a debate on Irish affairs, Fox again berated the ministry for continuing the "accursed, diabolical, and cruel American war" which had already resulted in "wasting forty millions of money, and sixty thousand lives" and "caused us to be deserted by our friends and allies, and despised and trampled on by our enemies." He also referred to "this increasing, this alarming influence of the crown," which alone "against all Britain" was propping up a discredited ministry, one that would, if not removed, "terminate in the ruin of the empire."[44] Two days later, Fox asked Germaine "whether the war in America was to be an offensive or defensive one." When Germaine answered "as far as he knew the American war was not abandoned," Fox described his answer as "equivocal" and recommended the withholding of funds until more information was forthcoming.[45] And in the budget debate of March 1780, Fox gave his enthusiastic support to the war against France and

Spain, "our natural foes," but warned that "every penny" voted for the "damnable and detested war" against America was a criminal waste.[46]

On April 6, 1780, it appeared that Lord North's government was finally about to fall. On that evening, in spite of North's objections, the House of Commons approved, by a majority of eighteen, John Dunning's resolution "that the influence of the crown has increased, is increasing, and ought to be diminished." After midnight, the House also agreed that it was "competent . . . to examine into, and to correct abuses in the expenditure of the civil list revenues" and "to provide; as far as may be, an immediate and effectual redress of the abuses complained of in the [reform] petitions presented to this House."[47] However, on April 13, a bill disabling revenue officers from voting in parliamentary elections was defeated. And on April 24, when Dunning requested that the session not be ended before his resolution was implemented, the ministry was able to defeat his motion in spite of Fox's caution that "the grievances of the people would be heard, ought to be heard, nay must be heard."[48] Although Parliament continued to sit until July 1780, the Whigs never again were able to win a vote against the government. Moreover, the Gordon anti-Catholic riots of June were pointed to as an example of what might happen if the reformers should attain power. In September, the king, feeling that he could increase his majority in the House of Commons, dissolved Parliament although it had over a year to serve. Though the results were not quite as promising as he expected, Lord North's government still decisively maintained control of the House of Commons.

Fox, however, gave the ministry no rest. Even when General Cornwallis was winning victories in his southern campaign in America, he refused to support a parliamentary vote of thanks to him. Fox gave two reasons for his reluctance: "Every [former] gleam of success had been the certain forerunner of misfortune" and "he hated and detested the war . . . the fountain head of all the mischief and calamities which this miserable country laboured under at this moment."[49] In January 1781, when the king informed Parliament that war with Holland was imminent, Fox prophesied (correctly, as it turned out) that only an early end of the American war could prevent the entry of Russia, Sweden, Denmark, and Portugal into the growing alliance against Great Britain.[50] In April and May, he unsuccessfully advised the House to hear a petition calling for parliamentary reform and an end to the American war.[51] And at the end of the following month, Fox reviewed the course of negotiations with the United States and accused the ministers of prolonging the war to ensure "their continuance in power," even at the risk of "the interests, and perhaps the existence of their country." He also berated the members of the House of Commons for the "credulity, the servility, and the meanness" they exhibited by keeping this government in power. He credited Lord North's staying power to the false fear he had inculcated in the king that the loss of America meant "his power would end" and the bribery of members of Parliament with "the disposal of places, and pensions."[52] Fox continued at length in this vein. He blamed the American Loyalists, particularly Joseph Galloway, for misleading Parliament and the public about conditions in America and described "the American war to be as unjust in its principle and as abused in its prosecution as it would be ruinous in its consequence."[53]

In June 1781, Fox moved that a committee study the American war with the purpose of concluding peace as soon as possible. He based this request on the dispatches of General Cornwallis, which, he claimed, proved that even temporary victories could not lead to an ultimate conquest of America, but was once again outvoted.[54] Next, Fox fought again unsuccessfully for better treatment of American prisoners of war, who were receiving smaller rations than foreign prisoners of war. He maintained that Americans should receive better, or at least equal, treatment or not only would it "excite the indignation of all Europe against us, but bring down the horrors of retaliation on our subjects, prisoners in America."[55]

Even the king's announcement in November 1781 at the opening of Parliament of "the loss of my forces in that province [Virginia]," the surrender of General Cornwallis, at Yorktown, did not at first change George III's mind about continuing the war. Fox retorted that the address should not "be considered the speech of the King, but of his ministers" for otherwise the king would have to be characterized as "arbitrary, despotic, hard-headed, and unfeeling." He would have wished the king to declare

> that he had been deceived . . . that in consequence of his delusion, the parliament had been deluded, but that now the deception was at an end . . . therefore he requested of his parliament to devise the most speedy and direct means of putting an end to the calamities, and restoring peace, security, and happiness to his dominions.

But instead of this, Fox continued,

> the men who had brought us to our present situation, and reduced us from the splendor, and the strength, and the happiness which we enjoyed, to the disgrace, the weakness, and the danger in which we stand at present [are] determined to persevere in the American war.[56]

He took credit for the consistency and correctness of Whig opposition to the war from its inception and implored the members of the House "to do their duty" and vote to end the war. However, he was able to persuade only

129 members against the ministry's 218. Undaunted, Fox voted for delaying military appropriations, derisively maintaining that the present ministers, if not actually receiving French bribes, "deserved to be paid" by France and asking "how could he trust an army to the present ministers unless he wished to see it surrendered up to Washington?"[57] But the main Whig attack came on December 12 with two specific motions:

> that the war carried on in the colonies had proved ineffectual . . . [and] all further attempts to reduce the revolved colonies to obedience are contrary to the true interest of this kingdom.

Fox spoke only briefly on these motions, which were defeated by a somewhat closer vote of 220 to 179.[58]

Whig strength continued to grow when the British fleet in the West Indies failed to intercept a French convoy. In January 1782, Fox requested an inquiry into the navy's lack of success during the war, particularly during the year of 1781. He blamed Lord Sandwich for "gross mismanagement" and demanded his removal. Two votes were taken on Fox's motion and it was defeated by narrow margins of twenty-two and nineteen votes. Lord Sandwich was saved but Lord George Germaine, whose desire to pursue the American war aggressively was an embarrassment to the ministry, resigned after being granted a peerage.[59]

Thus encouraged, the Whigs once again moved on February 22, 1782, to end the American war. Fox and Burke spoke eloquently but the motion was defeated by a single vote. Fox immediately gave notice that it would be reintroduced. Five days later, the House of Commons passed the resolution by a majority of nineteen votes. The king was notified and on March 4 replied that he would "take such measures as shall appear to me to be most conducive to the restoration of harmony between Great Britain and the revolted colonies." Feeling that this response was "not quite so explicit" as it had hoped for, the House then approved General Conway's resolution that it would consider any ministers who continued to advise or prosecute an offensive war against the United States "as enemies to his Majesty and this country." Fox could not forbear to point out again that the king's tepid response was really the ministers' and not his own.[60]

The attorney general then presented a bill giving parliamentary permission to conclude a peace with America. Fox recommended that "sovereignty over America ought to be totally renounced" but that a "substantial connection might still be negotiated." However, when the attorney general spoke of repealing the laws to which the colonists had objected and reopening trade with them as a preliminary step toward peace negotiations, Fox called his proposal "ridiculous and farcical." He doubted whether Americans would treat with the present ministry and offered to involve himself in the negotiations. The House agreed to the bill but the North ministry was not destined to see it through.[61]

On March 8, it defeated a vote of censure by ten votes. During the debate, Fox implied what measures a Whig government would follow: (1) peace with America, (2) exclusion of placemen contractors and pensioners from the House of Commons, and (3) annual or triennial (rather than septennial) Parliaments. A week later, the North government again survived by nine votes. With the threat of another, almost certainly negative, vote facing him, Lord North announced that *"his Majesty's ministers were no more"* [italics in original]. Fox still demanded a motion of censure because "the House could not place any confidence in the word of the minister." North reiterated that *"his Majesty had come to a full determination to change* his ministers"(italics in original) and requested an adjournment so that the king could "make the necessary arrangements for a new administration." Fox thereupon relented because it was now clear that the nation had repudiated North's administration, its goals, and its methods. The House agreed with him and agreed to a brief adjournment.[62] The negotiations for forming a new government were complex. Suffice it to say that the new government was divided between the followers of Lords Rockingham and Shelburne. The fall of the North ministry is the appropriate breaking point at which to end this chapter though we shall be meeting Fox again when peace negotiations with the United States begin.

Notes

1. Sir John Fortescue, ed., *The Correspondence of King George the Third from 1760 to December, 1783,* III, no. 929.

2. Lord John Russell, ed., *Memorials and Correspondence of Charles James Fox,* I, p. 143. Hereafter referred to as *Fox Memorials.*

3. R.C. Simmons and P.D.G. Thomas, eds., *Proceedings and Debates of the British Parliaments Respecting North America, 1754–1783* (hereafter referred to as *Parliament Debates*), VI, pp. 396–397.

4. Ibid., pp. 426, 458.

5. Ibid., p. 504; William Cobbett, ed., *Parliamentary History of England, from the Earliest Period to the Year 1803* (hereafter referred to as *Parliament History*), XVIII, col. 1332.

6. Simmons and Thomas, *Parliament Debates,* VI, p. 594.

7. Thomas W. Copeland et al., *The Correspondence of Edmund Burke* (hereafter referred to as *Burke Correspondence*), III, pp. 111, 291.

8. Ibid., p. 294; Russell, *Fox Memorials,* I, p. 146.

9. A. Francis Steuart, ed., *The Last Journals of Horace Walpole During the Reign of George III from 1771–1783,* I, p. 584; Copeland et al., *Burke Correspondence,* III, p. 299.

10. Cobbett, *Parliament History,* XVIII, cols. 1429–1431.

11. Ibid., cols. 1431–1433.

12. Ibid., cols. 1436–1439.

13. Ibid., cols. 1448–1449.

14. Ibid., XIX, cols. 10–13, 21, 48–51.

15. Ibid., cols. 136–139, 154–155.

16. Ibid., cols. 249–251.

17. Ibid., cols. 431–433.

18. Ibid., cols. 34–36.

19. Copeland et al., *Burke Correspondence,* III, pp. 381–384; Russell, *Fox Memorials,* I, pp. 159–161.

20. Cobbett, *Parliament History,* XIX, cols. 512–513, 522–524, 532.

21. Ibid., cols. 533–534, 540–542.

22. Ibid., col. 560.

23. Ibid., cols. 583, 592, 620–623, 644–647.

24. Ibid., cols. 671–683; Steuart, *Last Walpole Journals,* II, p. 99; Russell, *Fox Memorials,* I, pp. 167–169.

25. As quoted in Loren Reid, *Charles James Fox—A Man for the People,* p. 79.

26. Russell, *Fox Memorials,* I, pp. 179–194.

27. Corbett, *Parliament History,* XIX, cols. 707, 718–721, 725.

28. Ibid., cols. 762–766.

29. Ibid., cols. 767–769; Steuart, *Last Walpole Journals,* II, pp. 115–117.

30. Ibid., cols. 777–778, 784, 786.

31. Ibid., cols. 909–910, 952–953, 958, 1082–1085.

32. Ibid., cols. 1132, 1134–1136, 1170–1172, 1196, 1218–1221.

33. Russell, *Fox Memorials,* I, pp. 199–200; Cobbett, *Parliament History,* XX, col. 82.

34. Russell, *Fox Memorials,* I, pp. 206–223, 226–227, 240; Copeland et al., *Burke Correspondence,* IV, pp. 39–41, 144, 154–157, 160–161; Paul Langford, ed., *The Writings and Speeches of Edmund Burke,* III, pp. 449–453.

35. *Cobbett, Parliament History,* XIX, cols. 1322–1330, 1370, 1374; XX, cols. 51, 76–77, 79, 129, 139–142, 160, 162.

36. Ibid., cols. 174–203. Preliminaries of the debate are found in XX, cols. 63, 76, 89–90, 129, 140–142, 144–146, 148.

37. Ibid., cols. 204–239, 331–359, 372–406.

38. Ibid., cols. 129, 1302–1304, 1371–1374, 1378–1381; XXI, cols. 1–72, 78–79, 91–96, 105–106, 136–137, 151–152, 208–217, 285–287, 292–293, 295, 309.

39. Ibid., XX, cols. 716–720, 723, 725, 734–737, 750, 753–755, 757, 759, 770–774, 830–831, 839–842, 900.

40. Ibid., cols. 915–917, 933–940, 962, 1013–1015, 1017–1018.

41. Russell, *Fox Memorials,* I, p. 235; Fortescue, *Correspondence of King George III,* V, nos. 3099–3101; Cobbett, *Parliament History,* XX, col. 1936.

42. Cobbett, *Parliament History,* XX, cols. 1116–1125.

43. Ibid., cols. 1118–1120.

44. Ibid., cols. 1221–1222, 1225–1226.

45. Ibid., cols. 1249, 1253.

46. Ibid., XXI, cols. 161–162.

47. Ibid., cols. 347, 367.

48. Ibid., cols. 403–414, 494–533.

49. Ibid., col. 833–837, 906–907.

50. Ibid., cols. 1102–1104.

51. Ibid., XXII, cols. 97–98, 168–189.
52. Ibid., cols. 342–343.
53. Ibid., cols. 346–350.
54. Ibid., cols. 435–443, 500–516.
55. Ibid., cols. 609–616.
56. Ibid., cols. 636, 688–707, 729, 743–745.
57. Ibid., cols. 754–756.
58. Ibid., cols. 802–803, 825–826, 831.
59. Ibid., cols. 878–898, 904, 915–923, 932–934, 946.
60. Ibid., cols. 1028–1031, 1035–1041, 1045–1046, 1048, 1064–1085, 1093–1097.
61. Ibid., cols. 1101–1109.
62. Ibid., cols. 1114–1150, 1170–1200, 1214–1232.

15

"Peace, Peace, When There Is No Peace"

Nothing came easily to the new Rockingham administration. Shelburne and Fox served as the two secretaries of state: Fox in charge of foreign affairs, Shelburne of colonial affairs. Technically, until independence was recognized, negotiations with America were in Shelburne's jurisdiction. Shelburne, though expressing interest in David Hartley's "Breviate," passed him over as his representative, even though Hartley was eager for the position, probably because of the latter's previous ties with the North administration. Instead, Shelburne named Richard Oswald, a seventy-seven-year-old Scottish merchant. The cabinet, however, authorized Fox to send a representative, Thomas Grenville, to Paris. Obviously, this arrangement was bound to create friction. As Fox wrote to his friend, "Shelburne . . . is ridiculously jealous of my approaching on his department, and wishes very much to encroach upon mine." And Grenville wrote Fox, "I cannot fight a daily battle with Mr. Oswald." Benjamin Franklin was quick to take full advantage of this situation in order to obtain the most favorable terms possible for the United States, including the annexation of Canada.[1]

The British bargaining position was further weakened by a basic divergence in policy between Fox and Shelburne. Fox believed in immediate and unconditional recognition of American independence, while Shelburne wanted to make it conditional upon the signing of treaties with France and Spain. Fox's strategy was based on two premises: It would, hopefully, convert the United States into a friend and possible ally of Great Britain, and would force France and Spain into either signing favorable peace treaties with Great Britain or else leave them to face a British army and navy unencumbered by the necessity of fighting in America. Shelburne, in contrast, believed that the grant of American independence could be used to force France and Spain into signing more favorable treaties with Great Britain than they otherwise would, and should not be given away in advance. The Americans, of course, preferred Fox's plan. As John Adams wrote, Fox "has shown himself a profound statesman, Shelburne, a selfish and equivocal character."[2]

In May 1783, the cabinet at first supported Fox's view and Fox instructed Grenville "to propose the independency of America in the first instance, instead of making it a condition of a general treaty." However, Shelburne refused to give in and eventually was able to convince the cabinet at the end of June to reverse its decision. Fox was furious and threatened to resign. It was at this juncture that Rockingham died and the king immediately selected Shelburne as chief minister. Fox was in a quandary; he still had some hope that Shelburne might change his mind but, in spite of Burke's advice to remain at least temporarily, he finally decided to leave the cabinet. The duke of Richmond and General Conway decided to remain in office, though the duke left soon after. When Benjamin Franklin heard of Fox's resignation, he doubted that it resulted from a difference of opinion with Shelburne over unconditional independence but made it clear to Oswald that it was a necessary preliminary to successful negotiations.[3]

In a parliamentary debate shortly after his resignation, Fox, lest he be accused of jealousy of Shelburne, attempted to make his position clear. "When he found himself in a cabinet divided upon points which he considered of utmost importance . . . It was his immediate duty to retire from a situation on which he could no longer act with honor to himself, as he could no longer act with service to his country." When Conway claimed that Shelburne favored American independence and had even converted the king to that point of view, Fox retorted that the cabinet must once again have changed its mind since he left and he was "satisfied if the sacrifice he made to his principles should ultimately be serviceable to this country."[4]

Fox was, therefore, out of power while Oswald continued the negotiations that resulted, on November 30, 1782, in the signing of a preliminary treaty of peace between Great Britain and the United States. Nevertheless, his influence on the acceptance of the treaty was crucial. The king in his opening address to Parliament on December 5 stated that he

> offered to declare them [the United States] free and independent states, by an article to be inserted in the treaty of peace. Provisional articles are to be agreed upon, to take effect whenever terms of peace shall be finally settled with the court of France.

Did this mean that the recognition of American independence was unconditional or did it depend upon the signing of a peace treaty with France?[5]

When the question arose in the House of Lords, Shelburne frankly denied that "unqualified, unconditional independence" had been given to America. He went on to state that the "offer is not irrevocable" and quoted the king's statement above to support his contention. The king had never, contrary to General Conway's wishful thinking, agreed to unconditional independence and was still not reconciled to the "dismemberment" of his empire. In the House of Commons, Fox, at least, chose to believe that the independence grant was unconditional. Later, when he and Burke expressed some doubts, William Pitt (the Younger, the Chancellor of the Exchequer) assured him that the recognition of independence was "unqualified." Fox and Burke were not satisfied and demanded additional confirmation. The only response came from the ever-optimistic Conway, who believed that "the provisional agreement was a full, absolute, and irrevocable recognition of the independence of America." In truth, Shelburne was giving the "authorized" version and both he and the king were critical of Pitt for assuring Fox that American independence was unconditional.[6]

But the debate was far from over. A week later, in the House of Lords, a peer commented on the "extreme difference in the explanation ... of the King's speech here, and in another place [the House of Commons]." Shelburne attempted to evade the question by maintaining vaguely that "He was bound by his office to keep the secrets of the King," a response that satisfied virtually none of his colleagues. In the Commons, Fox moved that the ministry produce the articles of the provisional treaty that "relate to the independency of the said [United] States." David Hartley supported the motion because knowing Shelburne's past record, he feared "that the American war was not finally put to an end." In spite of Fox's prediction that if unconditional independence were recognized, "all [American] doubts would vanish, all jealousies would expire, the bond which tied them to France would lose its energy ... America would agree to a separate peace," his motion was defeated by a vote of 219 to 46 because Lord North's followers (about 120 in number) voted with the ministry.[7]

On January 27, 1783, however, the government presented copies of the provisional treaties of peace with the United States, France, and Spain to Parliament. Debate in both Houses was prolonged and wide-ranging. The Lords approved them by a bare majority of only thirteen votes, but in the Commons it soon became obvious that Shelburne did not control the required number of votes. He would have to enter an alliance with the ninety Rockingham Whigs, or Lord North's followers. However, Fox refused to join a ministry headed by Shelburne, and North could not promise unequivocal support for the treaties. Worse yet, from his point of view, Shelburne discovered that his efforts had brought about a coalition between these two old enemies.[8]

The new coalition showed its strength on February 17, when the Shelburne forces attempted to pass a resolution that would merely have expressed satisfaction with the peace treaties. North and Burke (believe it or not) agreed that Shelburne had surrendered too much to France, Spain, Holland, and America. They objected to the cession to America of the Ohio Valley (technically part of Canada since the passage of the Quebec Act), the granting of the right of Americans to fish off the Grand Banks, and particularly to what they viewed as a betrayal of the Loyalists. Fox began his remarks by admitting that he was in a delicate position. As the foremost parliamentary advocate of peace with America, any criticism of the treaty from him might appear to be motivated by "personal pique . . . envy . . . jealousy [or] ambition." Yet, though he had not changed his mind about peace, he considered these particular treaties "more calamitous, more dreadful, more ruinous than war could possibly be."[9]

Then Fox turned to the political realities. "I am accused of having formed a junction with a noble person [Lord North]; whose principles I have been in the habit of opposing for the last seven years of my life." He refused to apologize for this coalition. "When a man ceases to be what he was, when the opinions which made him obnoxious are changed, he is then no more my enemy, but my friend." The two new "friends" were able to marshall 224 votes to the government's 208 and the treaties were not approved.[10]

The coalition returned to the attack on February 21, 1783, when it introduced a series of resolutions, the most important of which stated that the concessions made to the erstwhile adversaries of Great Britain were "greater than they were entitled to." In his remarks on this occasion, Fox pointed out those aspects of the treaties (primarily with France and Spain) that he found deleterious to British interests and denied the charges that his opposition to the treaty was politically motivated or that there was anything disgraceful about the new coalition. The coalition resolutions were approved by a vote of 207 to 190 and Shelburne resigned on February 24.[11]

The Fox-North ministry did not assume power until April 2, 1783. The events of the preceding month were bizarre. The king was eager for William Pitt, or almost anyone else but Fox, to succeed Shelburne. On March 2, he reluctantly offered the position to Lord North, who refused it but expressed willingness to serve in a cabinet that would also include Fox and some of his supporters. The king was willing to accept this arrangement only if he could name the chief minister. Fox commented on this point in the House. He agreed that the king had the right to choose his ministers but argued that, when doing so, he should be influenced by "the sense of the

Parliament, and the sense of the people."[12] By March 18, the House of Commons was becoming restive. A Mr. Coke announced that he would move an address to the king on March 21 (then postponed to March 24), unless a new government assumed office. On that date (no government having been formed), he requested the king to form "an Administration entitled to the confidence of the people." Fox spoke fervently in support of the motion but requested that it be postponed because negotiations for a new ministry were complete. (It nevertheless passed with virtually no dissent.) On March 31, the earl of Surrey made a similar motion, which he withdrew when assured by Fox and North that it was unnecessary. The king had capitulated by accepting the duke of Portland as the titular head of the ministry and Fox and North as secretaries of state. But the king was so exasperated that he contemplated abdicating in favor of his eldest son and moving to Hanover![13]

As secretary of state for foreign affairs, Fox was now completely in charge of concluding peace. At this late stage, the best he was able to obtain from France, Spain, and Holland were minor modifications of the provisional treaty. Although the American negotiators in Paris began by expecting Fox to treat them with "liberality," they were soon complaining of his "indecision and timidity," which they blamed on the weakness of the coalition government.[14] Interestingly enough, the man chosen by Fox to conclude the final American treaty and negotiate a commercial agreement between Great Britain and the United States was our old "friend," David Hartley.

Since 1782, Franklin had been joined in Paris by John Adams and John Jay. Jay had no previous contact with Hartley. He expected him to propose that the British and American people "shall have all the rights of citizens in each [country]"—a suggestion that he tended to favor. Adams regretted Shelburne's fall and expected the appointment of Hartley to prolong the negotiations, even though he believed him to be "liberal and fair." Franklin wrote that he "could have been content to have finish'd [the negotiations] with Mr. Oswald"; Henry Laurens, who was unofficially representing the United States in England, was also disappointed but considered Hartley an "honest man."[15] Hartley arrived in France on April 24, 1783, with the best of intentions. He not only supported a liberal peace treaty with the United States but advocated a reciprocal trade treaty, which would allow American goods into Great Britain and the admission of English manufactured goods into the United States on the same basis as before the war. He was willing to allow American ships to trade with the British West Indies as long as they carried only certain American goods. Hartley also pledged an immediate evacuation of British troops from the United States. He hoped that this conciliatory policy would result in a virtual Anglo-American union—military as well as commercial.[16]

Fox had no difficulty in agreeing to the evacuation of British troops. However, the reciprocal trade had to wait upon the passage of parliamentary legislation. Before his resignation, Shelburne had prepared an "American Intercourse Bill," which was introduced on March 7, 1783. This bill provided that, until a permanent treaty was concluded, American products would be imported into Great Britain as they had been before the war and American ships could carry American goods to, and export goods from, British colonies in the West Indies. In return, British goods exported to the United States would receive the same benefits as they had before the war. The bill met immediate opposition. Burke compared it to a courtship in which "Great Britain was extremely fond in her wooing, and . . . was ready to give largely: whereas . . . America had nothing to give in return." And Fox warned that its provisions might be violations of Britain's commercial treaties with Russia and Denmark. In the debate a few days later, even Hartley (who had not as yet been named peace commissioner) described the bill as "wholly inadequate" and predicted that it "would lead to infinite mischief and inconvenience."[17]

The main opposition to the bill came from British merchants who feared American monopolization of the West Indies trade and the attendant decline of the British merchant marine. These views were represented in Parliament by Lord Sheffield, who also wrote an extremely persuasive pamphlet, *Observations on the Commerce of the United States*. Fox, whether convinced by Sheffield's arguments or bowing to political realities, decided to make only limited concessions to the United States. He expected American trade to continue to flow to Great Britain and hoped that Canada could assume the role of provider of goods to the West Indies (previously played by the Thirteen Colonies). When he came into power, therefore, he requested a four-week delay (really a burial) of the American Intercourse Bill until a treaty could be negotiated. But he did promise to remove all technical "difficulties in the way of our trade with the Americas."[18]

On May 14, an Order in Council opened British ports to American agricultural products without payment of any duties, and in June certain manufactured goods received the same privilege. However, by now Fox was adamant on the West Indian trade question. Unfortunately, he neglected to inform Hartley (whose original instructions had permitted him to allow American ships to bring their own produce to trade with the West Indies) of this change in policy.

The American commissioners had always had doubts about Hartley's authority to conclude a commercial treaty and, perhaps as a test, requested completely free trade between Great Britain and the United States. Hartley warned them that British political realities made this impossible but even he was unprepared for the British proclamation of July 2, 1783, which restricted trade between the United States and the British West Indies to British traders using British-built, -owned, and -manned ships.[19] According to Jay, Hartley continued to hope that this restriction would be lifted, but neither he nor the other American commissioners were sanguine. From the time that their free trade proposal was rejected, Adams was predicting that no commercial treaty would be negotiated; after the proclamation was issued, he was convinced of what he had long suspected, that "Mr. Hartley appears not to be in the secrets of his court." Sharing Adams's misgivings, Franklin decided to accept the preliminary peace treaty of 1782 as the definitive one and forego any attempts at a commercial pact.[20]

Hartley faced the facts and proceeded to secure his government's acceptance (subject to parliamentary approval) of the preliminary treaty as the final one. The American commissioners signed the treaty on September 3, 1783. (An official signing was scheduled for the following year.) The signing took place at Hartley's residence rather than at Versailles, in deference to his instructions not to leave Paris. (Actually, this was to minimize the importance of the French role in the negotiations.) The American commissioners, though disappointed by the lack of a commercial treaty, were still highly appreciative of Hartley's efforts on behalf of their nation. As Franklin wrote Fox, Hartley possessed the "frankness, sincerity, and candor which most naturally produces confidence, and thereby facilitates the most difficult negotiations." And Hartley wrote the American commissioners on the day after the signing of the treaty that he still hoped to "renew the discussion of those points of amity and intercourse" that remained unrealized.[21]

When Parliament reconvened in November 1783, the king was able to announce that peace negotiations had been concluded with France, Spain, and the United States. Even the ministerial address of thanks had to admit that these treaties were "in substance the same as the preliminary articles of peace" but continued that the changes that had been made were "beneficial to the country." The opposition was quick to point out that these treaties were "almost exactly the same" as those they had "reprobated" earlier in the year. Pitt echoed these sentiments and wondered why Hartley "after having exerted all the inexhaustible resources of his genius" had been unable to negotiate the commercial treaty promised by the Fox-North government.[22]

Fox responded by declaring that there were "great and essential differences" between the preliminary and final treaties. As for the lack of a commercial agreement with the United States, he averred that the Orders in

Council had lifted trade restrictions between the two nations. Fox praised Hartley for his "extensive knowledge of the interests of the two countries" but thought that a commercial agreement would be "better carried on in London or Philadelphia than in Paris." The coalition's opponents never had any intention of utilizing the treaties as a means to overthrow the government and, at the conclusion of the debate, the treaties were approved unanimously.[23]

Before the end of the year, however, dissension over the bill to reorganize the East India Company afforded the king the opportunity to dismiss Fox and North and place William Pitt at the head of his ministry.[24] Still in his early thirties, Fox did not realize at the moment that he would spend most of the remaining twenty-three years of his life in opposition. Nevertheless, he distinguished himself by contending for parliamentary reform, the removal of religious disabilities, and the abolition of the slave trade. Perhaps the most fitting tribute to him was expressed by Benjamin Franklin at the time the peace treaty was completed: "I really think him a Great Man"[25] [italics in original].

Hartley was encouraged by the fall of the Fox-North coalition and the rise to power of William Pitt, who had spoken in favor of a relation of trade barriers between Great Britain and the United States. Hartley's hopes were raised even higher by his appointment as British representative at the formal ratification of the treaty, which was to take place in Paris. He arrived at the French capital in April 1784 and remained even after the formalities were completed in June. As Franklin wrote, "Mr. Hartley seems to have some expectation of receiving instructions to negotiate a Commercial Treaty.... I have not much dependence on this."[26] Once again Franklin was proven correct. The new ministry was no more inclined than the old to take steps that it felt might be detrimental to British commercial interests. Franklin left France in July but Hartley tarried despite repeated orders to return home, until his appointment was terminated on September 24, 1783.[27]

Hartley, however, still remained an ardent advocate of Anglo-American reconciliation. When Thomas Jefferson arrived in Paris, he showed Hartley a map of the United States that contained the boundaries of fourteen new states, which he hoped would be created by the Ordinance of 1784. Hartley transmitted a copy of this map to the British government, along with a glowing prediction of a strong and populous United States, whose prosperity would be underwritten by the sale of public lands to Americans and European immigrants. And Hartley concluded his report by predicting that the future greatness of the United States would force the British government, if only to protect its own territories in the vicinity of the United States, "to encourage conciliatory and amicable correspondence" with the new nation.[28]

Hartley continued an amicable correspondence with Franklin, Jay, Jefferson, and other American friends. And as late as 1785, Adams, then American envoy to Great Britain, reported that Hartley was again making overtures to him about an Anglo-American alliance.[29] However, the prior year of 1784 had marked not only the end of Hartley's diplomatic career but that of his political career as well. He lost his seat in the House of Commons and retired to private life in Bath. He took a lively interest in Irish affairs and in the course of the French Revolution, but most of his time was spent in scientific experimentation and philosophic speculation. Hartley died in December 1813, in the midst of the War of 1812. His views on this conflict are unknown, but it must have been a tragic occurrence to the man whom Franklin referred to on his departure from Paris as his "dear Friend [and] fellow laborer in the best of all works, the work of peace."[30]

Notes

1. Lord John Russell, ed., *Memorials and Correspondence of Charles James Fox* (hereafter referred to as *Fox Memorials*), I, pp. 316, 343–387. Franklin's account of the negotiations may be found in Albert H. Smyth, ed., *The Writings of Benjamin Franklin* (hereafter referred to as *Franklin Writings*), VIII, pp. 459–560.

2. Charles Francis Adams, ed., *The Works of John Adams* (hereafter referred to as *J. Adams Works*), VII, pp. 606–607. Additional reactions of Adams may be found, ibid., III, pp. 312, 317–319, 321–323, 325–326; VII, pp. 610–611, 613, 660–661.

3. Russell, *Fox Memorials*, I, pp. 357, 453–463; Sir John Fortescue, ed., *The Correspondence of King George the Third from 1760 to December, 1783*, VI, nos. 3824–3827, 3830, 3833–3834, 3847; A. Francis Steuart, ed., *The Last Journals of Horace Walpole During the Reign of George III from 1771–1783*, II, pp. 443–452; Smyth, *Franklin Writings*, VIII, p. 567.

4. William Cobbett, ed., *Parliamentary History of England, from the Earliest Period to the Year 1803* (hereafter referred to as *Parliament History*), XXIII, cols. 161, 165–171.

5. Ibid., col. 206.

6. Ibid., cols. 217, 231–237, 264–268, 279–282, 285–287, 291–293; Fortescue, *Correspondence of King George III*, VI, nos. 4014–4015.

7. Ibid., cols. 305–314, 320–322; Thomas W. Copeland et al., *The Correspondence of Edmund Burke*, V, pp. 55–58.

8. Russell, *Fox Memorials*, II, pp. 20–24, 28–40; Steuart, *Last Walpole Journals*, II, pp. 479–481.

9. Cobbett, *Parliament History*, XXIII, cols. 345–358, 435, 443–455, 466–469, 485–487.

10. Ibid., cols. 487–489, 493.

11. Ibid., cols. 498–503, 526–543, 571; Fortescue, *Correspondence of King George III*, VI, no. 4130.

12. Fortescue, *Correspondence of King George III*, VI, nos. 4133, 4150, 4153, 4156–4158; Cobbett, *Parliament History*, XXIII, cols. 595–596.

13. Cobbett, *Parliament History*, XXIII, cols. 658–661, 664–668, 676–678, 685–709; Fortescue, *Correspondence of King George III*, VI, nos. 4259–4260, 4268; Steuart,

Last Walpole Journals, II, pp. 494–513.

14. Francis Wharton, ed., *The Revolutionary Diplomatic Correspondence of the United States,* VI, pp. 359, 446–447, 463, 512, 553.

15. Henry P. Johnson, ed., *The Correspondence and Public Papers of John Jay* (hereafter referred to as *Jay Correspondence*), III, p. 42; Adams, *J. Adams Works,* VIII, pp. 54, 60; IX, p. 517; Smyth, *Franklin Writings,* IX, p. 32; Wharton, *Diplomatic Correspondence,* VI, p. 361.

16. Wharton, *Diplomatic Correspondence,* VI, pp. 366, 442–444.

17. Vincent T. Harlow, *The Founding of the Second British Empire, 1763–1793,* I, pp. 450–451; Cobbett, *Parliament History,* XXIII, cols. 612, 614–615, 640.

18. Wharton, *Diplomatic Correspondence,* VI, pp. 638–639; Cobbett, *Parliament History,* XXIII, cols. 724–725, 762–767.

19. Wharton, *Diplomatic Correspondence,* VI, pp. 396–397, 483–487, 491–493; Adams, *J. Adams Works,* III, pp. 369, 371–376; Fortescue, *Correspondence of King George III,* VI, no. 4293.

20. Johnson, *Jay Correspondence,* III, pp. 66, 79; Wharton, *Diplomatic Correspondence,* VI, p. 553; Adams, *J. Adams Works,* III, pp. 363, 372; Smyth, *Franklin Writings,* IX, pp. 38, 78.

21. Wharton, *Diplomatic Correspondence,* VI, pp. 662–663, 674, 704; Smyth, *Franklin Writings,* IX, pp. 86, 130; Adams, *J. Adams Works,* VIII, p. 157.

22. Cobbett, *Parliament History,* XXIII, cols. 1124, 1132, 1139–1143.

23. Ibid., cols. 1143–1149, 1156.

24. Fortescue, *Correspondence of King George III,* VI, nos. 4546–4547.

25. Smyth, *Franklin Writings,* IX, p. 87.

26. Ibid., pp. 198, 210–211, 225–226, 241–242; X, pp. 348, 352, 355, 357.

27. Harlow, *Second British Empire,* I, pp. 487–490.

28. The full text of Hartley's letter may be found in Charles Sumner, *Prophetic Voices Concerning America,* pp. 99–103.

29. Adams, *J. Adams Works,* III, p. 322.

30. Smyth, *Franklin Writings,* IX, p. 359.

16

Summary and Conclusions

The preceding chapters have analyzed the attitudes toward the Thirteen Colonies, and later the United States, of a diverse group of English politicians and intellectuals during the quarter of a century following the conclusion of the Seven Years' War in 1763. These attitudes were influenced by the philosophical and economic ideologies, as well as the more mundane struggles for political power, current in Great Britain during this period.

No better exemplar of ideology determining one's attitude toward America can be found than Josiah Tucker. Certainly, at first glance, no more unlikely candidate for the title "British Friend of the American Revolution" can be found than he. Tucker, along with the majority of British politicians and political thinkers, perceived the Empire as "unitary," with all powers monopolized by Parliament. Though an active member of the Whig party, Tucker was a staunch defender of the established political order and a bitter opponent of the philosophy of John Locke. In addition, his opinion of Americans and their leaders was anything but complimentary.

However, Tucker was, for his time, a sophisticated economist. He was a strong opponent of mercantilism. Although he did not advocate as complete a measure of free trade as Adam Smith and his followers were to develop later, Tucker abhorred monopoly in any form. A precursor of the Little Englanders of the nineteenth century, he had economic theories that made him a determined anti-imperialist. Tucker considered all colonies to be economic liabilities rather than assets. Throughout their formative period, colonies cost the mother country far more in outlays than was ever received in return. And when their economies finally did mature to a point where they might be profitable to the mother country, they were no longer willing to accept political domination. The Thirteen Colonies provided Tucker with, what he considered, a perfect example of this theory.

Moreover, in Tucker's thinking, the granting of independence to its

American colonies was an undisguised blessing to Great Britain. He was one of the few men of his time who was knowledgeable enough in economics to understand that a colonial *economy* does not automatically come to an end when the colonies win their *political* independence. As it turned out, he correctly prophesied that Americans would long continue to supply raw materials to, and buy manufactured goods from, Great Britain. And all this without the trouble and expense of colonial administration. No wonder, then, that Tucker braved ridicule and abuse for advocating American independence long before it was seriously thought of, even in the colonies themselves!

Thomas Pownall, in contrast, was a pragmatist rather than an idealogue. He was one of the first few men in Great Britain who might properly be termed a "colonial expert." In fact, he was the only one of the group studied here ever to have been in America before the Revolution. Pownall seems to have made good use of his American experience. His understanding of colonial problems was sound and often sympathetic. Moreover, he clearly foresaw the economic and military potential of North America.

Pownall was also far more astute politically than the vast majority of contemporary British leaders. He realized as early as, if not earlier than, any of the opponents—whether British or American—of British imperialist policies that the British empire was a "federal" empire with political powers divided de facto, if not de jure, between Parliament and the colonial legislatures. He deserves full credit for outlining a plan for a dominion type of government that would have formalized this arrangement and possibly prevented, and certainly delayed, the American Revolution. Unfortunately for Great Britain, the theories he developed in the *Administration of the British Colonies* were too advanced for the time and were not accepted as governmental policy until well into the nineteenth century, when they became the basis for the British Commonwealth of Nations.

Pownall was one of the first to recognize that the mishandling of the American colonies by Lord North, his political patron, (though he had begun his political career as a Whig), had made a dominion solution of the problem impossible. He then willingly sacrificed his seat in the House of Commons, and possible political advancement, in order to advocate complete political independence for the United States. It is greatly to Pownall's credit that he was finally flexible enough to exchange his hopes for British dominion of the Atlantic community for an alternative plan in which Great Britain and the other nations of Europe would lay aside their mercantilistic restrictions and trade freely with a group of newly independent American nations.

John Cartwright had neither the economic insight of Tucker nor the political foresight of Pownall. Nevertheless, he arrived at a solution of the colonial problem similar to theirs: political independence for any and all British colonies that desired it within a dominion-like organization. Cartwright came to this conclusion from the pseudo-Lockean premise that people have the right to change their form of government virtually at will. After suffering several rebuffs, Cartwright, unlike the other "friends," withdrew from the struggle for American independence in order to devote himself to the cause of domestic reform.

Cartwright's "Lockean" theories placed him in the company of the Real or Honest Whigs, who embraced (more accurately than he) the ideas of the Glorious Revolution. They felt that these ideas had been betrayed by the Whig politicians who had dominated Parliament since the accession of the Hanoverian dynasty. James Burgh, a leading theoretician of the Real Whigs, characteristically equated colonial quarrels with Great Britain with the ongoing battle to restore British rights and liberties. Both Burgh and his female counterpart, the historian Catherine Macauley, had strong republican sympathies and were contemptuous of, to their way of thinking, the politically motivated perfunctory gestures made by Whig politicians to solve both colonial and domestic problems. Burgh died before the outbreak of the Revolutionary War but Mrs. Macauley lived to make a triumphal tour of the United States and to exchange political views with its leaders.

Over the long run, the most influential of the Real Whigs was Richard Price. Price's interest in the reform of English political institutions led him to take his pro-American stance. His great fear was that if the British government were successful in depriving its subjects in America of their rights, it would not be too long before the same attempt would be made in the mother country. Price's writings were aimed primarily at warning his fellow citizens of this danger, with the hope that an aroused public opinion might persuade the North ministry to reverse its imperialist policy. However, when he realized that no change was forthcoming, Price became an enthusiastic and consistent advocate of American independence.

Richard Price and Josiah Tucker had certain ostensible similarities: both were born in Wales, both were clergymen, both were Whiggish in politics, both might be termed economists, and both supported American independence. But these similarities were more apparent than real. Tucker was an Anglican minister, Price was a leading dissenting minister. Tucker used his economic theories to attempt to prove that Great Britain had never profited from its colonies and would be better off without them. Price, on the contrary, claimed that the colonies had greatly benefited Great Britain and that their loss, as a result of the policies of the North ministry, would be a disaster. Tucker embraced the more moderate Whiggism of the mid-eighteenth century. He disliked and feared the ideas of John Locke. Price, in contrast, was a Real Whig, who sincerely embraced the ideas of the Glorious Revolution.

Certain comparisons and contrasts may also be drawn between Price and Pownall. Price, though eager for close Anglo-American ties, disagreed with Pownall as to the feasibility of a dominion form of government. He was afraid that, in cases of conflict between the mother country and one of its former colonies, the former would ignore constitutional guidelines and impose its will on the dominion. Later, however, Price did agree with Pownall as to the form that the government of the United States should take. Both men criticized the weakness of the Articles of Confederation and recommended many of the improvements that were eventually incorporated into the American Constitution. And Price, Pownall, and Tucker (as well as Tooke, Hartley, and Fox, who will be discussed below) were consistent enough to argue that having won their own liberty, Americans should next take steps to end the institution of slavery.

Closely allied with the Real Whigs in their goals but differing in methods were the urban radicals epitomized and led by John Wilkes. He and his followers viewed British (mis)treatment of America as a symbol and harbinger of an imminent suppression of traditional British rights and privileges. Wilkes's tactics and the overreaction of the authorities made him the personification of liberty in both Great Britain and America. Wilkes may be considered one of the "eighteenth-century commonwealthmen" who kept alive, and expanded, the ideas of the Puritan Revolution of the 1641–1660 period. Although unsuccessful in implementing his program of domestic reform, he remained a vigorous supporter of American rights and, later, independence, both as a London official and as a member of Parliament.

John Horne Tooke was one of Wilkes's partisans and, later, one of his most bitter adversaries. It is difficult to categorize Tooke. He, like Tucker, was an Anglican clergyman. But unlike Tucker, he revolted against this role and tried (unsuccessfully) to become a practicing lawyer. He can hardly be termed a politician, although at a much later stage in his career he did serve one term in the House of Commons. Tooke was an urban radical and, as such, a firm supporter of American rights. But perhaps he can best be described as an "agitator." This was a role in which he reveled and which he played again and again. During the earlier "Wilkes affair" and the later French Revolution, he escaped unscathed. But during the American Revolution, his collection of funds for relatives of those Americans killed at Lexington and Concord made him the scapegoat for an angry, confused government that needed a victim on whom to vent its frustration. Tooke was an ideal candidate because his idealism and extremism had alienated all but a handful of his friends. Thus, while Tooke can certainly not be classi-fied as a politician or theoretician in the battle for American independence, his "martyrdom" entitles him to inclusion with those other "friends" of the American Revolution.

We next turn to the Whigs who served in Parliament for all, or most of this period. Of these men, the closest in ideology to the Real Whigs was David Hartley. Like them, Hartley was a lifelong friend and political ad-mirer of Benjamin Franklin. Some have even dubbed him the "English Franklin" because he also combined successful careers in both science and politics. The two men worked closely together, even during the war, on the exchange of prisoners. And it was largely because of their friendship that the British government utilized Hartley's services first as an unofficial, then as an accredited, negotiator of peace with the United States.

Hartley conceptualized the struggle between Great Britain and its colo-nies much the same way as did Price. Hartley believed that America was both a testing ground and a base for the massive attempt to restore the power of the royal prerogative, which had been limited by the Puritan and Glorious Revolutions. If the North government were to succeed in its al-leged plans to consolidate colonial government and to raise a revenue in America that would be independent of parliamentary control, Hartley feared for the liberties of all English citizens.

Hartley, unlike the other Whig politicians, claimed that the Navigation Acts had always been unfair to the colonists. Nevertheless, at the beginning of his parliamentary career, he had hoped that the British government might be induced to return to the pre-1763 relationship. When this hope proved futile, he accepted Pownall's dominion theory as a possible solution to the problem. By 1777, after Hartley realized that events had made indepen-dence inevitable, he (again like Pownall) worked for the closest possible ties between the two nations, including dual citizenship and complete free-dom of trade. It is a tribute to Hartley's sincerity and sagacity that he continued to work for these goals even after peace was concluded between the two nations. Hartley also deserves credit, like other "friends" already mentioned, for coupling his support of the American cause with his opposi-tion to slavery. In fact, he brought the question of abolition before Parlia-ment even before his more famous colleague in the British abolitionist movement, William Wilberforce.

A hero in both Great Britain and America, William Pitt, later the earl of Chatham, was the most famous Whig politician, though he claimed to be above party. He led the successful campaign for the repeal of the Stamp Act. Pitt was a mercantilist who consistently maintained the legislative supremacy of Parliament over the colonies but adamantly denied that the legislative power included the right to tax. It was for this reason that he opposed the Declaratory Act passed during Lord Rockingham's ministry. This crucial difference of approach placed Chatham and his followers at odds with the Rockinghamites for years and helped, along with personality conflicts, to preclude a Whig alliance, which might have delayed and/or modified (though probably not thwarted) Lord North's punitive policy toward America.

By the late 1760s, when he accepted a peerage and his health, both physical and mental, deteriorated, Chatham's influence diminished greatly. Nevertheless, he was always a figure to be reckoned with when he was well enough to speak in the House of Lords or to be consulted on political strategy. Chatham's antipathy to the Rockingham Whigs increased by 1778, after they had become resigned to the idea of American independence. As the "father" of the British empire, he just could not accept its dissolution. Even after the Declaration of Independence and the signing of the Franco-American treaty, Chatham continued to believe that a return to the pre-1763 colonial policy and a slight relaxation of the Navigation Acts would effect a reconciliation between Great Britain and the Thirteen Colonies. The irrefutable proof of his sincerity was the literal sacrifice of his life to prevent the passage of a motion to recognize American independence, which, ironically, never had any possibility of passing.

Who were these Rockingham Whigs with whom Pitt had sometimes contested and sometimes cooperated for more than a decade? Their leader was, of course, the marquis of Rockingham, whose major accomplishment was to hold his disparate group of followers together to serve as the only "organized" opposition to Lord North's American policy. Rockingham was supported in the House of Lords by the duke of Richmond. The duke was a wealthy aristocrat but, from the time that he hurried back from France to cast his vote for the repeal of the Stamp Act until he made the motion that led, indirectly and tragically, to Chatham's death, he defended the American cause to the best of his ever-increasing ability. The duke also distinguished himself as an advocate of parliamentary reform.

Edmund Burke was the intellectual leader and preeminent orator among the Rockinghamites. As such, he exemplified all the contradiction in the group's tenets. Burke defended the Declaratory Act at the time of its passage and for a decade thereafter. Yet, though an advocate of complete parliamentary supremacy, he thought it inexpedient and a violation of liberty to exercise its power of colonial taxation. In 1774, in his speech on American taxation, Burke tacitly agreed with Pownall that colonial legislatures should deal with local concerns, including taxation, but differed from him (and Chatham) by insisting that if the colonial legislatures did not meet their financial obligations, Parliament, as the "imperial" legislature (as well as the local legislature of Great Britain), had the right to tax them.

This emphasis on taxation in Burke's thinking was the key to the weakness of the Rockinghamite approach to the American problem. By 1775, when he made his famous speech *On Conciliation,* Americans had rejected the theory of parliamentary supremacy and were not to be placated by qualified assurances of freedom from parliamentary taxation. Burke also idealized pre-1763 relations between Great Britain and its colonies, claiming cheerful compliance with the Navigation Acts and generous contributions of men and money during the Seven Years' War.

Yet, right from the beginning of the debate over colonial policy, Burke had appreciated the fundamental spirit of liberty that permeated the colonists' thoughts and actions and the utter futility of attempting to coerce or conquer them. And, as the war progressed, he came to realize, first, the necessity of abandoning the concept of parliamentary supremacy and, ultimately, the inevitability of American independence. Once convinced, Burke worked diligently alongside the last of our "friends," Charles James Fox, to bring about the fall of the North ministry and an end to the American war.

Fox's reputation, like other defenders of the American cause, has been at least partially obscured by that of Edmund Burke. Yet, although it was Burke who gradually converted him to the Whig cause, Fox had realized the justice of the American cause long before. And in the day-in-day-out, year-in-year-out, often discouraging, and exhausting struggle that was to take place before the North ministry was overthrown, the leadership role was undertaken by Fox, not Burke.

Fox was a practical politician who utilized the propaganda produced by the other American sympathizers studied here. Their efforts helped build up anti-North sentiment in Parliament and among the general public. Fox, himself, did a great deal to undermine the ministry. He was not only an expert political strategist, but also a gifted orator. Although often shackled by the constraints of Whig party strategy, Fox had no hesitation in drawing scathing parallels between events leading to the Puritan and Glorious Revolutions, and the attempt of George III to exert royal control over Parliament by means of influence, patronage, and outright corruption. This was the main reason that Fox became an advocate of parliamentary reform.

Fox was in a position of power for only a brief period. Even then, his options were severely limited by political considerations. Nevertheless, he was responsible for the official peace treaty that was signed between Great Britain and the United States. Fox was also originally in sympathy with men like Hartley and Pownall, who hoped to see the negotiation of a commercial treaty that would ensure virtual free trade between the two nations.

However, Fox was later more influenced by the theories of Tucker and others, who believed that Americans would almost automatically continue to buy from, and sell to, Great Britain and therefore felt that absolutely free trade between the two nations was premature. Still, Great Britain accorded the United States more favorable commercial privileges than any other foreign nation. Fox's abrupt dismissal from office makes it impossible to determine just how he would have ultimately handled the commercial problem. Nevertheless, his previous career amply entitled him to the respect of those who believed in liberty—whether for Britons or Americans.

One question remains: How much credit do our "friends" singly, or in common, deserve? Tucker, Pownall, and Cartwright were virtually ignored. Price and Macauley were ridiculed and abused. Wilkes and Tooke allowed themselves to be distracted by a variety of causes. Chatham fell a victim of his age and prejudices. Even the efforts of the coterie of Rockingham Whigs to unseat North proved unavailing for twelve long years. All this is not difficult to understand when one considers that accepted British constitutional principles and the weight of British public opinion not only applauded North's American policy but also condemned as treasonable (particularly after France's entry into the war) any opposition to it.

Yet, in spite of these handicaps and their own intramural squabbles, our "friends" were able to keep the spirit of dissent alive until events made the prolongation of the American war inconceivable. Then, they were in a position to negotiate a peace treaty with the United States that, except for the refusal to open the West Indian trade, was extremely generous. But, as the old proverb goes, "he who looks for faultless friends will have none!"

Bibliography

Primary Sources

Adams, Charles Francis, ed. *The Works of John Adams, Second President of the United States.* 10 vols. Boston: Charles C. Little and James Brown, 1850–1856.

Almon, John, ed. *Anecdotes of the Life of the Right Honorable William Pitt, Earl of Chatham.* 3 vols. London: J.S. Jordon, 1793.

"The Bowdoin and Temple Papers." Part 1. *Collections of the Massachusetts Historical Society,* 6th ser., vol. IX. Boston: The Society, 1897.

Braeman, John, ed. *The Road to Independence: A Documentary History of the Causes of the American Revolution: 1763–1776.* New York: G.P. Putnam's Sons, 1963.

Burgh, James. *Political Disquisitions.* 3 vols. Philadelphia: R. Bell, 1774–1775.

Butterfield, L.H., ed. *Adams Family Correspondence.* 2 vols. New York: Atheneum, 1965.

Cartwright, F.D., ed. *The Life and Correspondence of Major Cartwright.* 2 vols. London: Henry Colburn, 1826.

Cartwright, John. *American Independence the Interest and Glory of Great Britain.* London: H.S. Woodfall, 1775.

———. *A Letter to Edmund Burke, Esq. Controverting the principals of American Government laid down in the lately published Speech on American Taxation Delivered in the House of Commons on the 19th of April, 1774.* London: J. Wilkie, 1775.

Channing, Edward, and Archibald Cary Coolidge, eds. *The Barrington-Bernard Correspondence and Illustrative Matter, 1760–1770.* Harvard University Historical Studies, vol. XVII. Cambridge, MA: Harvard University Press, 1912.

Cobbett, William, ed. *Parliamentary History of England, from the Earliest Period to the Year 1803.* 36 vols. London: T.C. Hansard, 1806–1826.

Controversial Letters of John Wilkes, Esq., the Rev. John Horne, and their Principal Adherents. London: T. Herlock, 1771.

Copeland, Thomas W. et al., eds. *The Correspondence of Edmund Burke.* 10 vols. Cambridge: Cambridge University Press, 1958–1978.

Crane, Verner W., ed. *Benjamin Franklin's Letters to the Press, 1758–1775.* Chapel Hill: University of North Carolina Press, 1950.

Cushing, Henry Alonzo, ed. *The Writings of Samuel Adams.* 4 vols. New York: G.P. Putnam's Sons, 1904–1908.

Elsey, George M., ed. "John Wilkes and William Palfrey." *Publications of the Colonial Society of Massachusetts* XXXIV (1937–1942): 411–428.

Everett, C.W., ed. *Letters of Junius.* London: Faber & Gwyer, 1927.

Fitzpatrick, John C., ed. *The Writings of George Washington.* 39 vols. Washington, DC: Government Printing Office, 1931–1944.

Ford, Worthington Chauncey, ed. "Warren-Adams Letters." *Massachusetts Historical Society Collections* LXII–LXXIII (1917–1925).

———. "John Wilkes in Boston." *Massachusetts Historical Society Proceedings* XLVII (1913–1914): 190–215.

Fortescue, Sir John, ed. *The Correspondence of King George the Third from 1760 to December, 1783.* 6 vols. London: Macmillan and Co., 1927–1928.

Gurney, Joseph, ed. *The Whole Proceedings in the Cause of the Action Brought by the Rt. Hon. Geo. Onslow, Esq. Against the Rev. Mr. John Horne.* London: T. Davies, 1770.

Hartley, David. *An Address to the Committee of the County of York on the State of Public Affairs.* London: J. Stockdale, 1781.

———. *Letters on the American War.* 6th ed. London: J. Almon, 1779.

Howe, Mark Anthony DeWolfe, ed. "English Journal of Josiah Quincy, Jr., 1774–1775." *Massachusetts Historical Society Proceedings* L (1916–1917): 433–496.

Howell, T.B., ed. *A Complete Collection of State Trials and Proceedings for High Crimes and Other Crimes and Misdemeanors from the Earliest Period to the Present Time.* 33 vols. London: T.C. Hansard, 1809–1826.

Hutchinson, Peter Orlando, ed. *The Diary and Letters of His Excellency Thomas Hutchinson, Esq.* 2 vols. Boston: Houghton, Mifflin, and Co., 1884.

Isham, Charles, ed. "The [Silas] Deane Papers." *Collections of the New York Historical Society.* 2 vols. XIX–XXIII (1887–1890).

Johnson, Henry P., ed. *The Correspondence and Public Papers of John Jay.* 4 vols. New York: G.P. Putnam's Sons, 1890–1893.

Kennedy, John P., ed. *Journals of the House of Burgesses of Virginia, 1761–1765.* Richmond: Virginia State Library, 1907.

Langford, Paul, ed. *The Writings and Speeches of Edmund Burke.* 12 vols. Oxford: Clarendon Press, 1981–1996.

Lee, Richard Henry. *The Life of Arthur Lee, LLD.* 2 vols. Boston: Wells and Lilly, 1829.

Lewis, W.S., and Grover Cronin, Jr., eds. *Horace Walpole's Correspondence.* 48 vols. New Haven, CT: Yale University Press, 1937–1983.

Macauley, Catherine. *An Address to the People of England, Scotland, and Ireland, on the Present important Crisis of Affairs.* 2d. ed. London: E. and C. Dilly, 1775.

———. *Loose Remarks on Certain Positions To Be Found in Mr. Hobbes' Philosophical Rudiments of Government and Society with a Short Sketch of a Democratic Form of Government, in a Letter to Signor Paoli.* 2d ed. London: W. Johnstone, 1769.

———. *Observations on a Pamphlet entitled "Thoughts on the Cause of the Present Discontents."* 2d. ed. London: E. and C. Dilly, 1770.

Matthews, Albert, ed. "Letters of Dennys de Berdt, 1757–1770." *Publications of the Colonial Society of Massachusetts* XIII (1910–1911): 293–461.

Morgan, Edmund S., ed. *Prologue to Revolution: Sources and Documents on the Stamp Act Crisis, 1764–1766.* Chapel Hill: University of North Carolina Press, 1959.

Morrison, Samuel Eliot, ed. *Sources and Documents Illustrating the American Revolution, 1764–1788, and the Formation of the Federal Constitution.* 2d ed. New York: Oxford University Press, 1965.

Olson, Alison Gilbert. *The Radical Duke: Career and Correspondence of Charles Lennox, third Duke of Richmond.* London: Oxford University Press, 1961.

Peach, Bernard W., and D.O. Thomas, eds. *The Correspondence of Richard Price.* 3 vols. Durham, NC: Duke University Press, 1983.

Pownall, Thomas. *The Administration of the British Colonies.* 5th ed. 2 vols. London: J. Walter, 1774.

————. *A Memorial Addressed to the Sovereigns of America.* London: J. Debrett, 1783.

————. *A Memorial Addressed to the Sovereigns of Europe and the Atlantic.* London: J. Debrett, 1803.

————. *A Memorial Most Humbly Addressed to the Sovereigns of Europe, on the Present State of Affairs Between the Old and New World.* London: J. Almon, 1780.

Price, Richard. *Additional Observations on the Nature and Value of Civil Liberty, and the War with America.* London: T. Cadell, 1777.

————. *Observations on the Importance of the American Revolution and the Means of Making It a Benefit to the World.* London: T. Cadell, 1785.

————. *Observations on the Nature of Civil Liberty, the Principles of Government, and the Justice and Policy of the War with America.* London: T. Cadell, 1776.

————. *Two Tracts on Civil Liberty, the War with America, and the Debts and Finances of the Kingdom.* London: T. Cadell, 1778.

Priestly, Joseph. *A Discourse On the Occasion of the Death of Dr. Price.* London: J. Johnson, 1791.

Russell, Lord John, ed. *Memorials and Correspondence of Charles James Fox.* 3 vols. London: Richard Bentley, 1853.

Schuyler, Robert Livingstone, ed. *Josiah Tucker: A Selection from His Economic and Political Writings.* New York: Columbia University Press, 1931.

Simmons, R.C. and P.D.G. Thomas, eds. *Proceedings and Debates of the British Parliaments Respecting North America, 1754–1783.* 6 vols. Millwood, NY: Kraus International Publications, 1982–1987.

Smith, Charles C., ed. "The Bowdoin and Temple Papers." Part 2. *Collections of the Massachusetts Historical Society,* 7th ser., vol. VI, Boston: The Society, 1907.

————. "Pownall-Bowdoin Letters." *Collections of the Massachusetts Historical Society,* 7th ser., vol. VI. Boston: The Society, 1897.

Smyth, Albert H., ed. *The Writings of Benjamin Franklin.* 10 vols. New York: Macmillan and Co., 1905–1907.

Stephens, Alexander. *Memoirs of John Horne Tooke.* 2 vols. London: J. Johnson, 1813.

Steuart, A. Francis, ed. *The Last Journals of Horace Walpole During the Reign of George III from 1771–1783.* 2 vols. London: John Lane, 1910.

Stevens, B.F., ed. *Facsimiles of Manuscripts in European Archives Relating to America, 1773–1783.* 25 vols. London: Malby and Sons, 1889–1898.

Taylor, William Stanhope, and Captain John Henry Pringle, eds. *Correspondence of William Pitt, Earl of Chatham.* 4 vols. London: John Murray, 1838.

Thomas, D.O., ed. *Political Writings: Richard Price.* Cambridge: Cambridge University Press, 1991.

Thomas, George, Earl of Albemarle. *Memoirs of the Marquis of Rockingham and His Contemporaries.* 2 vols. London: Richard Bentley, 1852.

Tooke, John Horne. *The Diversions of Purley.* Philadelphia: William Duane, 1806.

————. *An Oration Delivered by the Rev. Mr. Horne at a Numerous Meeting of the Freeholders of Middlesex.* London: N.p., 1770.

Tooke, John Horne, and Richard Price. *Facts: Addressed to the Landholders, Stockholders, Merchants, Farmers, Manufacturers, Tradesmen, Proprietors of Every Description and Generally to All the Subjects of Great Britain and Ireland.* 4th ed. London: J. Johnson and J. Almon, 1780.

Tucker, Josiah. *Cui Bono? Or an Inquiry What Benefits Can Arise either to the English or the Americans, the French, the Spaniards, or Dutch, from their Greatest Victories, or Successes in the Present War?* 2d ed. Gloucester, England:: R. Raikes, 1782.

————. *Four Letters on important National Subjects; Addressed to the Right Honorable the Earl of Shelburne.* Gloucester, England: R. Raikes, 1783.

————. *Four Tracts on Political and Commercial Subjects.* 2d ed. Gloucester, England: R. Raikes, 1774.

————. *An Humble Address and Earnest Appeal to the Landed Interest of Great Britain and Ireland Respecting Our Present Disputes with the Rebellious Colonies.* Gloucester, England: R. Raikes, 1775.

————. *A Letter to Edmund Burke, Esq.; Member of Parliament for the City of Bristol, and Agent for the Colony of New York in answer to His Printed Speech said to be spoken in the House of Commons on the twenty-second of March, 1775,* 2d ed. Gloucester, England: R. Raikes, 1775.

————. *The Respective Pleas and Arguments of the Mother Country and of the Colonies, Distinctly Set Forth: and the Impossibility of a Compromise of Differences or a Mutual Concession of Rights Plainly Demonstrated.* Gloucester, England: R. Raikes, 1775.

————. *A Series of Answers to Certain Popular Objections Against Separating from the Rebellious Colonies, and Discarding Them Entirely.* Gloucester, England: R. Raikes, 1776.

————. *A Treatise Concerning Civil Government in Three Parts.* London: T. Cadell, 1781.

Tuckerman, Frederick, ed. "Letters of Samuel Cooper to Thomas Pownall, 1769–1777." *American Historical Review* VIII (January 1903): 301–330.

Wharton, Francis, ed. *The Revolutionary Diplomatic Correspondence of the United States.* 6 vols. Washington, DC: Government Printing Office, 1889.

Secondary Sources

Ayling, Stanley. *Edmund Burke: His Life and Opinions.* New York: St. Martin's Press, 1988.

Bailyn, Bernard. *The Ideological Origins of the American Revolution.* Cambridge, MA: Harvard University Press, 1967.

Bonwick, Colin. *English Radicals and the American Revolution.* Chapel Hill: The University of North Carolina Press, 1977.

Bradley, James E. *Popular Politics and the American Revolution in England: Petitions, the Crown, and Public Opinion.* Macon, GA: Mercer University Press, 1986.

Cannon, John. *The Fox-North Coalition: Crisis of the Constitution, '1782–1784.* Cambridge: Cambridge University Press, 1969.

Christie, Ian R. *The End of North's Ministry, 1780–1782.* London: Macmillan and Co., 1958.

Clark, Walter E. *Josiah Tucker: Economist.* New York: Columbia University Press, 1903.

Colbourn, H. Trevor. *The Lamp of Experience: Whig History and the Intellectual Origins of the American Revolution.* Chapel Hill: University of North Carolina Press, 1965.

Cone, Carl B. *Burke and the Nature of Politics: The Age of the American Revolution.* Lexington: University of Kentucky Press, 1957.

————. *Torchbearer of Freedom: The Influence of Richard Price on Eighteenth Century Thought.* Lexington: University of Kentucky Press, 1952.

Crane, Verner W. "The Club of Honest Whigs: Friends of Science and Liberty." *William and Mary Quarterly,* 2d ser., XXIII (April 1966): 210–233.

Derry, John W. *Charles James Fox.* New York: St. Martin's Press, 1972.

————. *English Politics and the American Revolution.* New York: St. Martin's Press, 1977.

Donnelly, Lucy Martin. "The Celebrated Mrs. Macauley." *William and Mary Quarterly,* 3d ser., 6 (April 1949): 173–204.

Donoughue, Bernard. *British Politics and the American Revolution: The Path to War, 1773–1775.* London: Macmillan and Co., 1964.

Gipson, Lawrence Henry. *The British Empire before the American Revolution.* 15 vols. New York: Alfred A. Knopf, 1939–1970.

Guttridge, George H. *David Hartley, M.P.—An Advocate of Conciliation, 1774–1783.* University of California Publications in History, vol. XIV, no. 3. Berkeley: University of California Press, 1926.

————. *English Whiggism and the American Revolution.* Berkeley: University of California Press, 1966.

————. "Thomas Pownall's The Administration of the Colonies." *William and Mary Quarterly,* 3d ser., XXVI (January, 1969): 31–46.

Harlow, Vincent T. *The Founding of the Second British Empire, 1763–1793.* 2 vols. London: Longmans, Green, and Co., 1952–1964.

Hay, Carla H. *James Burgh, Spokesman for Reform in Hanoverian England.* Washington, DC: University Press of America, 1979.

Hill, Bridget. *The Republican Virago: The Life and Times of Catherine Macauley, Historian.* Oxford: Clarendon Press, 1992.

Hinkhouse, Fred Junkin. *The Preliminaries of the American Revolution as seen in the English Press, 1763–1775.* New York: Octagon Books, 1969.

Hoffman, Ross J.S. *The Marquis: A Study of Lord Rockingham, 1730–1782.* New York: Fordham University Press, 1973.

Langford, Paul. *The First Rockingham Administration, 1765–1766.* Oxford: Oxford University Press, 1973.

Lovejay, David S. "Henry Marchant and the Mistress of the World." *William and Mary Quarterly,* 3d ser., XII (July 1955): 375–398.

Lutnick, Solomon. *The American Revolution and the British Press, 1775–1783.* Columbia: University of Missouri Press, 1967.

Maccoby, Simon, ed. *The English Radical Tradition, 1763–1914.* London: Adam and Charles Black, 1952.

Maier, Pauline. "John Wilkes and American Disillusionment with Britain." *William and Mary Quarterly,* 3d ser., (July, 1963): 373–395.

Morris, Richard B. *The Peacemakers.* New York: Harper and Row, 1965.

Namier, Louis B. *England in the Age of the American Revolution,* 2d ed. London: Macmillan and Co., 1963.

Namier, Louis B., and John Brook, eds. *The House of Commons.* 3 vols. London: Her Majesty's Stationery Office, 1964.

Olson, Alison Gilbert, and Richard Maxwell Brown, eds. *Anglo-American Political Relations, 1675–1775.* New Brunswick, NJ: Rutgers University Press, 1970.

Osborne, John W. *John Cartwright.* Cambridge: Cambridge University Press, 1972.

Peach, Bernard W. *Richard Price and the Ethical Foundations of the American Revolution.* Durham, NC: Duke University Press, 1979.

Pownall, Charles A. W. *Thomas Pownall.* London: Henry Stevens, Son, and Stiles, 1908.

Reid, Loren. *Charles James Fox: A Man for the People.* Columbia: University of Missouri Press, 1969.

Ritcheson, Charles R. *British Politics and the American Revolution.* Norman: University of Oklahoma Press, 1954.

Robbins, Caroline. *The Eighteenth Century Commonwealthman.* New York: Atheneum, 1968.

Schutz, John A. *Thomas Pownall—British Defender of American Liberty.* Glendale, CA: Arthur H. Clark Co., 1951.

Shelton, George. *Dean Tucker and Eighteenth Century Economic and Political Thought.* New York: St. Martin's Press, 1981.

Sherrard, O.A. *Lord Chatham and America.* London: Bodley Head, 1958.

Sosin, Jack M. *Agents and Merchants: British and Colonial Policy and the Origins of the American Revolution, 1763–1775.* Lincoln: University of Nebraska Press, 1965.

Sumner, Charles. *Prophetic Voices Concerning America.* Boston: Lea and Shepard, 1874.

Thomas, D.O. *The Honest Mind: The Thoughts and Work of Richard Price.* Oxford: Clarendon Press, 1977.

———. *Richard Price and America, 1723–1791.* Aberystwyth, Wales: D.O. Thomas, 1975.

Thomas, Peter D.G. *British Politics and the Stamp Act Crisis: The First Phase of the American Revolution, 1763–1767.* Oxford: Clarendon Press, 1975.

———. *John Wilkes: A Friend to Liberty.* Oxford: Clarendon Press, 1996.

———. *The Townshend Duties Crisis: The Second Phase of the American Revolution, 1767–1773.* Oxford: Clarendon Press, 1987.

Thomas, Roland. *Richard Price: Philosopher and Apostle of Liberty.* London: Oxford University Press, 1924.

Toohey, Robert E. *Liberty and Empire: British Radical Solutions to the American Problem, 1774–1776.* Lexington: University Press of Kentucky, 1978.

Tucker, Robert W., and David C. Hendrickson. *Origins of the War of American Independence.* Baltimore, MD: Johns Hopkins University Press, 1982.

Yarborough, Minnie Claire. *John Horne Tooke.* New York: Columbia University Press, 1926.

Index

About the Author

Dr. Jerome R. Reich received his Ph.D. from the University of Chicago and is professor of history at Chicago State University. His special field of expertise is the study of protest movements and rebellions of the colonial period. He is the author of *Jacob Leisler's Rebellion: A Study of Democracy in New York, 1664–1720; Colonial America;* and numerous textbooks and articles on United States, African American, and world history. This volume is the culmination of his research on conflicting political ideologies current in England and America during the second half of the eighteenth century and those English individuals who attempted—albeit unsuccessfully—to reconcile them.

This volume is the culmination of Jerome Reich's research on conflicting political ideologies current in England and America during the second half of the eighteenth century and those English individuals who attempted — albeit unsuccessfully — to reconcile them. These short chapter studies profile a dozen British men and women who, for diverse reasons, consistently, sincerely, and successfully opposed the policy of the British government toward its thirteen colonies before and during the American Revolution and helped prepare the way for the recognition of the United States as an independent nation. Organized roughly chronologically, the chapters depict the actions and motivations of

★ a former colonial governor,
★ an Anglican dean,
★ a dissenting clergyman with a mathematical bent,
★ a distinguished scientist,
★ a rakish descendant of King Charles II,

and a half dozen other British "friends" who were influential in establishing a climate that helped place the emerging American constitutional government on a solid footing.

Reich demonstrates how a mixture of political expediency, constitutional scruples, and a desire for reform at home led prominent British politicians, economists, and leaders of public opinion to sympathize with the colonial point of view after 1776.

This book is ideal as a supplementary text for courses in colonial American history, the American Revolution, and U.S. constitutional history.

Jerome R. Reich received his Ph.D. from the University of Chicago and is professor of history at Chicago State University. His expertise is in the study of protest movements and rebellions of the colonial period. He is the author of *Jacob Leisler's Rebellion: A Study of Democracy in New York, 1664-1720*, and *Colonial America* (4th ed., 1998), as well as numerous textbooks and articles on U.S., African-American, and world history.

Cover Design: Salsgiver Coveney Associates

M.E. Sharpe
Armonk, New York
London, England

ISBN 0-7656-0074-5

9 780765 600745